Ethics for European Psychologists

Geoff Lindsay
Casper Koene
Haldor Øvreeide
Fredi Lang

Library of Congress Cataloging in Publication

is available via the Library of Congress Marc Database under the
LC Control Number 2008927621

Library and Archives Canada Cataloguing in Publication

Ethics for European psychologists / Geoff Lindsay ... [et al.].

Includes bibliographical references.
ISBN 978-0-88937-357-0

1. Psychologists--Professional ethics--Europe. 2. Psychologists--
Professional ethics. 3. Psychology--Moral and ethical aspects.
I. Lindsay, Geoff

BF76.4.E818 2008   174'.915   C2008-903555-0

© 2008 by Hogrefe & Huber Publishers

PUBLISHING OFFICES
USA: Hogrefe & Huber Publishers, 875 Massachusetts Avenue, 7th Floor, Cambridge, MA 02139
           Phone (866) 823-4726, Fax (617) 354-6875; E-mail info@hogrefe.com
EUROPE: Hogrefe & Huber Publishers, Rohnsweg 25, 37085 Göttingen, Germany
           Phone +49 551 49609-0, Fax +49 551 49609-88, E-mail hh@hogrefe.com

SALES & DISTRIBUTION
USA: Hogrefe & Huber Publishers, Customer Services Department,
           30 Amberwood Parkway, Ashland, OH 44805
           Phone (800) 228-3749, Fax (419) 281-6883, E-mail custserv@hogrefe.com
EUROPE: Hogrefe & Huber Publishers, Rohnsweg 25, 37085 Göttingen, Germany
           Phone +49 551 49609-0, Fax +49 551 49609-88, E-mail hh@hogrefe.com

OTHER OFFICES
CANADA: Hogrefe & Huber Publishers, 1543 Bayview Avenue, Toronto, Ontario M4G 3B5
SWITZERLAND: Hogrefe & Huber Publishers, Länggass-Strasse 76, CH-3000 Bern 9

Hogrefe & Huber Publishers
Incorporated and registered in the State of Washington, USA, and in Göttingen, Lower Saxony, Germany

Printed and bound in the USA
ISBN 978-0-88937-357-0

About the Authors

Geoff Lindsay practised as an educational psychologist and now directs the Centre for Educational Development, Appraisal and Research at the University of Warwick, UK, where he also chairs the faculty research ethics committee. He is a past president of the British Psychological Society (BPS) and past chair of the BPS Investigatory Committee. He is currently a member of its Professional Conduct Board and its Ethics Committee. Geoff Lindsay was an original member of the European Federation of Psychologists Associations (EFPA) Standing Committee on Ethics and is the current convenor. He has researched ethical dilemmas and lectures in the UK and abroad on ethics for practitioners and researchers.

Casper Koene practised as a clinical psychologist in the care of people with learning disabilities, sheltered employment, and outpatient psychiatry. As an advisory psychologist and policy maker, he served The Netherlands' Ministry of Social Affairs and Employment for many years. Nowadays he practises psychotherapy in private practice. For over a decade, Casper Koene was a board member and chair of the Advisory Council of Professional Ethics of the Dutch Psychologists' Association (NIP). He was an original member of the EFPA Standing Committee on Ethics and its previous convenor. Casper Koene teaches professional ethics at several post-Master's professional education programmes in The Netherlands.

Haldor Øvreeide is a clinical child psychologist practising in his private institute for family and relational development. Apart from his own direct clinical work, he teaches and consults colleagues in the Nordic countries on therapeutic communication with children and families, and on professional ethics. He has served as chair of the Ethical Board of the Norwegian Association for Psychologists and is a longstanding member of the EFPA Standing Committee on Ethics. He has convened two governmental committees on developing the role of and quality in being an expert witness in child protection and custody matters. He is author and co-author of several books.

Fredi Lang practised as a health and organisational psychologist in the areas of AIDS and addiction. He is now director of professional affairs in the head office of the Association of German Professional Psychologists, and also a member of the association's Board of Professional Ethics. Fredi Lang is the current convenor of the Ethic Committee of the Federation of German Psychologists' Association (BDP and DGP) and has been a member of the EFPA Standing Committee on Ethics since 2002.

Table of Contents

Preface

This book developed out of the work of the European Federation of Psychologists Associations Standing Committee on Ethics (SCE). The development of a Meta-code of Ethics was designed to guide and bring uniformity to the ethical codes of associations within EFPA. This proved a great success and attention was then given to developing other guidance for associations. Again, this proved successful. At this point, attention switched to supporting the development of national associations, both the organizations themselves and also their support for individual psychologists.

The development of a book on ethics for European psychologists is a unique venture. This book provides the first comprehensive attempt to examine ethical practice, its basis and execution from the experience of European psychologists and within the context of the culturally rich and varied countries of Europe. It is practice oriented, making it a useful resource for psychologists, whether applied practitioners or researchers. The book also explores basic issues in ethics and the wider societal context. Although firmly grounded in Europe, the principles explored within these pages have a wider applicability.

The idea for this book developed as a means to support the development of ethical practice by psychologists, drawing upon the experience of psychologists in many countries, and recognizing the need for consistent ethical principles to guide practice but also the fact that practical implementation occurs within a multicultural world in which the mobility of psychologists increases along with everyone else's. It grew out of earlier work by one of the authors, Haldor Øvreeide, who published a book aimed at Nordic psychologists. The SCE supported the development of a book based on EFPA's Meta-code (revised 2005). Although written by the four named authors, all current or recent members of the SCE, the book has benefited greatly from the work of the Standing Committee on Ethics as a whole, from the tremendous expertise of its members, who represent countries across Europe – from North to South and East to West. The current membership comprises: Victor Claudio (Portugal), Derek Deacey (Ireland), Henk Geertsema (The Netherlands), Jurg Forster (Switzerland), Hana Junova (Czech Republic), Yesim Korkut (Turkey), Fredi Lang (Germany), Alain Letuvé (France), Geoff Lindsay (United Kingdom), Polona Matjan (Slovenia), Pierre Nederlandt (Belgium), Haldor Øvreeide (Norway), Vito Tummino (Italy), and Wolf-Dietrich Zuzan (Austria).

We hope you enjoy and benefit from reading this book.

Geoff Lindsay
Casper Koene
Haldor Øvreeide
Fredi Lang

Chapter 1

Professional Ethics and Psychology[*]

Geoff Lindsay

The practice of psychology, whether as a scientific discipline or as a service to the public, is based upon two main foundations. The first foundation comprises a body of knowledge and skills which have been built up from research and from the practice of psychology. The second comprises the ethics of developing that knowledge and skills base, and of the actions taken when applying it to meet demands for services to be delivered to the public. Professions have these elements in common, but there are variations in each. For example, psychology is firmly grounded in scientific enquiry, with a strong basis in certain approaches such as experimentation, and in attempts to enhance objectivity and replicability of findings. At the same time meticulous observation, description and reflection of unique and naturally occurring events are important for scientific development in psychology.

In this book we focus on the ethical basis of psychology. We intend this to be a practical book that will help individual psychologists, at different stages of their careers, from the undergraduate starting out on a scientific subject at university, to the trainee professional psychologist or new researcher, to the experienced psychologist. In short, we consider that ethical practice is not something that is only learned at the start of a professional career. Rather, it develops as experience grows and new challenges arise.

Although primarily aimed at individual psychologists, this book is also intended to provide support to those engaged in the development of the profession. As psychology becomes a more popular and influential scientific discipline at universities across the world so new associations of psychologists are formed. Furthermore, as those countries develop their psychological science they also lay the foundation for professional practice. This development will require the further elaboration of thinking about ethics at the level of the national psychological association.

But what should be the basis or the organising principle for a book on ethics for European psychologists? Is it not the case that the rich diversity of cultures across Europe (and indeed across the world) effectively renders any attempt for commonality an impossible dream? Our answer is a resounding NO! We base this response not on prejudice or a "feel good" factor of pro-Europeanism. Rather, our opinions and our commitment to this project born out of the practical experience of having worked together over many years developing ethical guidelines for European psychologists and

---

[*] This chapter is based on a previous article that first appeared in the UNESCO-sponsored *Encyclopedia of Life Support Systems (EOLSS)* (see www.eolss.net), used here with permission.

their professional associations. This work has been in the Standing Committee on Ethics of the European Federation of Psychologists Associations (EFPA), in conferences and through the delivery of invited workshops in various countries.

In the first chapter I "set the scene" in two ways. Firstly I examine the nature of psychology and the impact that has on the development of an ethical code. In particular I consider that psychologists may be primarily professional applied practitioners (e.g., clinical psychologists, educational psychologists, forensic psychologists) but many are also researchers *not* directly engaged in providing services to the public. However, each group comprises *psychologists*. Should an ethical code apply to both or only the applied practitioners?

Secondly I briefly describe the development of the EFPA Meta-code of Ethics. The EFPA Meta-code forms the framework for chapters 3–7 of this book. It has become very influential as all member psychological associations of EFPA are required to ensure that their ethical codes are compliant with and certainly not in conflict with the Meta-code.

In the next two sections the nature of psychology as both a science and as an applied profession will be discussed: are there common or different ethical issues for those who psychologists who practise the science (researchers) compared with applied practitioners?

Psychology as a Science

Psychology has much in common with other sciences. Research in psychology may include either human or non-human participants. This raises questions about the generalisability of models of species and their location in an ethical hierarchy. Put simply, should our ethical concerns for researching humans differ from those when researching earthworms or rats? If so, on what basis will this be justified; is there a scale from lower to higher animals (including humans)? If so, where does each species sit, and what is appropriate or inappropriate for each?

This issue has led to differing positions which highlight two aspects. First, ethics and hence the determination of appropriate behaviour by psychologist researchers' is grounded in values. Second, values are themselves linked to and determined by factors including religion, beliefs and culturally influenced expectations. This being so, it is necessary to undertake research within a framework which has acceptability within the host society. Such acceptability may change over time and differ between cultures.

As a discipline psychology cannot be viewed as "value free". While some research may raise relatively few and fairly minor ethical issues other research may concern substantial and contentious ethical questions. An example of the former might be conducting reading tests with 11-year-old students, while the latter might comprise the investigation of religious beliefs, sexual behaviour or patterns of voting in elections: these are all essentially personal and private matters. With respect to research, the ethical issues concern the topic, the arrangements for conducting the research, publication and dissemination of results, and interaction effects.

The topic

Psychology as the study of behaviour and the mind covers a vast range. Consequently, the context of each particular research study will raise different ethical questions. It is not easy to categorise which topics are likely to pose fewer or more ethical problems, and these judgements might change over time. For example, research has been conducted which has examined basic cognitive processes, how these relate to each other and how they are applied in natural settings. While laboratory studies of reasoning may pose little ethical concern, the results of studies collectively may pose serious challenges. This is exemplified by findings which indicate mean differences between racial or ethnic groups in cognitive abilities. The scientific issues concern the rigour of the studies, and validity and usefulness of the findings (Phinney, 1996). In this example, the concept of race is now seen as contentious, affecting the scientific validity of findings. This in turn raises ethical questions regarding dissemination of findings from such studies. But there is a further ethical concern: should such research be undertaken at all? The work of Jensen and Eysenck, for example, was attacked not so much for the pure science but for the implications that might be drawn and consequent impact on, in this case, relations between different groups (e.g., Eysenck, 1971). This raises the sensitive issue – are certain topics for research to be avoided *not* on scientific grounds but because they are socially sensitive?

Conducting the research

Research methods in psychology cover a very broad field. At one end of the continuum there are invasive surgical procedures, e.g., planting electrodes in the brains of animals in order to examine the relationship between behaviour, thought or perception with brain activity. Here the technique is invasive and undertaken for the purpose of the experiment. This may be compared with research into brain activity in patients undergoing surgery for therapeutic purposes.

At the other end of the continuum may be placed interpersonal experimental techniques. One with a low degree of invasiveness is the completion of questionnaires, particularly in a large group. Compare this with a study by individual interview where the researcher asks probing and challenging questions about the participant's personal behaviour and views.

These examples imply at least two dimensions: physical–interpersonal and low–high intrusiveness. Hence, intrusion may be conceptualised as either physical, e.g., surgery, or by questioning. Each of these has implications for the well being of the participant, which may also be considered with respect to physical and psychological health. That is, not only does physical intrusion pose potential ethical questions, so also does questioning.

An example, which also suggests how attitudes to what is permissible in experiments change, concerns an experiment by Landis in 1924 in the US (described in Crafts et al.,

1938). Twenty-five "subjects," mainly adults but including a 13-year-old boy, and a hospital patient with high blood pressure, were exposed to various conditions to produce emotional responses, the purpose being to assess facial expression of emotions. The 17 situations included the playing of jazz, reading from the Bible – probably regarded as fairly benign depending on one's views of jazz or the Bible in a predominantly Christian country. However, other conditions included deception, e.g., sniffing ammonia rather than the "syrup of lemons" as indicated by the experimenter. Other tasks involved asking the person to cut off a rat's head; and requesting the participant to put their hand into a covered bucket, without looking, and feel around. The bucket contained several inches of water and live frogs, and a strong electric shock was delivered.

A third dimension implicit here is the vulnerability of the participant, with respect to their developmental status, both age and intellectual ability, and their physical and psychological health and resilience – in this case boy and a hospital patient.

Ethical consideration of the conduct of research therefore requires attention to several different dimensions concerning the participants, and indeed the experimenters. In addition there are ethical concerns regarding the practicability of research, including consent, verification of the participant and the validity and reliability of measures. While these may often be seen as technical matters, they have an ethical dimension: invalid data pose potential problems for the competence and integrity of the research findings and reputation of the researcher.

Publication and dissemination

Dissemination of research findings takes various forms; e.g., reports to sponsors, journal articles for other researchers or professionals, and presentations in the media. There are ethical considerations which apply to all of these, but there are also variations. In each case there is a requirement of *integrity*, characterised here by accurate, truthful and comprehensible presentation. At its most basic, data should not be fabricated or ignored if they confound the researcher's preferred outcomes. An example of where this was open to question concerned Sir Cyril Burt, an eminent British psychologist who was the country's first educational psychologist. After his death it was alleged that his influential work on IQ, using data from twins, was suspect: it was suggested that he had fabricated findings, and even made up at least one researcher worker, in order to bolster his views on the heritability of intelligence (Kamin, 1974[1]).

While blatant fabrication may be unequivocally unethical, other examples may be less straightforward. Psychologists may legitimately report the findings of a study which lends support to their theories: however, not to consider opposing findings, or not to conduct studies which might challenge the findings would not be ethical. Consequently, in reporting one study, not to contextualise its worth with reference to the findings of other studies would represent a lack of integrity.

---

[1] For a fuller discussion of this *cause celebre*, see Mackintosh (1995).

The nature of the medium represents a further ethical challenge. Different expectations are required if the recipient is a researcher or member of the public. These relate both to the medium of publication, and also the style of representation. While journal articles are generally carefully written in measured prose, a television programme or tabloid newspaper may accentuate, possibly distort, meanings. The responsibility ultimately is always with the psychologist, even if the (mis)representation is by another person or agency. This applies not only to deliberately questionable representation, but also to ensuring the avoidance of misunderstanding by the audience. Hence, ethical consideration includes not only honesty but clarity. The issues raised here apply also to the other main method of dissemination: teaching. There is the dimension of audience, e.g., the expert postgraduate seminar through to the invited presentation to a community group. In each case there is an ethical requirement to seek to communicate effectively not only on grounds of good science but also on the ethical basis of seeking to avoid misinformation being acquired.

Interaction

Finally it is necessary to consider the interaction of these three elements and of these with psychologists" personal values. For example, it may be argued that some research is unethical in itself, but its effects are beneficial – the "end justifies the means" argument. One example is the work of Milgram on conformity (e.g., Milgram, 1963). In a classic experiment he required people to give shocks to a "subject", positioned out of sight, if wrong answers were given to questions. The intensity of shocks delivered increased. Hesitation or reluctance led to a white-coated supervisor insisting the person continued. Despite increasingly apparent signs of distress, it was found that the participants did deliver these increasingly severe shocks, a finding which was interpreted as conformity in the setting and in the presence of an authority figure giving commands. It is difficult to imagine such an experiment being allowed now, yet it could also be argued that this experiment was a significant contribution to our understanding of an important social psychological phenomenon. A similar example is the famous Stanford Prison Experiment carried out by Zimbardo and now reported in detail for the first time in his book *The Lucifer Effect* (Zimbardo, 2007).

A different issue concerns the potential biases which may impact on any or all three of the elements above and consequently lead to a cumulative disposition to bias of the discipline. For example, it has been argued that psychology lacks socio-political diversity and that most psychologists are politically liberal, with conservatives being underrepresented in the discipline and profession. Research topics are chosen which, it is argued, are salient to the values of psychologists: these may be interpreted with a liberal bias; the findings may be reported within the values domains of the researcher. In such a case, there is a potential bias from start to end of the research process. This may not be intentional, but is rather a subtle manifestation of the psychologists' individual value systems. The problem is confounded if, as is argued for psychology, the members of the profession have a high level of homogeneity of values.

Psychology as a Profession

The need for psychological associations

Organised psychology has only been around for a hundred years or so. It was towards the end of the 19th Century that laboratories for the study of psychology were established, but these did not necessarily represent psychology as an independent discipline. For example, in the university in the UK where I took my Bachelors degree it was well after the 2nd World War before a department of psychology was established. Before then there were lecturers in psychology in the department of philosophy. Such developments occurred at different rates within as well as between countries. Indeed, even now it is of little if any interest to some psychologists whether or not they practise within an organisation which is "psychological", whether a university department, a public service, industry, commerce or private practice. Others are most concerned to be recognised personally as psychologists, and to operate within organisations or subsections of psychology.

Of more relevance to the present discussion therefore, is the development of formal organisations of psychology. The oldest are the American Psychological Association (APA), and the British Psychological Society (BPS), both over 100 years old. These have always been organisations of *psychologists*. That is, membership is open to those who meet certain requirements with respect to training in psychology.

These organisations have been central to the development of ethical codes as it is within these bodies that discussions have occurred, and ultimately where decisions have been made on the nature and substance of any codes which have been developed. Also, being typically democratic bodies, such organisations have needed the support of members to approve policies and regulatory procedures including ethical codes. Consequently, the development of ethical codes is dependent upon the existence, strength and organisation of psychological associations as well as universities and groupings of practitioners, on the procedures to inform and gain the support of members, and on the views of members on ethical matters. These factors will be influenced by various elements, not least the general societal context. For example, the development of psychological associations since the fall of the old communist regimes in Eastern Europe has allowed previously restricted associations to develop their practice, and to develop new ethical codes.

The importance for psychological associations of the development of ethical codes is probably most clear in those countries which have been later in instituting the professional bodies. However, their role can also be seen when tracing the development of ethical codes within well established associations. In doing this it is necessary to consider: what is a profession? And why have an ethical code?

What is a profession?

Pryzwansky and Wendt (1999) argue that a profession may be characterised by the following:
- Existence of a formal professional member organisation
- Systematic training
- Body of knowledge "to profess"
- Code of ethics
- Regulation of the members who provide a service

However, these are not simple issues. For example, in many countries psychologists have practised with limited organisation. Also, until relatively recently, psychologists had no specific code of ethics. That of the APA, generally argued to be the first, was not approved until 1953, well over half a century after the APA was set up, and when large numbers of psychologists had practised for many years. Within Europe, many countries have developed their ethical codes following the initiative of EFPA which set up a task force to develop an ethical code in 1990[2]. Even now, there are psychological associations which do not have disciplinary procedures as one element of a regulatory system, a limitation recently addressed by the EFPA Standing Committee on Ethics.

The definition of professions, therefore, is complex. There are historical and cultural factors which challenge the generally agreed criteria. Furthermore, there are other factors to consider including:
- Specificity of knowledge and skills
- Level of skill application
- Self and societal interest

Psychology *par excellence* is a discipline which has contributed to a range of professions, including healthcare, teaching, social work, personnel and human relations and advertising, among others. Many, but not all, will have their own ethical code. For example, until recently there was no ethical code for school teachers in England and Wales, a limitation addressed by the newly instituted General Teaching Council.

The level of skill required may distinguish between or within professions. Again complexity is increased with overlapping sets of competencies. For example, a school teacher may train in educational measurement to a high level, but not have the breadth of experience of psycho-educational assessment of a school or educational psychologist. Hence *psychology* is applied by others as well as by *psychologists* – we must draw lines to define the *psychologist* in order to define who is competent and who is subject to an ethical code for psychologists.

The third issue concerns the nature of the work undertaken and the society in which it occurs. This is also problematic with the variation in private and state

---

[2] After the Meta-code was approved in 1995, the Task Force became the Standing Committee on Ethics.

provided practice and this varies across countries. Some argue that a primary orientation to community interest rather than individual self-interest is a characteristic of professional behaviour, but this is difficult to unpick. Traditional commitment to society
characterised by low wages and poor working conditions has been challenged by organised labour and changes in society's views of what is appropriate. Also, those in
private practice essentially have a degree of self interest inherent in their practice –
they need clients to survive. But more subtle pressures may be present for others, including those employed by the state or a voluntary agency. For example, critiques of
special education have argued that professionals may maintain the system out of self
interest as their livelihoods are implicated. Interestingly, such critics tend not to apply the same allegation to themselves, whose professional careers may be based on
promulgating such critiques.

In summary, the question of what is a profession is problematic and contentious.
However, for present purposes the primary focus will be on the development of an
ethical code, and the regulation of professionals' behaviour.

Why Have an Ethical Code?

Ethical codes are characterised, implicitly or explicitly, by two elements: a set of ethical principles and statements of practice typically written as enforceable standards.
Ethical codes, therefore, are means of translating beliefs regarding necessary behaviour into statements which specify how the professional may act appropriately. These
principles are derived from general moral positions including values. But why have an
ethical code at all?

This question may now seem absurd, but in the development of the first APA code
there was an active debate in which the argument for not having a code was put force-
fully by Hall (1952). This was not an argument against ethical behaviour, but Hall
argued that there was no need to have a formal code. Rather, he argued, ethical behaviour should be assumed of psychologists and, he argued, the institution of a formal
code was a retrograde step as "I think it plays into the hands of crooks on the one hand
and because it makes those who are covered by the code feel smug and sanctimonious
on the other hand" (p. 430).

This view did not prevail but the point made is important. Firstly, it distinguishes
ethical behaviour from a formal ethical code, but implicitly it raises the issue of training.
Hall's position was based upon a belief in the goodness of right thinking psychologists,
but was silent on how they achieved their right thinking behaviour: "decent mature people do not need to be told how to conduct themselves" (p. 430) – experience shows this
view to be naïve. For example, each year both the BPS and APA publish statistics regarding complaints made about their members. Although in percentage terms these are
not high rates, the numbers are not insignificant. In 2006, the BPS received 109 complaints, appointed 20 panels to investigate complaints, and seven complaints went to a

full Conduct Committee hearing. The APA reported that 82 complaints had been received and 29 new cases had been opened[3].

A further issue concerns the range and *comprehensiveness* of any code, and its impact on the members of a profession. Ethical codes are typically designed to apply to *practitioners*. Psychology is unusual in its large number of psychologists who do not offer services to the public, namely researchers and educators. In typical professions the overwhelming majority of members will be practitioners, (e.g., medical practitioners, nurses). Ethical codes therefore are directed towards practice with clients. Psychology, however, has a substantial proportion of those who develop the discipline through research and disseminate through education.

One approach could be to limit ethical codes only to those members who offer services to the public. This was not the line taken by the major national societies in Europe or the APA. While there are practical factors, separating out members into distinct groups, there is also a tradition of bringing science and practice together. This can be exemplified by the situation in the APA at the end of the 1940s, early 1950s. At that time practitioners in psychology *developed from* researchers in that the doctorate was seen as the key qualification. This position was debated and challenged, and the Boulder conference of 1949 was an important event which firmed up the notion that clinical psychologists should be trained with a grounding in basic research and that clinical applications should follow from and be built upon this foundation. This approach often called the "scientist-practitioner" model has been followed in other fields of applied psychology (Lindsay, 1998) but continues to be a matter of contention (Rice, 1997). These debates took place at the same time as those about the first APA code of ethics and researchers, some of whom would have been in practice with clients, were important contributors. This policy of inclusiveness by psychological associations may not be matched by licensing authorities which may typically not require researchers or teachers of psychology to have a license to practice. These psychologists will therefore fall outside the remit of licensing authorities, and hence the psychological association must provide the necessary investigatory and disciplinary procedures, as well as ethical guidance.

This issue of coverage is important as there are different implications for ethical codes. When considering practice (e.g., as a clinical psychologist) an ethical code must address the behaviour of the psychologist with a client, an individual. On the other hand, research requires consideration of individuals who are not clients in the same sense (e.g., research participants) but also there is a need to address a more abstract concept, namely the body of knowledge of the science. This is not to argue for a simple dichotomy, the concept of client, for example, is complex (see chapter 3). Researchers may have clients in the form of organisations that provide finance, while those providing services may have multiple clients, or different orders of clients as with a child within a family, or workers within a company. Nevertheless, there is

---

[3] See the British Psychological Society's Annual Report www.bps.org.uk and the special issue of the *American Psychologist* published each August.

a legal position in many countries which acknowledges the particular relationship, and hence obligations, between a professional and identified client. This may be considered as a special duty of care for the welfare of one's clients or patients. However, such a duty of care may also be attributed to the researcher, with respect to research participants in particular. Hence, ethical behaviour should be expected of *all* psychologists, and systems to ensure this occurs must address this full range, including researchers and educators.

The development of the EFPA Meta-code

The European Federation of Psychologists Associations (EFPA) was founded in 1981 as the European Federation of Professional Psychologists Associations (EFPPA), and changed its name in 2001. EFPA is a federation and hence has limited power over member associations which comprise a single body from each member country. It is the national associations that exercise direct power over individual members. The position of psychology in Europe is highly varied and this is matched by the nature of the associations. While some bodies are fundamentally scientific and/or professional associations, others are trades unions/syndicates. Also, while some countries (e.g., UK) have one predominant association for all psychologists, others (e.g., France) have many associations. Consequently, while the UK is represented by the British Psychological Society (BPS), France is represented by ANOP, a federation of associations.

These political realities are important when considering the development of a common ethical code. This was identified as a key aim in the very early stages of EFPA's existence. A Task Force on Ethics was set up in 1990 with the aim of producing a common ethical code for psychologists in Europe. Given freedom of movement within the European Union (which covers much but not all of Europe) there are benefits in common procedures. There was concern that a psychologist disciplined in, say, Portugal could move to UK without this being known. This is not the case in the US and Canada where the Association of State Psychology Boards facilitates communication.

It was evident at the first meeting of the Task Force in Copenhagen 1990, however, that this aspiration was unrealistic. A number of associations had their own codes, but not all. These codes had much similarity (Lindsay, 1992) but there were also a number of significant differences, mainly with detail rather than principle (see Table 1)[4]. Nevertheless, each had been devised by the association in question to meet their specific requirements, and a common code might not ensure this occurred. Furthermore, in many cases (e.g., BPS) a vote of members was needed to change the code. Hence, it was decided that a common code was too difficult to achieve.

---

[4] Since this analysis there have been developments of the ethical codes of these national associations.

Table 1.1. Contents of ethical codes of six European countries and the United States

	Nordic	Germany	Spain	Hungary	Austria	UK	US
1. Responsibility, general principles	✓	✓	✓	✓	✓	✓	✓
2. Competence	✓	✓	✓	✓	✓	✓	✓
3. Relationships with clients	✓	✓	✓	✓	✓	✓	✓
4. Confidentiality	✓	✓	✓	✓	✓	✓	✓
5. Psychological methods, investigations and statements, including research reports	✓	✓	✓	✓	✓	✓	✓
6. Public statements, advertising	✓	✓	✓		✓	✓	✓
7. Professional relationships	✓	✓	✓	✓	✓	✓	✓
7a. Relationships with employers					✓		
8. Research, teaching	✓	✓	✓	✓	✓		✓
9. Professional designation, title, qualifications	✓	✓	✓	✓		✓	✓
10. Training		✓					
11. Fees and remuneration			✓				✓
12. Working conditions				✓	✓	✓	
13. Personal conduct						✓	✓
14. Obtaining consent						✓	✓

From: Lindsay, G. (1992), p. 195. By kind permission of Continuum.

The alternative model was to devise a Meta-code. Rather than a code for psychologists, the Task Force devised a Meta-code for the national associations. This set out what the code of each member association should address, but left it to the associations to produce specific codes and elements within codes. This approach was successful and the Meta-code of Ethics was approved by the General Assembly of EFPPA in 1995. It is the EFPA Meta-code (as revised in 2005[5]) that sets the framework for this book.

The development of the Meta-code is of interest as it represents a specific inclusive strategy designed deliberately to attain maximum generalisability and acceptance. An early analysis, mentioned above, had indicated similarities but also differences between the codes of different national associations of psychologists. Furthermore across Europe at that time it was known that some associations had no code or were in the process of developing their code. Consequently there were variations in stage of development; in content, to varying degrees, when codes existed; in the size and status of different national associations; and differences in language with the possibility of conceptual and linguistic challenges in producing one Meta-code. Furthermore, it was also important to recognise the variations between nations (at the socio-political rather than psychologist association level) including culture, history and politics as well as language(s).

The success of the Meta-code can be attested to by two main sources of evidence. Firstly, it was approved by the 1995 EFPA General Assembly. Secondly, associations without codes or developing their code used the Meta-code as their template, as intended. Thirdly, the 2005 revision was successfully achieved with few amendments.

The process that led to this success was straightforward. Member associations were invited to send one member each to the Task Force on Ethics. From its beginning, membership consistently comprised at least 10 countries from the full range of Europe from the Nordic north to the Latin south, and including post-Communist Eastern Europe. The Task Force considered different models that existed in their own countries as well as those from non-European associations, particularly the APA code and the Canadian Psychological Association (CPA) code. The latter was particularly attractive because of its strong educative orientation with an accompanying extended manual with vignettes (Sinclair & Pettitfor, 2001).

The Task Force drew on a range of material but from the start was committed not simply to replicate another code, however positively that was viewed. The structure of ethical principles followed by more specific standards was agreed to be appropriate but the Task Force decided, after much debate, to structure around four principles rather than, for example, the five that characterised the then current version of the APA code. That decision was partly influenced by a wish not simply to follow the APA – a determination that this should be European – but more importantly there was disagreement with the APA's 5-principle structure (the current APA code has four principles).

The exact specification of the principles and of the different standards took place over several years, with the Task Force meeting twice a year. An early decision by the group was crucial in simplifying the process: the code should be written in English. By this decision the Task Force was able to focus on a single version. However, this also allowed a relatively straightforward approach to deal with linguistic variations. At

---

[5] See www.efpa.eu and Appendix 1.

each point the English text would be considered by Task Force members to identify potential problems for the different national languages. The policy was for each association to translate the English version into their language(s) so a straightforward route that prevented ambiguity following translation was required. This process demanded much discussion but this was productive.

There were very few major concerns about the English text. The most important was a discussion of the English word *confidentiality*. In South European countries the common term would be translated into the English equivalent of *professional secret* and there was much discussion as to whether these terms were of equivalent power. Otherwise, the development of the Meta-code was challenging but ultimately successful with the Task Force's proposal being accepted by the 1995 General Assembly of EFPA.

Subsequently, the Task Force on Ethics was replaced by a Standing Committee on Ethics (SCE). The SCE spent the next few years developing other guidance including the evaluation of complaints. It was then decided that a 10th anniversary of the Meta-code in 2005 would be an appropriate time for the EFPA General Assembly to receive a revision. The basis for this decision was that revisions tend to be necessary over time. Certainly the APA code had undergone a series of revision over its 50 years of existence, some being substantial.

The SCE initiated the review as a committee but also sought comments from national associations. Two symposia were organised in Prague in 2004 and 2005 attended by representatives of national associations as well as the SCE. A rigorous review of the content of the Meta-code was supplemented by consideration of current ethical issues and dilemmas, such as the use of the internet (for which the SCE had also provided separate guidance). As a result of this work the revised Meta-code[6] was approved by the 2005 EFPA General Assembly. Interestingly, this intensive interrogation of its content led to very few changes being required, suggesting that the original structure and content was sound, fit for purpose, and likely to remain so for some time.

Other ethical guidance

In the period up to the 2005 revision the SCE developed other ethical guidance as well as the Meta-code. For example, the SCE developed guidance on how a national association might deal with complaints of alleged unethical conduct by a psychologist (see chapter 9). Consequently, the revised Meta-code was able to make reference to the need for procedures to deal with such complaints. Note that the approach is not simply punitive. Complaints need to be evaluated but, there are various approaches. One – mediation – seeks to avoid the formal dealing with complaints, replacing what is essentially a quasi-legal or even legal process by a lower key approach to settling disagreements – where appropriate (see chapter 9). In some cases disciplinary sanctions are necessary as the alleged unethical conduct is so serious but often – perhaps even

---

[6] For the remainder of this book, the term "Meta-code of Ethics" refers to the 2005 revision.

always? – what is also of importance is to seek to ensure that the psychologist improves their behaviour in the future whether or not any disciplinary action for the past unethical behaviour is deemed appropriate.

Outline of the Book

In this chapter the Meta-code of Ethics has been introduced, contextualised within a discussion of the nature of psychology and the range of psychological practice. The Meta-code was designed to apply to *psychological associations* and is written as such – see Appendix 1. However, our experience has been that many individual psychologists have found the Meta-code helpful also in guiding their own practice. In the following pages we shall show how the Meta-code can be used in this way.

The following chapter (chapter 2) presents a wider background for consideration of the Meta-code. The danger of a code is that a psychologist uses it simply as a cook book and expects to find "an answer" to every question simply by looking up the appropriate "recipe". That is not our view, and was not the basis of the Meta-code. Rather, the Meta-code provides a *framework*, a *stimulus* to thinking. More is needed and in chapter 2 we present a consideration of ethical discussion and dimensions.

Chapter 3 introduces the Meta-code by focussing on the general issues, those that cut across specific content. These include the definition of the client and the nature of the relationship between psychologist and client or others. chapters 4–7 address each of the four ethical principles in sequence: Respect, Competence, Responsibility, and Integrity. In each case we explore both the principle and the specifications and standards for each.

Chapters 4–7 address each of the four ethical principles in sequence: Respect, Competence, Responsibility, and Integrity. In each case we explore both the principle and the specifications and standards for each.

Following this discussion of the Meta-code we turn to implementation. In chapter 8 we consider the nature of decision-making and ethical dilemmas while in chapter 9 we explore approaches to dealing with complaints. Finally, in chapter 10, we take a brief look into the future. The Meta-code has been very useful for European psychologists so far but will we need to consider new ethical challenges in the future? For example, does the internet pose particular challenges? Does the so-called "War on Terror" and the focus on "national security" in European countries lead to different expectations of ethical practice? The basis for ethical practice is firmly embedded in the four ethical principles we discuss here but in a changing world we must all continue to reflect on and learn from the challenges posed by developments, whether within psychology as a science, psychology as an applied practice or society as a whole.

Chapter 2

Ethical Discourses and Ethical Dimensions

Haldor Øvreeide

This chapter on different ethical discourses and dimensions is not directly related to the text of the Meta-code. It might, however, give some concepts of relevance that can deepen the understanding of the text, and so also be useful for solving ethical dilemmas and challenges. The topics discussed are not discrete, independent entities that add up to a comprehensive ethical theory, or perspective on ethics. They are more to be understood as ways of looking at the same questions from different social and intellectual positions.

Ethical discourses

Moral questions are at the base of all small or larger social projects and conflicts. Morals are therefore both core and unavoidable complementary issues in all political and social processes, in the single dyad, as well as in larger social systems and societies. All human interactions are thus embedded in discourses on ethics – *What will be the right thing to do? How do we achieve the good and the best? How do we share and distribute resources? How do we relieve pain and avoid harm?* and *How do we evaluate what happened in a moral perspective?* These discourses are practised on many different areas, and one is when psychologists are developing their sectional, professional ethics. Many of the most important ethical discourses often take place without us being really aware that this is so, since they are embedded in all kinds of social problem-solving.

As humans have different needs, interests, dependencies, loyalties and other differences in our relationships and contextual frames, so we also often arrive at different answers to these questions. We still have to keep up the dialogues and discourses because we also have mutual dependencies and common interests and goals, in groups and as humanity in general. The formulation and awareness of ethical principles, and when established the continuous discussion of how they are to be understood and applied at different times and in differing situations, are necessities for cooperation and coherence within human systems. In the following sections some typical areas for ethical discussions and developments will be described. These are discourses that might be relevant when we as psychologists establish ethical principles and discuss and monitor our practice accordingly.

Moral philosophy

Moral questions have been the most central issue in philosophy. Intellectual pondering on ethical questions has been an important base for scientific as well as social and educational programs, and thus the development of society. On the other hand, moral philosophy can be seen as a reflection of social processes that already are in movement. It is, however, putting words, concepts to the process and offering critical perspectives and a moral description of the moral phenomena that exist and which are central themes in contemporary, as well as historical social processes. Important philosophical texts and discussions on morals flourished, for example, in the aftermath of The Second World War, and older philosophical contributions were revisited and criticised. Both intellectual and political endeavours contributed to the formulation of international declarations of human rights, important formulations also for the professional ethics. None of the then existing professions came through the war-times without flaws in their professional integrity.

Developments in other sciences and scientifically based professions are important contributors to unravelling the phenomena and processes that are of interest to philosophers. The Adorno studies on the authoritarian personality had impact on philosophy, as well as the Milgram study, described in chapter 7. In another context, Psychology's discovery of the socially competent baby is also beginning to catch the interest of philosophers thinking about moral questions. When dependencies, as well as personal competence, are central in a relationship, right from the child's first cry, dialogue is necessary to solve the ethical challenges, so also in developmental support. Albeit philosophers had foreseen some of the later discoveries of dialogical processes in their discussions on the moral appeals and contradictions that exist in the human encounter (Arendt 1978, Levinas 1981). Sometimes it can be said that philosophy poses questions, and other sciences "see" and describe the phenomena foreseen and advised by philosophy, as well as the other way round. Without an input from moral philosophy to scientific progress and practice, science loses an important compass for its development as legitimate and valuable social practice. That does not mean that the compass always is right: it must always be tested and criticized.

Intellectually marvellous moral ideas and constructs can go terribly wrong when they are seen as *"The Solution"* and put into practice. Religious texts have important intellectual contributions to understanding and solving moral dilemmas, and historically many important philosophical contributions, both from eastern and western cultures are hybrid philosophical texts on religious and moral questions. The problem when moral text and thinking are too closely connected to religion and political ambitions is that they often imply or are accompanied by intolerance for other perspectives.

At the edge of moral philosophy are art and literature which also often examine moral questions. An important part of the intellectual consciousness and development of moral questions are found in the works of artists, novelists and authors, and the later intellectual discussions of the texts and artistic expressions. Dostoyevsky, Ibsen, Kafka and an endless line of other authors and artists have made important contributions to the moral discourse and to our understanding of ethical dilemmas, our human failures and successes.

It is important that the ethical principles formulated by the profession and the practice that follows has resonance in moral philosophy so that the practice has an intellectually well founded background. An intellectual reasoning and arguing for practice is needed to lift it from the flaws of feelings and fades.

Common Ethics

While moral philosophy can be seen as an intellectual basis to answer general ethical questions in-depth, there is always an ongoing here and now discussion in the papers, on Internet, in schools, in the Parliament, at the work place etc. All these discussions will be mirroring ad hoc moral issues, what might be called the *common ethics* in groups, in social classes and in society. Everybody will have a say in common ethics.

The common ethics comes close to the timely ethical problem-solving in society at large. It is the here and now moral context for ethical problem-solving, a continuous evolving of consensuses and divergences on value questions. It is embedded in the actual attitudes, prejudices and meanings at a certain place and time, and shows what issues are in front and how the moral thinking, the ethics, is reflected in these discussions. In contrast to what later is called *personal ethics*, common ethics discourses can be seen as the striving for moral consensuses at a given time and place. It is situated in a "now" and in a definable social context. As such it can be observed and empirically studied. It reflects how people feel, think and behave in relation to certain values. Political campaigns, elections, polls and many different social studies can be seen as catching and exposing the common ethics at the time: Likewise essays, columns and debates in the papers, blogs on the Internet, all expose thinking and feeling on how different issues are related to values.

These diverse common discourses are of interest for the profession and the individual psychologist to be aware of. This is because: *These will be the discourses that the clients will engage in and out of which they understand their own moral position, rights and responsibilities.*

Personal ethics

Personal ethics can be seen as the result of the individual's socialising and experiences related to moral issues. It contains both a cognitive structure of social stances and not the least, an emotional inclination for responding to what is "right". All behaviours, both in private as well as in professional practice will be related to personal attitudes and moral tendencies for responding; to what feels right, what fosters inclusion or rejections, and to what generates guilt and shame as well as feelings of coping and success.

This means that due to differences in upbringing, sub-cultural standing and individual experiences moral values will be ordered in differing personal hierarchies and dispositions. These individual dispositions will apply both in private as well as professional settings. One will be notably sensitive to the Other's needs for caring, a second will be acutely conscious of respecting the integrity of the Other. The third may be occupied with avoiding negative consequences for the Other, while the fourth is seeking the long-term best interests of the Other, and for the fifth aesthetics and convention in the relationship to the Other are important. Individual differences in temperament and reactivity can also be expected to influence one's moral inclinations.

In professional practice it will be important to be aware of how one's personal values and tendencies are aggregated and how they may enter and affect practice. Since personal ethics are largely a set of emotionally organised dispositions and as such largely unconsciously triggered, it can be a challenge to bring them in to reason and intellectual scrutiny. Thus it can come to interfere with a sound ethical assessment of a professional challenge.

Personal ethics should, however, first of all be seen as a resource. The emotionally based sensitivity for values and moral issues is necessary for catching ethical dilemmas and relevant questions. One "feels" a value in a social encounter as much as it can be intellectually deduced, and in the last instance one "feels" if the action was "right or wrong". This without it necessarily being the best action taken according to common ethics or when considered from the perspective of professional ethics. Professional ethics, its principles and specifications, are important for balancing, correcting and advising the impulses from personal ethics which always will be the base for ethical acuity and responding. The first impulse will however need support or correction from reflective consideration. Thorough knowledge of professional ethical codes and discourses will be essential when entering the professional context. Discussing ethical dilemmas and options with colleagues are important ways to counter-balance the first impulses to act; impulses that often stem from a personal value system.

Sector ethics and professional ethics

Sector ethics refers to when certain values and practices are highlighted within a special social grouping. It can be within a firm, a religious grouping, a sports organization, and a professional group etc. Specific guidelines or norms for the members' behaviour are discussed, developed and formulated by and for the members or practitioners of the group or organization. To become a sector ethics, apart from the more free-floating processes in common ethics, the values and principles for practice must be highlighted by the members within the sector themselves. It is thus the discourses within the group concerning members' own behaviour and practice that constitutes a sector ethics and not what might be specified through laws and regulations by governments or other sources of external constraints. Sometimes, however, processes concerning ethical issues within the sector might bring forward statutory regulations, and then ethics and outside directives might to some extent become paralleled. Professional ethics for psychologists is a typical sector ethics, which due to issues and competence of societal importance also have brought forward governmental regulations for the profession in most European countries.

When psychologists associations formulate ethical principles for their members, two main motives can be explicated. First the profession wants to signal that the practice to be expected will be in line with important social values contained in the common ethics of the time, so as to secure trust in and legitimacy for the profession. As in the relation to moral philosophy, there must be a resonance between professional ethics and the common ethics. In the professional encounter with the client it is necessary to understand the moral position of the client in order to respect and communicate on important issues. The client will be embedded in the streaming discourses on common ethics.

That does not mean that professional ethics should be seen as, or be a simple derivative of or extract from common ethics. Quite the opposite, professional ethics should include, but at the same time, from the professional perspective, take a critical stand regarding common ethical solutions and practices, as well as with respect to the imperfection of personal ethics, as discussed above. How do both personal and common ethics enhance or limit reaching the profession's goals and how do they support or undermine the trust and legitimacy of the profession?

Example 2.1

The client of a psychologist wrote a furious letter to this author when serving as chair of the ethical board for psychologists. The board had intervened in a couple of cases where colleagues had sexually abused clients. These cases had also come to the notice of the tabloid press. In her letter the woman argued strongly that she felt that the ethical board was behaving unethically when reprimanding therapists for having sex with their clients. She was a responsible adult and what happened between consenting adults was their right to engage in as long as no one else was damaged. Somewhat similar views appeared in readers' columns.

This example brings out the second and possibly the most important motive for formulating sectional ethics for psychologists. This motive is an awareness that the profession itself must take the responsibility for the practice that is derived from the specific and privileged knowledge that psychologists uphold. It is not obvious that outsiders will understand the limitations, effects and the range of consequences of professional practice. This example shows that there are not always mechanisms of counter-power protecting clients from exploitation and repressions. It is not for all clients, like the woman in the example, to understand the power differences and its risks in the psychologist-client relationship. By focussing on the ethical issues that are not obvious to outsiders, professional ethics has an important function to regulate situations where the client could be at hazard for deliberate as well as fortuitous abusive or degrading practices from the psychologist. The potential ethical pitfalls connected with psychological practice must be pondered by the practitioners themselves, preferably in a proactive process and always by an ethical evaluation of the effects of the ongoing practice. This is what ethical discourses and development of ethical codes and regulations within the profession are about.

Section ethics – like common ethics – how it is understood and practised, can be observed, registered and empirically assessed. For example: What cases are filed for ethical complaint and how are they reacted to by the ethical boards? – What ethical dilemmas do psychologists experience in their practice, what do they seek consultation on and what issues with ethical components are discussed in the different professional forums? However, unlike for common ethics, more explicit codes advising practice are developed by the profession and thus serve as the standard for evaluating actual practice.

Although meant for advising and disciplining psychologists, psychologists' sectional ethics will also be a contribution to common ethics. When professional ethics is exposed outside the professional sector, both by its codifications, and when shown as a base for practice and analysis – in articles, reports, how clients are met and described in cooperative settings with other professionals and the like – it contributes to general ethical awareness. This awareness is first of all relevant for the psychologist's relationships but can often be generalized and be relevant for others to reflect on. The challenge is for psychologists to maintain the self-reference in ethical assessments and evaluations and not fall into moralizing. The psychologist is no moral expert, but strives towards an ethical application of psychological knowledge and its professional practice.

Ethics and law

One special subject matter to discuss and understand is the relationship between ethics and law. The two often apply to the same situations, may be practised concurrently and may raise similar questions. Consequently they are not always easy to keep apart. It is however important to separate the two as they have different bases for legitimisation, different coverage and should pose different challenges.

Psychologists have both legal obligations and ethical obligations. Simply put: Ethics challenges us to come to a personal, responsible decision of what is right or best to do. Law obliges us to be aware of and find what behaviour the lawmaker or law-enforcing authorities would expect in the present situation. Professional ethics, when formulated in codes, are a somewhat mixed entity. As earlier pointed out it also, like law, gives a set of norms by which actual professional behaviour can be evaluated. However, it comprises self-enforced norms which are, as we will see in later chapters, first of all formulated as guiding principles of high generality and not as specific rules for practice. The evaluation of an ethical dilemma resides with the practitioner even if it later might be re-evaluated by an ethical board after a complaint. The ethical norms laid down in professional codes might also be used for a legal evaluation of a psychologist's behaviour – for an evaluation of "good practice". It will however still be the text of the law to be enforced that has the final word – for example in withdrawing a licence, for deciding on a reimbursement of fees etc.

It is also to note, as later explained, that an ethical evaluation will often present the challenge of balancing several ethical principles, while complying with law is a more simple process of finding if the rule set by law applies to the situation or not. Most law texts strive to have a high degree of specificity.

In example 4.10. (chapter 4 on Respect), a psychologist who gets to know about a child being maltreated finds that he has the obligation by law to inform child protection authorities. His own ethical evaluation according to the ethical principles of the profession came to the same conclusion. However, the ethical evaluation adds much to his practical solution, for example how and when to inform his client. This is not specified by law but advised by the ethical principles of respect and responsibility. At other times one can come close to, or even come to an opposing ethical conclusion compared with the legal position.

Example 2.2

The client of a psychologist was a depressed man of 55, with the secondary sequels of divorce, social isolation, a drinking problem and problems with staying at work. His only daughter had been molested and killed some years ago, and that was when his life-problems all started. Now, after a period with stomach-pain his condition was diagnosed as cancer. He then came to the psychologist revealing suicidal plans. He could not bear the thoughts of going through harsh treatments and being left to be cared for by strangers. He felt he had responsibility to nobody, and would not want to be a burden on anybody. He explained how he was planning a quiet and un-dramatic exit.

The psychologist found the man's suicidal intent to be very realistic. He discussed the client's options and admitted that the client had a very strong and appealing case for his right to decide if and how he could end his life. On the other hand, as a health professional the psychologist had the legal responsibility to protect life; an obligation that gave no options. On the basis of the information the client had given, and his own evaluation of the probability of a suicidal episode, he decided to take action to submit the client to secure ward. After three weeks in a protective ward, the therapeutic relationship survived, and so did the client for half a year. The client refused life-lengthening, but accepted pain relieving treatment, and he came to reconciliation with his ex-wife.

As in this example one can easily follow the psychologist's ethical evaluation and share his appraisal of the client's appeal for the right to decide to live or not, thus respecting his right to self-determination, but at the same time this would be in conflict with the legal responsibility. Acting on a legal obligation gives high legitimacy for the decision taken. However, the ethical evaluation undertaken by the psychologist will always be important for the relationship, whether it is in line with or at variance with the legal requirement. Sometimes, like here, a differing ethical evaluation of the legal imperative might save a relationship, although the psychologist here acted on the legal obligation.

Many laws and statutory regulations can be seen as solutions to ethical dilemmas that have gone from ethical considerations to become explicit legal norms – a problem area is assessed, a proposal is raised, a democratic process is initiated and a legitimate body makes a decision and a law regulating the problem area is established. It is through a democratic process that the solution is found to what you should or not do. You just have to follow the law. If uncertain you have to get it explained to you by a person or body competent on law, and assess if it applies to the situation you are in. The moral thinking, the ethics, is done by the lawmakers, or assessed by courts and the like, you have not much to say but to obey, or oppose with the legal consequences that may come.

Say the psychologist in the above example had not acted on the client's suicidal plans and they were carried out. On ethical grounds the psychologist considered that the existential situation for the client was such that he found that no other values could be weighed in favour to intervene on the client's plans, after having given him a chance to discuss the options. The cancer specialist, or the client's ex-wife, might have charged the psychologist for not acting according to his legal obligation, and he may have been reprimanded for this, or even be punished in some ways. That does not mean that his ethical evaluation was wrong. The psychologist had however weighed ethics heavier than the legal requirement. This might in some instances be the best moral stand, but that does not free the psychologist from the consequences of not following legal demands.

Following the law instead of following a divergent ethical appraisal, can also be self-protective for the psychologist; a motive that is relevant in the legal domain, but not within ethics. While many laws and regulations have moral challenges as primary intents, others are self-protective and interest based. For example laws regulating imports and immigration are often explicitly self-protective. Professional laws also have elements of protecting the interests of the profession. In this way there is a fundamental divergence from ethics. Ethics are solely aiming at the best interests of the Other – setting the Other first. That does not mean that own interest should not also be weighed, if the behaviour and claims of the Other are too invasive and exceeding the limits and recourses at hand. In such situations laws and other protective measures are important to lean on. But use of such instruments is not part of an ethical evaluation, but might be legitimate and necessary as no one has the right to threaten or damage others.

From one point of view law can be seen as yesterday's solutions to moral problems. An ethical problem has arisen, and as pointed out, a democratic process has brought forward a decision that in the aftermath must be obeyed, also by the minority that might have been in opposition to law. This might also be said to be an ethical problem with laws enforcing behaviour and overruling interests and respect for minorities. This is for example well illustrated in the discussions and, in some countries, lawmaking that forbid girls to wear the veil at school. On other issues it might be more subtle repressive structures in laws and regulations, like on social security issues.

When a law is enacted, then the general discussions of the moral issues will usually lessen, at least for the time being, although there might be a lot of battles in court on how the law is to be understood and applied. Law is thus foremost a conservative social element and when first instituted discussions mostly go on among legal representatives and experts. Ethical evaluations are on the other hand freer and can catch the dilemmas of the here and now as well as trends for the future by discussing and assessing situations, without relying on the conservative element of the democratic and legal system, to say what is right. Ethical discussions might sometimes be about the archaic structures in laws which do not match the information and challenges of today. Such cases might result in a process that might after some time change laws that are found not to function according to new or a modern understanding of ethical dilemmas. It is for example not many years ago that homosexual practice was forbidden and punished in many European countries. It took a long time, however, from the vigorous raising of the ethical problem until laws were changed. Certainly, ethical discussions will be held about laws and legal practices of today that are discriminative when seen in the aftermath of laws being implemented. For example laws keeping immigrants for years in camps or as illegal work resources, excluding them from workers rights, education and health services, as is the practice today in many European countries, will presumably not survive without change or turmoil.

This does not mean that there are no norms in the ethical discourse. From the ethical perspective norms change and are found in the dynamic and open discourses in common ethics in a democratic society; so also in the discussions and in the formulation of the ethical codes and declarations, both general and sectional. Like law, established codes are norms but they are principles with high generality and strive to be close to universal adherence – no one should be excluded, as can be done by law-enforcement.

Two last remarks on the relationship between law and ethics. First, there can be many things that are legal, or rather, not illegal but might be unethical to do. Ethics thus helps to advise and regulate relationships to a much wider extent than law does.

Example 2.3

The psychologist coaching a group of leaders in a firm was attacked by one of the member for the way he handled the group process. The psychologist answered by giving a rather sarcastic remark and went into a more open conflict with the group-member, and the trust in the psychologist was reduced for the whole group. He did not manage to get out of it and the engagement came to an early end.

Of course, such behaviour is far from being illegal; it was, however, unethical to respond sarcastically towards a client – more to the stupid side isolating the psychologist and undermining his work.

Secondly, when a person feels he has or is given a formal legal right, the refusal or denial to fulfil this right will for most people be felt abusive. The psychologist's knowledge of the client's legal rights and behaving with respect and line with these are important to prevent strain in the professional relationship. This connects to the preventive idea in law. For example laws defining violence and abuse within the family and to be protected by society in private relationships, will heighten the acuity and reactivity when such violations happen. Through the formal formulation of a right you may be helped to understand and register when you are abused or exploited. The development and proliferation of patients' legal rights within the health-system will help psychologists' clients to be more aware of, and able to react when meeting unethical procedures and behaviour.

Ethical Dimensions

The rest of this chapter will highlight some ways or dimensions to consider in order to find the best ethical solutions. In many instances none of these will alone be adequate when faced with an ethical dilemma. It may be necessary to give differential weight in the consideration and final choice.

Ethics of intention

Ethics of intention can be seen as taking a pro-social position – to put the Other first. It means to have the best intentions and to be non-judgemental and accepting in the relationship with the Other. All ethics are based on a willingness to see and meet the Other's needs and interests, and to be committed to the Other even if it should demand to abstain from one's own needs and interests. As such, ethics of intention are a starting point for "willing to do good and best". This position will for most persons be connected to their personal ethics where attitudes and personal prejudices might jeopardise attaining a pro-social stand in all situations. But as indicated earlier, personal ethics can be seen as traits and competences that can mature and develop: for example by being critical and reflective on our social encounters and experiences. The pro-social challenge might be a question of having integrated the "right" values, virtues and characters. This will again connect to the individual's socialising and the cultural expectations of what are "right". Intentional ethics are thus not independent of the next dimension – *ethics of duty* -to be discussed later.

Professional ethics do not exist outside the person – they should be well connected with our personal ethics. Our personal ethics must therefore be scrutinised for prejudices that might hinder being able to have the pro-social, positive intentional starting point in our professional relationships. The individual psychologist's intentional ethical stand can be seen as a competence that can develop through teaching, training and collegial reflection and discussions on ethical dilemmas, so that the pro-social intentions become generalised, and well integrated in professional practice.

As indicated, ethics of intention might be seen as primary, and a premise for ethical awareness; that one has an inclination and willingness to relate moral values to one's behaviour. However, ethics of intention draw attention to the actor, not to the act or behaviour, nor to the relationship and its context. The question of intentions or moral character of the actor are thus not of much help in evaluating a dilemma. Most people will say, and probably experience, that they have the best intentions and a pro-social stand. If, however, these intentions have strong connections to norms and duties that are highly valued by the intending person, the individual "good will" can be arguments or excuses for transgressions and offence. For example a strong norm saying that children should behave respectfully in relationship to parents, might be an argument for belittling and offending a child's integrity – with the best intentions in the eyes of the offender. In professional practice "the good intentions to help" can end in becoming an ethical problem and offence.

Example 2.4

A psychologist worked in a child protection institution assessing the needs of the children and advising on placements in foster-care. After six months, a 5-year-old boy previously assessed by the psychologist came back to the institution after placement in foster-care. The foster parents had separated and neither of them wanted to go on taking care of the child. The psychologists felt very badly for the boy who already had experienced several grave rejections and traumas in his life. After discussion with his family they applied and became the foster family for the boy and he thrived. One year later the biological mother brought the child's placement into court. The psychologist's different roles came into focus in the proceedings and were attacked also by colleagues acting as witnesses. He was accused of having misused his position for his own interests. The boy was taken out of his care and brought back to a rather miserable situation with his mother and her new fiancé who was seen by the court as having a "caring potential". The boy lost all connection with the psychologist and his family.

When questions and criticisms are raised about behaviour and actions, it is not uncommon that the person whose actions are questioned responds by claiming to have had the best intentions. "I did not mean to----" is a rhetoric phrasing, or a tip of the tongue formulation that is early attained by the child and follows the person through life. By claiming the best intentions one tries to avoid rejection as well as other negative responses for the wrongdoing. When arguing with the best intentions, this is also an appeal for forgiveness that tries to divert the awareness from the wrong to the intended good.

When evaluating complaints for the Board of Ethics it was this author's experience that psychologists in response to the filed complaints often stated: "*It was absolutely not my intention ---*". It is, of course, not possible to argue against a person's intentions, or for that sake, to question them. In the aftermath the intention was a totally private, and bygone, state of the act. For ethical evaluations the claim for having had the best intentions does not help much as it will be unassessable by others. A statement of positive intentions can rather be seen as a manipulative act to divert the attention from the negative effects of the behaviour to a question of forgiveness – the offender or missdoer is issuing an appeal to the injured party.

Strong engagement, out of the best intentions, can as already pointed out, end in a process of transgression, which sets others aside who might have more legitimate qualifications to give support and care. In voluntary work, but also in professional practice, one can sometimes question whether or not helpers have a special purpose in demonstrating their good intentions. The helping project is a project for the helper also and showing off may be an important part of the motivation and dynamics. Helpers may promote themselves by their "best" intentions. In such instances the ego-related motivation may come to create unhealthy dependencies and cover up misuse of power; and "the best intentions" become a source of unethical practice. The best intention project alone can become a paternalistic position: *This is for your best interest!* If not the psychologist, many consigning instances may have this attitude to primary clients; either it is in contracting for the psychologist's assistance in reorganizing a workplace, or in referring a client for psychotherapy. For the psychologist it is important to try to communicate with the parties and to analyse ones own motives, so that the best intentions of others do not come patronize the individual client.

Paradoxically, the idea of *"having the best intentions and interests of the client"* in mind can foster distance from the client. One can come to oversee needs, feelings and the intentions of the individual and the professional position can even become cynical. It is often astonishing to register that personnel in institutions, especially when they are to administer restrictions in client's freedom, can come to develop degrading attitudes and illegitimate limitations on top of the legal restrictions they are to uphold. The whole staff can lose their ability to react on moral misbehaviour from colleagues. Lobotomy, sterilizing, isolation of disabled people etc, have been upheld in the not so distant past as being "in the best interests" of the individuals abused.

This discussion should show that the best intentions do not help the psychologist much in ethical assessment and evaluations. Quite the contrary: this approach can grow into an unethical position. On the other hand, having a pro-social and open mind to the needs of others can be seen as a prerequisite for being able to behave ethically. It will, however, require communication and other guiding principles to find the ethically best solutions.

Ethics of duty – ethics of nature

One widespread and central way of looking at ethics is the claim that there are some universal principles for human relationships that are mandatory for the individual to comply with. These principles have the status of being imperative in their conceptuali-sation: *you should/must/ought – should/must/ought not –* much in line with how laws and regulations are formulated. However, different from legal regulations which are democratically decided, the ethics of duty, or of nature, are seen as embedded in the human condition, and as such above humans to decide on. In religious contexts such principles are seen as given by God. In a more humanistic context, many of the same principles are seen as knowledge based implications. When reflecting on, and getting more knowledge about the human function and existence, our relationships and de-pendencies to our environmental context, some ethical issues and imperatives arise. As such they are given by nature and may also be called an *ethics by nature*. Such princi-ples of duty or of nature are formulated in religious texts, in the Koran and the Bible for example, in UN declarations and in different ethical codes. The Meta-code has some formulations of this character. For example: in the first principle of respect: *"The psychologist accords appropriate respect to, and promotes the development of fundamental rights, dignity and worth of all people".* As we see, there is no option, psychologists just behave in this way, and it is a fundamental duty to do so.

The human condition and our natural human premises can be said to be the base for an ethics of duty. Our common destiny and dependencies will demand and appeal to the individual to make efforts so that the necessary community and loyalties can be upheld, without which the individual will not be able to exist. There is a need for a basic human solidarity and this basic premise of human nature implies social duties from the individual. If you refuse to act on the appeals of others you lose your moral right to make appeals to others when you are in need; a position every human being will encounter.

While ethics of duty were earlier formulated by religious texts, the more modern versions are motivated by knowledge, understanding and a claim for respect for the "natural" preconditions for human life. They can also be seen as based on an eco-logical understanding of the individual human being. As such the ethical principles of duty can be argued by empirically derived information and a rational approach to human and inter-human phenomena and ecology. Acquired psychological knowl-edge about what conditions are necessary for healthy human development, for ex-ample by secure attachments, can be seen as information supporting an ethics of duties towards children and how they should be respected and treated.

Ethics of duty or of nature and derived principles will claim to be universal, but will also be under debate for their implications, interpretations, range of validity and application in different times and under different conditions. For example there is much debate and many disputes and conflicts within and between religious groups and traditions on how to apply imperative texts of duty within the context of modern living. So also are discussions on humanistic or secular principles of human rights challenged by different interpretations and contextual conditions. Globalisation and secularisation have fostered declarations and codes to secure reciprocal respect and care cross-culturally. At the same time this confronts traditional principles of duties embedded in local cultures and religions. What is seen as universal can be very different seen form differing local perspectives. One should always be careful when postulating anything to be universal.

As discussed earlier in this chapter on common ethics and on the relation between ethics and law, ethics of duties are often central in the discourse and disclose varying perspectives on how the guiding principles and the consequent duties should be understood and applied.

In modern media, single cases and events are often exposed in relation to how ethics of duty have been neglected or challenged. This often creates important discussions on values issues and how duties and responsibility for the individual's dignity are managed in the case that has been publicised, for example on issues including ethnicity, sex, childhood, immigration and the like. However, the problem with exposing ethical issues primarily by single cases, as the media often does, is that this can come into conflict with an approach to the same issue based on solidarity and may hide or repress group interests. Ethics of duty can become an overriding dimension that focuses on the single event. Many people can become occupied with the one media-exposed child victim of war, while the other children's faces in the shadow of that exposure are never recognized.

Ethics of duty are in modern discourses very much related to the rights and dignity of the single individual, and as such the multi-relational characteristics of human nature can become undervalued. Ethics of duty have a rather absolute character. However, if taken too literally other perspectives and valued interests can be set aside, and following only one "duty" might end in an unethical position. For example, as will be shown in later examples and discussion, there might be a tension between respecting the individual's freedom to choose and the protection of others. Therefore, all duties have their practical and timely domain of validity. If taken only on its intentional and aspirational level, and not evaluated on the practical level, ethics of duty, as with ethics of intentions, will lose their value as practical ethical guidance.

While ethics of nature have their motivation in scientific "truths", discussions will also arise on what these facts are. While religious and tradition based duties must be discussed and implemented according to the stage of development of the relevant society, so also will knowledge based principles be discussed according to the actual knowledge base available. Such discussions of the validity of ethics of duty or ethics of nature are embedded in what earlier in this chapter was named as the general discourse on common ethics.

Ethics of consequence and utility

An important corrective to the ethics of duty and nature is what might be called *ethics of consequence*. What are the possible or expected consequences of our professional acts and interventions? First of all we might think of what are the possible negative effects. From the age of Hippocrates, *primo non noccere – "First of all do no harm"* – is an old and primary principle in the ethical code of medicine. It has since been used as a principle of attention and vigilance in most professions, so also included in the Meta-code for psychologists. A proactive analysis of possible negative effects should also be central in psychologists' practice.

It is, however, a principle that can be misconceived as a principle of self-protection. As ethical guidance, ethics of consequence refer to the effects for the Other, not for the actor (psychologist). In professional contexts it is sometimes observed that the intention to be cautious is understood as: "I must see that I am not criticized". Being in a professional role, includes the possibility of being criticised, complained about and even sued, and this can lead one to an approach influenced or even driven by self-protection. This is not an ethical position, quite the contrary; it can lead to an unethical position if safeguarding oneself is the main motive in the thinking of possible consequences. In such a situation one will not be able utilize one's full potential as a professional in the interests of the client, as one's own safety is put first.

Example 2.5

"I try to avoid clients that are, or might be involved in legal matters. Then I don't do any harm. I hate being summoned as a witness and to appear in court. You never know, people like that might also one day sue yourself."

This statement from a colleague in a seminar on ethics raised a heated discussion on the balancing of the responsibility for clients against the interests of the psychologist: avoiding tasks that might be unpleasant for the psychologist. Avoidance, and not acting, can be unethical if you had the potential to act in a way that might enhance the wellbeing or reduce harm to the Other.

As ethical guidance, ethics of consequence are concerned with the optimisation of the utility and positive effects of the relationship and having awareness of, and acting to limit the possible negative effects for the Other. For the psychologist this means the client. It is of course legitimate also to be aware of the possible consequences for oneself in the assessment; it is the weighing of utility or negative effects and who is given priority that is the ethical issue. An important turning-point in the balancing of consequences and interests is when there is a threat to your personal integrity and legitimate position that might undermine your ability to uphold a professional role. For example by being threatened, or getting sick or burned out by the workload in the professional relationship. Sometimes however, taking risks and accepting personal strain can be part of acting on an assessment of consequence.

Example 2.6

During a family-therapy session a young girl discloses that her father had abused her friend during an over-night stay with the family. This had happened during one of the father's drinking periods and had become an unmentionable event within the family until now it was revealed. The girl was afraid that her friend should tell other friends about her father's drinking and what had happened. When the psychologist asks the parents what they feel they must do now that the story is out in the open, both parents say that nothing more needs to be done. The mother says she has talked with the child and told her that the father regretted very much what happened and that they all should forget about the incident. If anything more should be done they would sort it out them-selves. The psychologist then says that she has both a legal, and an ethical obligation to inform the appropriate authorities when having knowledge about a child being abused and under possible pressure. The parents strongly protest and claim to be pro-tected by the psychologist's confidentiality.

After some discussion the psychologist informs the child protection authorities. The abused child confirms the information disclosed and is protected from further contact with the family. Legal processes are started against the father and complaints about the psychologist's actions are filed. The psychologist is also for some time disturbed by nightly telephone calls with only breathing on the line.

The primary concern for the psychologist was to protect the probably maltreated girl from being threatened and possibly becoming re-victimised. This girl became an ethically relevant *"Third Face"* (see later discussions) in danger of negative conse-quences if the psychologist did not act. The total consequences of the psychologist's action were extensive: The family went into a crisis, the child protection authorities acted on two families, the father was jailed, the therapeutic relationship was broken, the psychologist was charged with breaking professional confidentiality, and the alleged abused girl was forced to disclose an experience she had until now kept se-cret. The parents of the girl reacted towards the psychologist claiming that their right to self-determination and confidentiality was broken. If, however, the psychologist had refrained from acting on the information, the alleged abused girl might have been further repressed and victimised by the abuser and his family. Giving ethical priority to the possible negative consequences for the abused girl did however have dramatic outcomes for others in the client-system and was an unpleasant process for the psychologist.

Ethics of consequence does not only address being attentive to minimize negative consequences. The primary goal of all professional practice is the expectation that it should have some positive consequence or useful effect for the client. For psychologists, their practice should be some scientifically describable effect. Utilitarian anticipations are thus implicit in professional practice. Some kind of evidence for positive effects is demanded and anticipated by clients, employers and assigners of contracts. The question then also arises – who is it to define what is useful, and for whom?

The first part of this question can be said to be scientific – are scientific established theory and methods available and valid for the effect sought and observed? When trying to answer this part it is important to keep in mind that scientific answers are always contestable as this is a key hallmark of scientific process. So also is the professional use of scientific evidence, an ability to understand the uncertainty in all scientific answers, to be critical to the answers and still to endure this and be able to apply the uncertain answers to solve practical problems and challenges. To maintain this professional stand can be difficult as professional methods and even scientific theories and "schools" are branded and marketed often with economic interests connected to the professional application and dissemination. To be critical of the understanding and the limits for generalisation of the effects and consequences observed is the responsibility of the professional and of the professional community.

The second part of defining utility or negative consequences is not a scientific question, however, but rather a question of values that must be assessed in the relationships of the individual involved. For example, can the relationship between a psychologist and client be valued highly by the client although no "objective" effect can be observed. No change, or stability, or even just an understanding human encounter at the right moment, can be valued as part of a professional practice. For the psychologist, it is however important that practices that are more open to what the outcomes may be and where the client has the most to say on the value of interacting with the psychologist, still have a scientific base.

In using ethics of consequence as guidance it may be important to separate the concept of utility from the concept of productivity. The latter may be of most interest to employers, funding agencies and governmental planning of services, while the first comes closer to assessing the usefulness, the good, for the individual client. It can come to a conflict between utility and productivity. While productivity is often seen in short-term and directly observable effects, utility may be seen in a more long-term and developmental perspective and the two can foster different and conflicting theories and practices.

A further question may be whether the observed or valued effects come about and whether they should be attributed to the privileged knowledge of the psychologist's interventions, or be attributed to the client's competence to make sense and use of the psychologist's expertise. It is not without ethical relevance how effects are explained. Psychologists (as other humans!) will have a tendency to attribute failure in getting results and obtaining negative effects to a lack of motivation, special personality traits in the client, or by other external factors. Similarly, positive results and successes are described as being in line with and attributed to the psychologist's theory, interventions and competence., What kind of evaluation of utility and evidence is this from an ethical perspective? It can be that it is the ethical qualities in the relationship between the psychologist and clients that are significant for the client in making use of the psychologist's competence. The question of utility is thus connected to how the effects are explained, and explaining is part of the power issue between client and psychologist. Thus, to optimise the ethical qualities of the relationship – high ethical awareness in general – might be an important way of fostering utility and avoiding negative consequences in professional practice.

A final point, however, even if the psychologist lets the client set goals, make priorities and evaluate outcomes, the responsibility for the process will reside with the psychologist. It is for the psychologist to see to that the approach to the problem and the goals set are reachable and within with the methods and competence of the psychologist; so also must the psychologist assess and explain limitations and possible negative outcomes. The practice must always be in a frame that can be supported by professional experience, evidence-based theory and ethical responsibility.

Ethics of procedure

Justice and what is fair are central issues in ethics. This is very often a question of distribution; how resources, goods, rights, needs and freedom to choose are distributed. Avoiding discrimination is important, but sometimes positive action or even discrimination is seen as fair, due to the lack of other opportunities – for example a exclusive parking-zone for disabled close to the entrance of a building, or a priority for immigrants for certain employment in governmental institutions. Both are processes which are carried out in some countries to bring about more equality on areas that have been closed or limited for some groups. Questions of justice are often central in political issues and debates – how resources and degrees of freedom should be distributed. It is typical for addressing such questions, either by democratic or bureaucratic process, that solutions are found in setting up some kind of fixed procedure for how the just distribution, or positive discriminations should be implemented.

Ethics of procedure can be relevant consideration when a special procedure based on specific criteria and rules is set up to reach what is seen as a fair reaction or a just distribution of goods that are limited or unevenly allocated. They are also relevant to procedures for exploring how positive effects might or should be enhanced and negative effects reduced. Ethics of procedure often have a base in ethics of duty or of consequence, and ethics of procedure is a method for reaching and upholding these values. One chooses to conform to a norm for behaviour solving an ethical challenge. As such it becomes an ethical method much in line with laws and legal regulations. There is however an important difference. While legal regulations have their legitimate basis in democratic representative decisions, ethics of procedure do not have such a base.

The basis comprises the norms set up by the practitioners themselves to solve ethical challenges. Surgeons, for example, will have some standard procedures do avoid accidental complications and the surgeons will have to bear the responsibility themselves for these procedures. It is the professional personally that must choose to comply in the specific situation. It is typical for professional practice where procedures are well developed that they relate to situations where the Other in the relationship is passive or has little opportunity to contribute – a comatose patient, an air flight passenger, a client tested and the like; the responsibility for what is to happen lies in the hands of the professional alone. If the client was invited to influence what should happen one would be unsure how the result would come out and how it should be interpreted. Uncertainty of outcome is reduced by not involving the client, and is for the interest of the client. *"Do not disturb the driver!* is the mantra.

The idea and expectations behind procedural ethics are that if over time and situations we meticulously follow a specified procedure this will us lead to obtain the best results. By extensive use of procedures for practice and interactions one does not have to rely on the single practitioner's creativity or imperfection, only on the practitioner's compliance with the procedure. There might, however, also be built into the procedure guidance on how to react if the unexpected situation arises The "human factor" is minimised.

As ethical solutions, procedures and rules will always be relative and must be argued and defensible in the specific situation in comparison with other ways of solving a dilemma. If one becomes used to solve challenges by procedures it can become a habit and the procedure gets its intrinsic value. However, one might lose the connection to the necessary values by developing the procedure. Our tendency to engage in repetitive, conservative and "safe" behaviours can be strong elements in procedural ethics. This means that we must have a double perspective when applying procedural solutions. One must both follow the procedure and at the same time be critical to its application and its consequences in the actual situation. For example, evaluate if there might be vicarious or self-protective elements dominating in applying the procedure. Although the responsibility for professional practice will always stay with the individual psychologist, using standardised practices can become a comfortable way to practise, a manner of avoiding personal responsibility by seeking safety within a generally accepted procedure.

One argument for using procedures for practice is the need for scientific and evidential support for theories and methods. This has been a steady argument within psychological professional practice in recent years when different funding agencies, especially the American MediCare system, have been setting criteria for the funding. Governmental institutions, insurance companies and other large firms with bureaucratic structure often use psychologists' expertise, contracting for larger or more limited tasks, assessments and interventions. The product delivered by the psychologist will often be part of procedures set up the contracting agency. One ethical quandary for the psychologist is to reflect on how ones own contribution fits into the total procedure in an ethical acceptable way. Consider the following example:

Example 2.7

A student with dyslexic problems applied to the national social security for a scholarship making it possible to have reading support and if necessary to extend the stipulated standard time for completing the curriculum for which she had been accepted. The student had excellent grades form the sixth-form college where she had been supported by special teaching programs. She had by good margins passed the inclusion criteria for the course. The social security office demanded that before evaluating her application she had to be tested by a psychologist to prove her intellectual capacity to cope with the curriculum. She felt offended as for a time she had felt misconceived as mentally retarded, being wrongly assessed by a school-psychologist when she was in her second grade. She hoped that the new psychologist would write a recommendation based on the diagnostic information about her dyslexia and her study-success so far. The psychologist, however, insisted on taking a full intellectual assessment as this was what he was asked to do and argued that this was standard procedures in such cases. The student felt herself to be discriminated against by the procedure and let herself be interviewed on the national television and she later complained to the ethical board for psychologists. The board found that the psychologist would have enough documentation to conclude that she had the capacity to manage further studies but that she would be in need for special support for the dyslexic problem. Further assessment of intellectual capacity could be seen as unnecessary, and understandably it might be experienced as unfair as other students who entered the course would not have to be tested. The student got her scholarship and the procedures with obligatory psychological assessment were changed.

This example shows that procedures that might have a general positive goal to secure that those in most need should receive proper support, might be inappropriate in specific cases. This is not an unusual contradiction in using procedures. It demands that when such an incongruity arises there is a sound assessment as to what ethical dilemmas are at stake. What in the next section is called *ethics by proxy* will be an important supplement when such situations arise.

Dialogical/proximal ethics[7]

It can be difficult to establish and maintain a dialogical connectedness with the client, and at the same to uphold a competing professional and scientific perspective on the client's behaviour, thoughts end feelings. The first perspective demands being in an interactive process with the client, the second require a detached position. The easiest

---

[7] The author has coined this *ethics of dialogue* (Øvreeide 2002) meaning that a central place for sorting out ethical issues and dilemmas is in the dialogical, dyadic process between people; between psychologist and client. This will also expose the multi-relational nature of the individual, both client and psychologist, further discussed in the text.

way is to take on the position of distance and to give answers and interventions that are based on psychological interpretations and explanations. This however, isolates the client as an object for the psychologist's study and interventions. However, the ethical position in a relationship requires letting the Other maintain the position of being a self-organised and self-determining subject in the relationship to the greatest extent possible. This means that to place the Other solely as an object in the relationship will be unethical In an ethical frame of relationships, the understanding and responsibility points to the individual and his actions in the person to person interaction. In this frame both are on the same human level; it is a question of how one reacts and respect the Other in the human encounter.

Dialogical ethics, or ethics of proximity, can be relevant when one tries to find the *right* or *best* choice in the actual and unique encounter. One can always see the human encounter as dialogically organised. It is through dialogue that distance and closeness and inter-subjectivity and mutual understanding are developed. This view looks at ethics in the actual closeness and dialogue that will develop in any relationship. This process will influence and determine what is *right* or *best* , because it is here, in the process of the relationship that needs, states of mind, initiatives, meanings and responses can and will be exposed, hidden or distorted; accepted or refused. A central philosophical perspective for this way of looking at ethics is that of Levinas (Levinas 1981 Bauman 1993) stating that in the human encounter *the Face of the Other* can not refrain to express itself: to convey an appeal in the human encounter. This encounter is characterized by mutual appeals; as feelings and sentiments exposed and reacted to by each other's face.

According to this view, it is the interaction and development of meanings in the relationship that can foster a mutual understanding of the demands and needs exposed; as well as misunderstandings and rejection. The point of departure and challenge for ethical behaviour is thus to come into an interaction that assesses the needs and states of the Other through the proximity of dialogue, face to face. Such an encounter and searching dialogue is not possible without mutual trust and safety. It is only within a trusting and non-rejecting relationship that one can expose oneself. This means that one cannot abstain from entering the emotional, not always understandable in a rational sense, emotional experience that all human encounters entail. In this process in which both parties will react on each other's emotional expressions. Trust is thus not something that can be demanded or given as a permanent state, but rather something that must be developed and upheld all the way during the interaction. The mutual trust will always be tested in the actual dialogue. *"Can I dare to expose myself?* – is a question permanently embedded in the exchange. If you try to control the Other's expressions this will be contrary to the goal of the dialogue. An open dialogue demands that the Other is respected as a self-organized actor, with the right to freely choose and form their own initiatives and reactions.

When ethics are seen like this, one can never know if one's initiative or action was ethically proper, until the Other has presented a reaction. However, as mentioned, openness must be based on mutual trust because being open and authentic also implies being vulnerable. Trust can only be achieved if being open is not exploited. Hidden power issues and dependencies are the most central threats to authentic self-exposure and unethical practice. Assessing and communicating about power elements in the relationship are therefore important for reaching sound and supportive ethical practice in any relationship.

At first glance, a proximal perspective on ethics can seem individualistic in its suggestions for solutions to challenges; *"what is good for us is right"*. If, however we look closer at what is implied in being open and authentic it will first of all be to expose one's dependencies and responsibilities to others. We are all in multi-relationships and the Third Faces, meaning our obligations in other relationships will enter and make demands in the actual relationship and its dialogical process. Shame, guilt, feelings of attachment, loyalty, love and responsibility all point to relevant third Faces in our encounter with the actual Other. The proximal perspective will thus reveal our multi-relationship identities and lives.

An individualistic or non-dialogical perspective on ethics can be seen as a distancing from the reality of our having many relationships that count in our lives. However, a proximal view on ethics confirms the responsibilities that also are relevant in the relationships to third persons. For example, if you listen to a leader complaining about his employees, the indirect appeal from them, the uneasiness that these people are not heard, will be part of the actual relationship and consultation. The depressed mother who feels worthless for her children will expose an appeal from her children.

Such indirectly exposed appeals from Third Faces can lead to moralizing and communicative problems in the dyadic process. *"What do you think your mother would say!!"* can be a representative phrase for this position that can arise. In this way we always meet our own, or the Other's others in the dyadic dialogue. One can say that dialogue is dyadic in process but triadic in consequence. What I do and expose in one relationship will be of relevance for other relationships of mine. This is the ethical challenge that the proximal ethical perspective helps us to uphold. It exposes the often experienced doubt and ambivalence in who should be given priority and how support should be weighed, handled and distributed. The psychologist who privatizes the relationship with a client will expose his disrespect for colleagues and undermine other clients' general trust in psychologists; but most of all it can hurt and damage other important relationships for the client.

Responsibility always follows the relationships we enter, so too is this clearly relevant in professional relationships where the roles, status and dependencies are clearly different. Therefore there will always be a need to find out what is the relevant responsibility to take that the relationship demands of the professional. The dialogue within the relationship, including the most relevant Third Faces, can uncover resources, contradictions, conflicting issues, needs and dependencies which are not obvious form outside the relation.

A proximal or dialogical ethical perspective can help to be attentive to the following concerns:

- *The unique* character of both who is encountered and the situation in which the encounter occurs, and the distinctive emotional appearance of the encounter. This is an important corrective to standardised classifications and methods that are part of a scientific approach to human phenomena. Encounters that imply, for example, diagnosing human behaviour, can be seen as unethical if simultaneously space is not given for the ones diagnosed to present themselves on their own conditions. All kinds of objectifying and generalising of the individual will entail an unethical potential that might reduce the unique humanity of the individual.
- *The basic human appeal;* a mutual need for respect and care where the most independent in the relationship will ethically be the most challenged. That person will have the greatest degree of freedom to choose to follow the appeal. For the more dependent, compliance or rejection will be the alternatives. An appeal and its response can only be issued individually – *from me to you, – I want, – I respond.* The appeal cannot be avoided, or avoiding it is also a response with its own consequence for the relationship. In the perspective of proximal ethics one can say that the appealing individual and the one to whom the appeal is issued, are bound in a joint destiny, both being in need for human relationships and thus in need for ethics for these relationships.
- *Dialogue* is the means for providing the possibility the relationship has to sort out needs, resources, values, and obligations that are relevant in the relationship. So also expectations and consequences for third parties to which the two in interaction have relationships. Dialogue gives the individual a legitimate space to express individuality and uniqueness. Dialogue underlines that authentic information about oneself, not catchable by the Other's observation, can only be expressed by oneself in a trusting relationship.
- *Power and responsibility* differences are central in relationships. In a professional relationship the most power and thereby responsibility will be with the professional. Through dialogue the power-issues can be exposed and sorted so that both parties can express themselves in understandable ways within a shared meaning of the contextual limitations and options. In this process appeals from relevant Third Faces will become visible as important elements of the context of the relationship and must be brought into the ethical assessments that the professional must undertake.

Concluding Remarks

This chapter presents a discussion of the broader ethical discourses that underlie the formulation of any ethical code. The basis in moral philosophy, common and personal ethics, sector and professional ethics are all relevant. Also, in all countries, there must be a relationship – perhaps and preferable a tension – between professional ethics and national laws. Finally, a series of ethical dimensions have been explored. These demonstrate the complexity of the exercise but also the importance of ethical *thinking*. Codes, and in the present case the Meta-code, are important but there is, fundamentally, a need also to consider the different issues discussed here. Hence, although our main focus in the book is on the Meta-code we are committed to psychologists addressing ethical concerns, challenges and dilemmas by a combination specific, codified guidance – in this case the Meta-code – and reflection on basic principles and the broader range of ethical concerns that are provided in this chapter.

Chapter 3

Introduction to the Ethical Principles – Content of the Code

Haldor Øvreeide and Geoff Lindsay

The four main principles and their accompanying specifications will be discussed in the following chapters. There are, however, some important introductory statements, before the principles of the Meta-code are described. They can be found after the Preamble, which we discuss first, under the headings *Preamble* and *Content of the ethical codes of member Associations*. These are important qualifying texts that are worth reflecting on before looking at the principles. The Preamble sets the scene by focussing on psychologists and their professional role. The respective roles of the European Federation of Psychologists Associations (EFPA) and the national associations is then explained with reference to ethical codes and the promotion of ethical behaviour by psychologists. The following introductory clauses underscore the importance of being proactive as well as reactive, in the ethical reflection on practice. Also highlighted is the frequent need to balance principles in order to build the best daily practice, as well as for solving more challenging dilemmas. This chapter on the introductory text gives guidance on how the principles and their more detailed specifications relate to practical situations that need to be evaluated. Knowledge of this introductory text is important in order to consider dilemmas and weigh differences and conflicts of interests, and so supporting ethical problem-solving.

First, the Meta-code is not written as a code for psychologists as such as is the case with national codes. Rather, the Meta-code was developed to provide guidance to psychological associations rather than individuals. As discussed in chapter 1, the Meta-code's purpose was to assist each national association to develop its own code. However experience has shown that many psychologists have found the Meta-code useful in guiding their practice. Second, it should be noted that the wording of the code is not in the form of *psychologists should* and *must*. On the contrary, it is phrased like *psychologists accord to, are aware of, respect, are obliged to,* and the like. The Meta-code, and the derived national codes, are therefore not to be seen as a set of fixed rules for psychologists' behaviour. As also pointed out in the Preamble, they are norms for professional practice. Consequently, should primarily be understood as texts for consultation and as references for practice and science within the collegial society of European psychologists. In addition, the Meta-code is an explication of what society, clients and authorities can expect as best professional practice of psychology.

According to the text in the Meta-code, professional practice is based on the expectation that the individual psychologist is: *conscious of, adheres to,* and, *weighs* the values, both explicit and implicit, in the text of the codes. Behaving ethically therefore is to be in an *active* process, engaging with the ethical principles and specifications. It is thus expected that a psychologist's practice includes ethical reflections to guide that practice, to be in accordance with these basic principles. If not, an explanation of the deviation might be demanded from the psychologist by clients, colleagues and relevant third parties. If such deviation from one or more of the principles cannot be defended on the basis of other legitimate values and ethical principles, the behaviour which is not in accordance with the principles of the code will be seen as an unethical practice.

The Preamble to the Meta-code

The Preamble to the Meta-code comprises seven paragraphs that "set the scene" but have different foci. The first paragraph specifies the range of practice of psychologists:

Psychologists develop a valid and reliable body of knowledge based on research and apply that knowledge to psychological processes and human behaviour in a variety of contexts. In doing so they perform many roles, within such fields as research, education, assessment, therapy, consultancy, and as expert witness to name a few.

As noted earlier in chapter 1, this range is unusual but central to the nature of psychology. There is a need, therefore, to have ethics guidance that covers the wider variation of practice both in science (research and teaching) and also within the various fields of professional practice.

The second paragraph is aspirational:

They also strive to help the public in developing informed judgements and choices regarding human behaviour, and aspire to use their privileged knowledge to improve the condition of both the individual and society.

Here the focus is not only on individual clients but society as a whole. This juxtaposition of concern for the individual and society in general is a central feature of psychology. Furthermore, implicit here is also the notion of "giving psychology away", of empowering others with whom the psychologist has a professional engagement. Psychological practice is not just about an expert (psychologist) telling or supporting a non-expert (lay client). Rather the nature of psychology is an engagement with other persons – e.g., clients, students, society as a whole – often referred to in this book as The Other. Note also, however, the recognition that psychologists have privileged knowledge by virtue of their expertise. Hence, psychologists recognise that any collaborative exercise is not equal – they will typically have greater knowledge in one sense (although not of an individual's personal knowledge). The main issue is that with this comes the need to take on greater responsibility.

Paragraph 3 is an administrative statement about EFPA:

The European Federation of Psychologists Associations has a responsibility to ensure that the ethical codes of its member associations are in accord with the following fundamental principles which are intended to provide a general philosophy and guidance to cover all situations encountered by professional psychologists.

This sets out the status of the Meta-code. It is to be the template and all member associations should match their codes to it. Not also the reference to "all situations" again stressing the universality of the Meta-code for all areas of practice. Recall, as explained in chapter 1, that the original purpose of the Meta-code was to guide national psychological associations when they devised or revised their ethical codes. This paragraph , therefore, is on limited relevance to this book where we are presenting guidance mainly to individual psychologists. Nevertheless, it is important to note the implicit pan-European nature of the Meta-code as its sphere of influence is specified as all psychological association members of EFPA, and hence all European psychologists who are members of associations that are themselves members of EFPA.

Paragraph 4 specifies the responsibility of national associations:

National Associations should require their members to continue to develop their awareness of ethical issues, and promote training to ensure this occurs. National Associations should provide consultation and support to members on ethical issues.

This paragraph has at its heart the need for continuing professional development (CPD) – see also chapter 5. There is a joint responsibility here: national associations should have procedures that require members to develop their awareness of ethical issues as well as psychologists needing to undertake this development. Further, national associations should be proactive in providing support for members. Some such as the Netherlands association (NIP) have a long history of providing such consultation whereas for other associations this is a developing area.

Paragraphs 5 and 6 specify the relationship between the Meta-code and national codes. Paragraph 5 specifies the comprehensiveness required of the national association's code:

The EFPA provides the following guidance for the content of the Ethical Codes of its member Associations. An Association's ethical code should cover all aspects of the professional behaviour of its members. The guidance on Content of Ethical Codes should be read in conjunction with the Ethical Principles.

Paragraph 6 specifies the nature of conformity required:

The Ethical Codes of member Associations should be based upon – and certainly not in conflict with – the Ethical Principles specified below.

This formulation allows national associations to develop their own codes with a certain freedom. The order of clauses for example and the amount of explication or differentiation may vary to meet local circumstances. Nevertheless, ultimately the national code must "be based upon" the Meta-code and not in conflict with the Ethical Principles.

Finally, the Preamble links the Meta-code of Ethics to other procedures:

National Associations should have procedures to investigate and decide upon complaints against members, and mediation, corrective and disciplinary procedures to determine the action necessary taking into account the nature and seriousness of the complaint.

We discuss these issues in chapter 9. However, it is important to state at the outset that our interest is primarily in education and hence the avoidance of ethical transgressions. We shall provide information and discuss the issues concerned "When things go wrong" in chapter 9. However, we strongly believe that the primary purpose is to try to prevent complaints about alleged unethical behaviour by supporting psychologists in their practice.

In the rest of this chapter we address several aspects of ethical codes that cut across the four Principles that are covered in chapters 4 to 7. These include the sometimes tricky issue of defining the client; the importance of recognising that psychological practice is embedded in relationships; the importance of recognising unequal power relationships, their impact on the professional relationship and the necessary responsibility on the psychologist as a result; and the relevance of the stage of the professional relationship. Finally, we also consider the inter-relationship of the four Principles. It is very easy to fall into the trap of taking into account guidance on one principle alone, that which seems the "obviously" relevant. However, as we argue below, this is a mistake as very often, indeed in most if not all cases, there are inter-relationships such that it is important both to consider the separate principles *and*, very importantly, consider how they relate: which, if any, should be given the most weight, for example.

Defining the Client

In the following Meta-Code the term "client" refers to any person, patients, persons in interdependence or organisations with whom psychologists have a professional relationship, including indirect relationships.

Usually, more than one person is included, engaged in and/or affected by a psychologist's work assignment. Dependencies, attachments and responsibilities will often be unequally distributed between the persons with whom the psychologist interacts in any particular case. It is therefore not always obvious who the client is. This definition in the Meta-code of who is the client is important for finding who might be relevant to include as having the status of being a client, and thus to whom the psychologist will have ethical obligations.

It is essential to note that, although the client might be a system or group, the ethical challenge always concerns the individual – *"any person"*. The single human being is always the subject in ethical evaluations, but there can be more than one. This means that psychologists can have several persons in the client-system with whom they interact and must always look to obligations that might apply to any person involved or affected by their work, as these obligations might differ (as shown in example 3.1 below).

The person that gives the assignment to the psychologist might not be the one with whom the psychologist has the most direct professional interaction. For example in organisational psychology, in forensic work, in child protection, occupational psychology and in many more areas of psychological practice, third parties may contract the psychologist, or receive the results of assessments, or expect the effects of the interventions. In such cases the psychologist's relationships will comprise rather extended and complex systems with individuals holding different types of "client" status, direct and indirect.

Even if the client-system is extensive, the obligations to the persons concerned and the consequences for each can be clarified. Thus confidentiality, informed consent and self-determination, as well as competence and responsibility can be sorted out with the persons involved. The contextual frames, and legitimate roles and contracts will form an important basis for the psychologist when trying to find what obligation applies to the different persons involved.

Sorting by primary and secondary clients in the client-system might a way of conceptualizing when analysing relevant obligations. In clinical, as well as in more general consultation work, there will often be a referring person, colleagues, next of kin and others involved, even if it is the best interests of a single, individual client is the target for the psychologist's work. This person can be said to be the *primary client*, and be the person whose interests will be most central for the psychologist to attend to: for keeping the information confidential, for expanding the freedom of consent etc. The primary person's rights in the relationship to the psychologist will be supported by the ethical principles, as will be discussed by many examples in the following chapters.

But often, for example in working with children, the psychologist will interact with more than one person both in the natural network of the primary person, as well as in the formal helping systems around the primary client. Interventions targeted for change in these person's relationships with the primary client might be necessary for the wellbeing and development of the primary client. These persons who might be affected in this way can be seen as *secondary clients*, to whom the psychologist also clearly will have ethical obligations. For example, it is normally the case that a child does not self refer. In such cases, the parent may engage the psychologist on the child's behalf. There is, therefore, a client relationship with the parent because of their role as *agent*. Furthermore, in this case, the parent is typically not just a neutral agent but actively and intimately concerned with the child's well being. The parent may also be judged by the psychologist to be a key person to contribute to action to support the child's development. In doing so, the parent will also benefit in fulfilling a role closely connected to identity and life-satisfaction.

There are however some instances where identifying who is the primary client, and the weighing of different interests are less obvious and might change during the working process. Consider the following example:

Example 3.1

A psychologist gives regular consultation to a young woman in charge of a preschool community project. On one occasion, while consulting on a specific child, the woman suddenly starts to cry and asks if, under strict confidentiality, she can confide a personal issue and challenge. The psychologist accepts, thinking that it might be linked to some impasse in the case being discussed.

The woman reports that for five years she had a sexual relationship with the charismatic principal of the church she attends. He was married and the relationship started when she was just under the age of 15. He terminated the affair when she was 20. She then went into a depression, had a lot of agony and periods with suicidal thoughts but gradually regained her balance. She had never before told anybody about what happened.

Her distress now is that she suspects the principal is having a similar relationship with a 14-year-old girl in the congregation. She knows the girl very well, had spied on them and had heard through the door that they had sex. She now asks the psychologist for advice.

There seems not to be a direct impasse related to the actual case that led to this consultation. The woman had gained trust in the psychologist and this had given her the opportunity to come out with her anguish. When accepting, the psychologist had entered a new professional relationship with the woman, shifting from a work issue, to a personal issue.

Such shifts in focus as in this example are rather common in psychological practice, but it is extremely important to be aware when such shifts are made, as they call for changes in contracts and obligations. The system of clients and consequent obligations and responsibilities are changing at the same time (see also Example 4.11). In this example the 14-year-old girl is now also a person indirectly concerned possibly in profound ways, by the psychologist's advice.

The psychologist made a separate appointment to discuss the woman's challenge. Different options were analysed. The psychologist tried to motivate the woman to inform the parents of the girl, but she decided that her first step would be to confront the principal with her suspicion.

When the psychologist met the woman again for the regular consultation, she did not herself mention the issue. When the psychologist asked, she thanked him for the consultation and said that he matter was taken care of and solved for the best interests of the church. More she would not say.

Now the psychologist was in distress. He felt responsible for the girl, being afraid that the principal now controlled the situation and that the abuse might still be going on. His questioned himself: Do I indirectly have a client relationship with the girl, through the relationship I entered with the woman on her personal problem? – and what can I do?

He decided to ask for a new meeting with the woman, arguing that he had a professional obligation after being informed about a person under age who might be abused. As he suspected, the principal had promised to end the relationship with the girl and also pleaded his love for the woman, missing her, and pleading with her not to go further with the information as that would ruin the church and many people would suffer.

After some discussion the psychologist and the woman agreed that they would approach the girl's parents together. The psychologist took care to inform them about his obligations, and the bravery of the woman in coming forward to help their child.

The Psychologist Is Defined by a Relationship

Psychologists' professional behaviour must be considered within a professional role, characterised by the professional relationship.

Being a professional psychologist means taking roles based on the knowledge, competence and licences achieved. In the example above, the psychologist is aware of how the professional relationship changes and monitors his behaviour according to the responsibility that resides with the role. When being asked, and in responding according to the expectations of being a psychologist, a professional relationship is established and the obligations of the role are activated. On the other hand, the psychologist is not obliged to, and should not enter a relationship, before an assessment of the task and the contextual conditions are cleared. In the example above, the psychologist could have declined to enter a relationship regarding the woman's personal problem, and perhaps a referral to a colleague would have been the best solution. But when he, perhaps too quickly, accepted, the relationship and a new set of responsibilities were established.

As a person, you have both the status and responsibilities defined by being a psychologist, but also a private domain which is not bound by the ethical expectations laid down in the ethical principles. This does not mean that you might not uphold the same ethical standards for your private life. Still, it is important for the integrity of the professional relationship that the psychologist draws a clear line between the professional and the private domain (See Example 4.7). This will hinder that intentional, as well as unintentional exploitation and rejection might happen. It is however, also important for protecting the psychologist's private sphere and interests. Safety and integrity is fundamental for being able to deliver competent professional service.

In friendships, among the family and in collegial relationships there will of course be small-talk and social interactions where your self-presentation is private, but where the expectations will also have some components that refer to your professional standing. This should not be seen as a big problem, being aware of the tendency for a process of gradual sliding from a private to a professional role; as well as the converse, which is more problematic, where the sliding is from the professional into a private role; or even more importantly, sliding into double roles that can be problematic to close down without damaging the professional role. Consider the following example:

Example 3.2

As part of an introductory small talk in a session the psychologist mentioned to his client that he and his family were looking for a summerhouse by the coast. A few weeks later he was called by a property developer, a friend of his client, inviting him to be among a priority-group for choosing a property, and getting extra price reductions in a new resort he was developing in a popular area. The psychologist and his family were very happy suddenly to become the future owners of a perfect holyday-residence. It became, however, somewhat annoying to the psychologist, that his client now was happy to have provided this opportunity for his therapist, and he felt that the distinction between his private life and the professional role had become unclear.

Inequalities of Knowledge and Power

Inequalities of knowledge and power always influence psychologists' professional relationships with clients and colleagues.

A professional relationship will always comprise a complementary dyad of roles. The privileged knowledge and status given to the psychologist will be the basis for influence, intended to be for the benefit of the client, or for some other legitimate interest, such as the vital protection of others. Thus, inequality is a central aspect of any professional relationship. The professional relationship is therefore also a dyad with difference in power. This implicit difference in authority will therefore impose a correspondingly greater responsibility on the psychologist.

This must not be understood as the psychologist having responsibility for the life and choices of the client. The psychologist's responsibility concerns the working process and interaction with the client and the consequences thereof. The clear line that the psychologist draws between the professional role and his private life, being reluctant to enter all kinds of double roles, is crucial in managing the power issues inherent in the relationship. As discussed earlier, being a psychologist requires taking a clear and legitimate role.

Within professional relationships with colleagues knowledge and power might also vary. That makes it important to monitor how inequalities might affect the working process. Especially when there are line management and/or supervisory elements, and thereby differences in dependencies in the relationships, clear contracts and separation from other roles might prevent unhealthy consequences of the power-differences. Unforeseen and illegitimate effects of power differences are prone to happen unless one, and preferable both colleagues in the relationship are aware of the power elements and of the responsibility that each carries. There is often a tendency to look at collegial professional relationships as more symmetrical than a contextual and systems analysis would show. The not so exceptional collegial conflicts in work-groups might stem from lack in communicating and acknowledging the power differences in collegial relations.

Range of Responsibility

The larger the inequality in the professional relationship and the greater the dependency of clients, the heavier is the responsibility of the professional psychologist.

As shown above, the Preamble declares that psychologists enter a wide variety of roles and assignments, probably more so than many comparable professions. The impact of the psychologist's work thus ranges from a single episode of advice with no commitment and dependency on the part of the person asking for the advice, to an assessment that might lead to a person's imprisonment for life, or providing the vital intervention that helps the suicidal person to choose life. A professional relationship can likewise vary from existing for a few minutes to be a relationship for years. It is thus obvious that the consequences of the psychologist's actions, assessments and interventions will be correspondingly varied, and consequently the weight of the psychologist's responsibility will vary.

In some instances the question arises; what is the professional responsibility when the formal professional relationship is terminated? Is the road then open for entering a new relationship, for example an intimate, private relationship? Consider the following example in two versions:

Example 3.3

A young university professor in psychology is teaching a group of graduate students on research methods. He is very attracted to one of his students, who he gets to know is, like himself, gay. They exchange glances.

For his doctoral thesis, the student asks if the professor would be his supervisor. The professor refuses and declares that he has become too attracted to the boy, and that would be a problem for them. The student accepts, and finds another supervisor, but the student and the professor become lovers. They keep their relationship discrete, unknown by staff and students.

In addition to exchanging glances, the professor approaches the student and proposes that he would like to be his supervisor for the student's doctoral thesis. He says he finds the theme the student has chosen very interesting. The student is flattered as the professor is known as a very competent supervisor. After some time during the supervision process, the professor declares his love for the boy, but that they for ethical reasons must wait to consume their love until the student's thesis is finished. He helps the student much and even rewrites some passages in the thesis.

This example shows that the existing dependencies during a professional relationship might open up opportunities for exploitation. The inequalities and differences in power will probably still exist after a professional relationship is terminated and a new relationship is entered. The possible sexual exploitation of the student could be expected to be more profound in the second version of the example. Here the professor approaches the student, well aware of his sexual interest. His behaviour can clearly be seen as unethical as the dependency is heavy and the professor seems to have used his professional standing to bind the student with the intent to enter an intimate relationship. It is no excuse that the intimate behaviour is postponed until termination of the formal relationship.

In the first version the professor seems to understand that his private feelings for the student will confound the professional task, and declines to enter a new professional relationship with the student. It can still be questioned, even if there is no direct formal relationship, if a professor would not be in danger of using his position for exploitation when entering an intimate relationship with a student, even if the student was taking the initiative. Rule of the thumb: do not look for private relationships in professional relationships; there will always be inequalities that can foster both intentional as well as unintentional exploitations and conflicts.

Stage of the Professional Relationship

The responsibilities of psychologists must be considered within the context of the stage of the professional relationship.

All affiliations have developmental processes, so also professional relationships. Dependencies are often part of the professional working alliance, although some level of independence might be the goal of the professional relationship. This means that the responsibilities will differ at different stages, and according to what other support that may exist in the client's context. In example 3.1, we see that the psychologist's responsibilities change as the contract changes. When the psychologist understands that the young girl might be without contextual support, his responsibility for knowing about the girl's probable situation, becomes acute.

The above formulation about changing responsibility also highlights that when dependencies, power-issues and involvements are extensive, so also are responsibilities. That responsibility might reside after formal termination of the relationship; these post-relationships will also vary with the degree of the earlier involvement. In one situation it might not be a significant challenge to enter another type of relationship after termination of the first. In other relationships might any later non-professional relationship, at any stage, have the potential for being exploitative or repressive? Consider:

Example 3.4

Five years after terminating a two-year therapy, the therapist approaches her former client. She declares her love for the client and states that she has patiently waited until she now felt the time had worked in their favour.

Remember that when evaluating situations like this, clients have exposed themselves in a personal, often vulnerable situation, while this is not the case the other way: The psychologists have not been so exposed for their clients and therefore there will reside an imbalance in the relationship. This can be expected to have effects, at least unintentional, in favour of the psychologist if conflicts of interests should arise. Such conflicts that normally occur are often sorted out according to the dependencies and power-issues that also exist in any private relationship. An earlier professional relationship can accentuate such power-differences in a later private relationship.

Interdependence of Principles

It should be recognised that there will always be strong interdependencies between the four main ethical principles with their specifications.

The four principles will be outlined in the following chapters. However, the above formulation reminds us that the principles and their specifications will highlight different aspects of the same basic question: – how to do right? – how to find the best ways to obtain this meta-goal in professional practice? All four principles can therefore be relevant for assessing a particular situation. In the above example (3.3), the professor's integrity in the second formulation is unclear as he seems to have hidden motives, he is using his professional standing for exploitation and

thus not respecting the student's integrity, he is not responsible for how his engagement might hamper the student's career by over-involving himself in the student's
thesis, and questions about his competence may also be raised by his behaving with
such ethical negligence.

*This means for psychologists that resolving an ethical question or dilemma will re-
quire reflection and often dialogue with clients and colleagues, weighing different
ethical principles. Making decisions and taking actions are necessary even if there are
still conflicting issues.*

The above text points to the very important issue of communicating with others
when seeking to find the best ethical solution. It is by bringing ethical dilemmas into
the open, that the best assessment and the best solution can be found, either by directly discussing the dilemma with the client, or by consulting colleagues, or both.
However it is important to be aware that an ethical solution to a dilemma can never
be a solution based on consensus. The responsibility for acting and for the consequences of the action always resides with the psychologist. Discussing dilemmas
with clients can easily slide into giving the client responsibility for what the psychologist comes to do. This will be a misuse of the principles of informed consent
and self-determination in the relationship with the psychologist, to be discussed in
later chapters. Consensus and acting in agreement with the client should be valued,
but they can never be used as an ethical argument for the psychologist's actions.
Quite the contrary, asking for consensus can be an appeal to the client so that an
unethical situation can continue, as in the second version of example 3.3. The concepts of agreement and the like are not to be found in the Meta-Code. Informed consent and self-determination point to the client's right to make their own independent
decisions in the relationship with the psychologist. Agreement would imply a full
insight, shared responsibility and mutual integrity, while consent implies acceptance
and trusting the other to take his responsibility.

As will be shown later, in discussing the principles and their specifications, different
precisions of the principles can be derived. By the help of the qualifying text from the
Meta-code discussed in this chapter, the principles and specifications can be extended
even further. They can be rephrased and studied to find how they might apply to specific
areas of professional practice, as well as to the specific ethical dilemma encountered.
Pondering the text and juxtaposition of the principles, together with evaluations of dependencies, variations and stages of the relationships, are often necessary to find a
solution for the specific situation and dilemma.

By using all principles for assessing a situation for ethical dilemmas and solutions, the most nuanced picture of the ethical challenges emerges. In both versions
of the example above (3.3) the professor uses ethical arguments, but the assessment
is too limited, and hides other unethical ethical behaviours for the student, his client.
Using only one ethical principle for guidance can thus result in unethical practice,
when it might be in conflict with others.

In many situations a multi-dimensional ethical assessment will strengthen the action first chosen from the first principle found relevant. In other instances the principles might point to conflicting actions. Then it can be said that a real ethical dilemma exists.

When a contradiction between principles, or rather between values embedded in the principles exists, an impetus to withdraw from the situation might arise, or a stalemate can be established where nothing happens. Then a weaker party might suffer in the system of interactions where the professional relationship exists, or a crisis will build up. Example 4.10 and many others of the examples in the book will have a similar complexity of contradiction of values in the same situation: Consider the following example:

Example 3.5

An industrial psychologist is coaching a group of leaders in a firm. The managing director who has hired the psychologist agrees the contract together with the group. The work progresses as planned and the group as a whole give good evaluations. One of the leaders, however, is often attacked aggressively by some of the others, including the managing director. The psychologist tries to intervene in these discussions, trying to soften the obvious scapegoat process in the group. He never brings this issue out in the open, as he feels that the group as a whole finds his contributions valuable in their strategic decision-making for the firm. After a while, the scapegoat is on sick-leave. The psychologist receives a letter blaming him for having contributed to an unbearable situation. The scapegoat claims that the psychologist had indirectly legitimated the aggressive behaviour from the colleagues, making his position impossible in the firm. A copy of the letter was sent to the managing director, and in the next session the group also blamed the psychologist, saying they had expected the psychologist to take care of such processes.

In this example the psychologist works in a complex social situation where several dilemmas arise; project success vs. negative consequences, hierarchy, integrity in the group process, and responsibility – who has what responsibility?, respect for the individual vs. group interests and so on. By not bringing these dilemmas into the open the psychologist ends up trying to compensate for the behaviour of the clients and thereby takes over responsibilities that should reside within the client system. The individuals in the client system thus come to rely on the psychologist to take care of how they treat each other. When the negative consequences become clear the psychologist himself ends up attacked and a scapegoat.

The example illustrates the importance of the last sentence in the qualifying and introductory text to the ethical principles; the subject of this chapter: *"Making decisions and taking action is necessary even if there are still conflicting issues"*.

Conclusions

Conflicting issues are the essence of ethical dilemmas and will not go away by not addressing them. Consciousness and reflection on the ethical principles outlined in the following chapters will give a base for addressing and communicating about such dilemmas. Reflection on ethics enhances the professional competence and gives a solid base for psychological practice of whatever speciality and in varied contexts.

Chapter 4

The Principle of Respect

Haldor Øvreeide

Psychologists accord appropriate respect to and promote the development of the fundamental rights, dignity and worth of all people. They respect the rights of individuals to privacy, confidentiality, self-determination and autonomy, consistent with the psychologist's other professional obligations and with the law.

This principle is elaborated in the following specifications:

• General Respect
• Privacy and Confidentiality
• Informed Consent and Freedom of Consent
• Self-determination

This first basic principle of *Respect for Person's Rights and Dignity* in the Meta-Code has two components. The first clause states the general expectation that professional psychology has an *aspirational* aim, not only to respect the rights, but also to *promote* the fundamental rights of human beings. Reference for these fundamental rights will, for example, be how they are defined by international declarations, such as the UN Declaration of Human Rights, and the UN Declaration of Children's Rights. By accepting the Meta-Code as guidance for practice, psychologists thus claim not only to adhere to such values but, in addition, to promote these basic rights. Showing respect to individuals is fundamental, but it is also expected that psychologists are active in supporting and providing premises for adherence to the basic human rights, within their professional context.

This ethical principle of Respect thus takes the stand that psychologists have a *moral goal* in their professional practice, not only to comply to the ad hoc moral expectations, but within their practice to contribute to a society of psychologists that are caring and practising in line with fundamental human rights, without any discrimination and prejudice.

The psychologist's professional work is the domain where this aspiration should be fulfilled. Many psychologists do voluntary work and engage privately within organisations such as Amnesty International, Red Cross and the like. These are valuable contributions and to be respected, but this is not what is expected from the text of the Meta-Code. The Meta-Code primarily applies to the *professional relationships* that the psychologist enters into. The aspirational expectations are linked to the daily practice, meaning that psychologists should ensure that the routines and other contextual issues, within which they practise, are respectful and without prejudice. For instance, that the personnel of whom the psychologist is in charge adhere to a respectful practice. The relevant ethical scope is thus broader than just how a single individual client is directly affected by the psychologist's work.

Referring to how "client" is defined (chapter 3), it is expected that the psychologist has a broader social and systemic perspective than just his/her relationship with the single individual client. The aspirational expectation is not fulfilled if the psychologist treats individual clients with respect, while colleagues or routines in the psychologist's organization treat clients in degrading and disrespectful ways. According to the aspirational aim, the psychologist is expected to address disrespectful structures and practices within the work context, so that these can be corrected. "Whistle-blowing" can thus be seen as an ethical requirement for psychologists. (See example 4.3)

This basic formulation of the Principle of Respect draws a clear line to exclude practices that might have manipulative or exploiting properties or goals, be they deliberate or by accident. It demands that ethical questions about how human rights and dignity are respected must always be raised when the services of psychologists are sought. Some areas of practice might especially raise the sensitivity for these questions, for example in opinion-making, marketing and entertainment, and of course, in all situations when practising and advising on legal restraining of people's rights.

Can ethical questions on these grounds be raised in the following two examples?

Example 4.1

Two developmental psychologists do market analyses for products where children are consumers. Using surveys designed on the basis of evidence from developmental psychology they give advice on the presentation and marketing of a broad range of products, toys, food, and clothing. The criterion, on which they recommend marketing campaigns, is to what extent the children persistently draw the parents' attention to the product. The presentations that produce the most insistent and repeating hassle and demand are recommended for use.

Here the psychologists are using their psychological competence for intervening on young children's consumer-behaviour in subtle ways. They try to influence the children to put strain on their parents. Predicting that parents will give way to a pressure that is built up by psychological influencing of the children through marketing: behaviour that neither the child nor the parents can be expected to be aware of and how they are influenced. As such the psychologist's practice can be seen as one of exploitation.

Example 4.2

A clinical psychologist is approached by a TV-producer. A new entertainment program of the "big brother" type is to be launched. The program has an interactive element where the viewers can comment electronically directly on the screen and criticize the participants who will be expelled or continue in the program on the basis of the viewers' remarks. Young people with no experience of being in the public focus are recruited as participants.

In their contract the participants have to declare absolute confidentiality about what they get to know about the production and they are obliged not to criticize any aspect of the program and staff. The contract also states that the production company has no liability for any damage that might arise from participating in the program. On the other hand each participant will be given 10 hours of free professional psychological support and consultation within one year after participation. The producer wants to contract the psychologist to give the participants this service. On ethical grounds the psychologist refused to take on the task.

On what ethical grounds? This example might pose a dilemma for the psychologist who is asked. Helping people coping with stress and psychological difficulties are both areas in which the psychologist has competence and as such a legitimate task to engage in. On the other hand the psychologist becomes part of, and thereby indirectly co-responsible for, the strain that the participants might come to experience. The total concept for the entertainment program seems to use young people's engagement and willingness to exposure, without taking the full responsibility for the probable negative outcomes that might come for some of the individual participants. The psychologist seems to have come to the conclusion that participating would be to be part of a project that could have exploitative elements. As such he would be part of a practice dis-respecting the integrity of the participants. He weighed avoiding this to be most valued for his practice.

The second clause of the basic Principle of Respect draws our attention to the fact that psychologists have a set of obligations. Legal obligations are often obvious, while others, such as those to persons in relationships and dependencies might be more challenging to handle. For example, the advice a psychologist gives to a client reflecting on divorce will affect the client's children. Collegial obligations and the like might have more subtle and indirect influence. For example, a psychologist on sick leave might not want to be troubled with questions from colleagues about his/her clients and projects. The interests of the client and the colleague could then be conflicting.

All such diverse and sometimes conflicting obligations will influence psychological practice. This demands consciousness of the relevant obligations for finding the best balancing of the simultaneous diverse interests. In solving the possible dilemmas, informing and open communication with the client about the concurrent obligations are of outmost importance. The *Principle of Integrity* (chapter 7) is therefore an important supplement for advice in order to pay due respect to the rights and the dignity of the person when differing demands are at stake.

Persons have both moral and legal *rights*. These two domains are not always overlapping. Often the moral rights will be more general and global than how the legal rights are formulated (see the discussion of the relationship between the moral and legal domain in chapter 2). From an ethical perspective both domains are equally relevant for the professional psychologist to pay attention to. They might be overlapping, as many laws and regulations can be seen as solutions to ethical issues that have prevailed. However, when laws come into effect new dilemmas can arise which were not foreseen, and over time there can develop discrepancies between moral and legal rights. Those instances, where there is a discrepancy between what is seen as a moral problem and the legal rights, might challenge the aspirational issue of promoting fundamental human rights.

In the above examples the question of exploitation can be raised. In the first, developmental psychology can be said to be used to influence children. They can not be expected to have the competence to understand how they are affected by the marketing to which they are exposed. Some countries have taken legal measures to forbid or restrict advertising aimed at children. Such activity is seen as against the moral rights and that children have to be protected from exploitation. In the aftermath, psychologists who have contributed to marketing aimed at children can be seen as not having had an ethical awareness in line with the requirements of this first principle of respect. On the other hand, psychologists, who on professional grounds have been arguing for the weak position of children as consumers, can be said to have had an aspirational aim on ethical grounds, and to have been successful when these rights are confirmed by law.

Revisiting old dilemmas and solutions might over time give new solutions due to changing contexts, new knowledge and the development of moral thinking (see chapter 2). Every dilemma must thus always be freshly evaluated

The example shows that the applications of human rights are changing and often emerging issues in complex societal processes and communication on ethical issues. The moral rights as such might not change. However, the areas and in what instances they might apply can change quickly when new information arises. Psychological science and practice bring forward such information that can change the moral perspectives and where and when the human rights are relevant for guidance. Psychologists can contribute on the basis of the unfolding psychological knowledge and experience from practice. This can be done by pointing to where psychological information has ethical relevance, especially when it comes to forming the psychologist's own practice. For example, parents' right to discipline their children physically is still a legal right in some European countries, while many will see this as an appalling practice offending the integrity of the children, having negative psychological and developmental consequences. The rights of parents and the dignity and protective needs of children in such circumstances are conflicting.

This introduces *dignity*, the second important concept related to the Principle of Respect. While rights are easier to define and listed as "rights to do---, rights to have ---" etc., dignity can be more difficult to assess. Dignity is a more subtle value expected to regulate the direct human encounter, as well as how we talk about. name and describe each other's life and qualities. This is an activity which is an important part of psychological practice.

The issue of dignity is to take care not to underestimate and offend the self-worth of others, so as not to elicit feelings of degrading and marginalization. Meeting a person with dignity is also to give the person worth in the eyes of others. But more than that, as an aspirational goal, its purpose is also to give worth and full human status to all persons, no matter the situation and distance in the relationship, so as to enhance positive feelings of worth. As such, taking care of the dignity of persons is a fundamental premise for establishing communication and cooperation.

As mentioned, a central part of the profession of psychology is to name and describe others; their characteristics, capabilities, limitations, history and development. This is to be done by theory and methods developed on scientific grounds. This narration often comes close to issues connected to person's feelings of self-worth. How we as psychologists discuss, understand and take care of the dignity of the persons we meet, assess, intervene with, and describe, will be the central question for finding the best ways to behave in an ethically proper and acceptable way. Guidance for this important ethical issue will not be found in laws and regulations. It will depend on our own ability to develop sensitivity for the client's feelings and self-understanding in relation to our commenting about them and their lives. Remember that a psychologist's description of a person's personality and traits will have high credibility, built as it is on privileged knowledge and is therefore difficult to contest by others.

Example 4.3

The new psychologist at an institution for rehabilitation for youngsters with a criminal record observes that the personnel on one of the wards often make degrading comments to some of the clients, sometimes close to racism. The psychological climate in the ward seems to foster group processes that isolate and marginalise some of the young boys. From time to time explosive episodes appear that trigger anxiety in both personnel and clients. The personnel complain that they often get the most difficult youngsters to handle on their ward.

What can be seen as the psychologist's ethical challenge in this situation, as one of his tasks is to act as a consultant to the ward personnel, as well as to assess the clients and develop individual plans for their rehabilitation?

Specifications of the Principle of Respect

The basic Principle of Respect is given 15 specifications under 4 headings; 1) *General Respect*, 2) *Privacy and Confidentiality*, 3) *Informed Consent and Freedom of Consent, and* 4) *Self-determination*. In this and the three following chapters, the number system for each section and clause will follow that of the Meta-code to aid cross reference.

General Respect

i) *Awareness of and respect for the knowledge, insight, experience and areas of expertise of clients, relevant third parties, colleagues, students and the general public.*

As helpers, scientists and experts, with privileged knowledge, psychologists can come to be self-content and defining of others in ways that undervalue resources of clients or others among the client's relationships. The first specification highlights this pitfall. It is also an important corrective to the often objectifying, problem- and weakness-oriented psychological assessments and interventions. The formulation points to the psychologist's responsibility to enhance the self-respect of the client and others, as well for psychologists to be aware of the limits of their own competence, and to give priority and space to the competence of others, especially those of the client himself.

Caring for the dignity of persons is central in this specification. The client's self-respect is first of all promoted by an active acknowledgement by the psychologist of the client's competences and experience. This requires that the psychologist is able to relate to the client and other professionals in ways that give them right and opportunity to present themselves more wholly, and not to restrict their self-presentation only to problems and limitations. To assume this perspective is also important for advancing the client's right to self-determination (see the later specification 3.1.4). The complementary structure of roles in professional relationships, in most instances, gives most power and privileges to the professional. This demands a special sensitivity for the psychologist to be aware how this difference in power can make the client conform and be compliant, and thereby in subtle ways limit initiatives for self-presentation (a discussion of this issue is found in chapter 3).

Example 4.4

A journalist calls his old acquaintance from school; a psychologist he knows is working with anorexic male clients. The journalist is working on a series of articles on eating disturbances. Now she wants to get in contact with a male patient and she also wants to interview the psychologist as an expert on men's eating problems. The psychologist asks one of his clients with longstanding symptoms if he would like to present his condition in an article about eating problems. The client agrees immediately and contact is established with the journalist. Some months later the client's rather miserable story appears in the paper. This is followed by general statements given by the psychologist and other experts about such conditions; among others, the article refers to the tendency for clients to have been over-compliant in attachment-relations.

The client drops out of therapy and in a later therapeutic relation he reveals how uncomfortable he was with being exposed in this way as "a big problem". The comments and "sympathy" he got from friends and relatives became more than he felt were pleasant. Everything had gone so fast and he had been afraid that his former psychologist could feel offended if he had refused to cooperate with the journalist.

Communication and dialogue are necessary processes to face many of the ethical challenges, especially those covered by the Principle of Respect. Otherwise "respect" is derived from the psychologist's ideas of what is respectful behaviour, not giving space and acknowledge the self-presentation and reactions of the other person (the Other). Without this dialogical frame respect can otherwise end in paternalism and even repression. Having privileged information must not be misunderstood by the psychologist as a right to take, or to be appointed "one-upmanship" to others. This applies in the relationships with clients, as well as in co-operation with colleagues and other professionals. Differences in power and responsibilities must have well-defined sources of legitimacy, such as legal limitations and responsibilities in work assignments, or otherwise clearly be stated in the contracts that are regulating the relationships at stake.

The formulation can also be seen as a corrective, not to monopolise professional activities, but so as to give way to others to seek the most nuanced knowledge and interventions in the best interest of the client.

ii) Awareness of individual, cultural and role differences including those due to disability, gender, sexual orientation, race, ethnicity, national origin, age, religion, language and socio-economic status.

The cultural frames and limitations of assessment instruments, as well as for theory, can be a challenge for psychologists, as for other sciences. What are seen as universal phenomena at one point in time often come out as culturally and historically limited by later scrutinising. It has not always been the development of psychological science itself that has changed professional perspectives, but more general societal changes and moral developments. The psychological understanding of race, ethnicity, age, sexuality and how different forms of disabilities should be understood and reacted to have in many ways changed fundamentally over relatively short periods of time. These changes have been fought and brought forward by single persons and groups that have felt that both society, well supported by the professions in power, have been repressive and have misunderstood their character and capabilities.

There is no reason that we, at our point in time, do not have similar cultural, interest and value related blind spots in our understanding of human phenomena. Psychology must always be prepared to be de-masked on ethically questionable information and practice. But of course, a proactive critical discussion within the profession of what might be our culturally and hidden prejudices in science and recommended practice, is important. This is needed for many reasons, not least for building the trust that is necessary to uphold the status and credibility of the profession in society.

Example 4.5

A 5-year-old girl was referred by school nurse to the psychologist working at a community mental health service. The girl was suspected to have a grave attachment disturbance, as she seemed to prefer to relate to other adults, rather than her parents. The girl was the daughter of a student couple, coming from Africa studying biology and pharmacy at the local university in a European city. They were in their second year of studying abroad. The parents did not seem to understand that their child had a problem and a tension had arisen between the preschool teachers and the parents. The psychologist's observations of the child and assessment information from the pre-school showed that the child met some of the criteria for having an attachment problem, according to the diagnostic manuals. On the other hand, at interview the parents revealed that in their local African village a small child should primarily be reared by the extended family of the father. After weaning, the mother should keep distance and a close relationship to the biological parents should be avoided during the first years. The girl should not have come with them for their study-period abroad, but due to the death of the father's sister and his mother's illness, it was a last minute decision to bring their daughter along. Within their frame of reference their child's behaviour was normal and to be supported.

The psychologist's assessment, based on the scientific consensual frame for reference, could label the girl's behaviour as pathological. However, this psychologist had the integrity to take a critical stand to her own contextual position. She was able to see the limits of this position and thus establish a relationship with the girl and her parents, taking their cultural frame into account. By informing and consulting from this broadened perspective the teachers and parents could work jointly to support the child's development without using a pathological reference.

iii) Avoidance of practices which are the result of unfair bias and may lead to unjust discrimination.

This clause also draws our attention to the inherent biases that could stem from our cultural frames of reference, from loyalties and bindings in our different relationships, and from our personal interests that might not always be obvious. We are always embedded in frames for interpretations, relations, interests and loyalties that can come to offend both clients and relevant third persons. The specification can be seen as an important reference to our responsibility for the potential consequences of our practices. Following "the best intentions" alone, can easily lead to practices that can come to offend others, if this is not combined with a contextual critical analysis of consequence – primary *"non nocere" (first of all, do no harm)*.

Example 4.6

In a custody conflict the mother was supported by a psychologist who also was politically active on women's rights. The psychologist had been a bystander in the mediation possess that did not work out. The dispute was brought to court and the psychologist was summoned as a witness. When the mother's attorney asked the psychologist if she, as a professional, would give her understanding of the conflict, she answered: "Based on the mother's information and what I myself have observed during mediation and otherwise outside the court building, it is my professional impression that the father has some underdeveloped personality traits, including a limited capacity for empathy". The judge stopped her from continuing, stating that she was summoned as an ordinary witness and had not been appointed by the court to assess the persons as an expert witness. Later the father complained to the ethical board of psychologists, claiming to be offended by the psychologist who without his consent, observed, and offered a description of him as a person. He argued that the psychologist might have ruined their mediation possibilities without his knowing how she had intervened.

This example underscores how important it is that the role and practices of the psychologist are open and have a clear and legitimate base and, as often as possible, to be accepted by those involved in and affected by the psychologist's practice. Otherwise the practice can be seen as biased and coloured by interests and a sense of obligation to the individual client, in opposition to other people's interests. The psychologist can come to act on behalf of, instead of in support of a client, and can become thus part of the conflicts and of more private domains of the client. Double or unclear roles arise (see chapter 7). The example also underscores the interdependence of the ethical principles. In this case, the failing integrity of the psychologist and the possible dual relationship between the psychologist and her client resulted in an experience by a relevant third party, the father, of not being respected.

Privacy and Confidentiality

The maintenance of confidentiality and the protection of the privacy of clients and subjects for research might be the most valuable tool psychologists have in their work.

Whether it is in consulting, therapy, assessment or research, the obligation to respect privacy to the greatest extent possible is of outmost importance to build the trust necessary for working alliances. The client's confidence in the psychologist is based on the explications of what generally can be expected in terms of how the client's self-exposure will be managed by the psychologist; and secondly whether the psychologist is actually behaving according to these expectations. The general expectation that psychologists have high standards of confidentiality is also an important part of giving professional psychology a legitimate role in society.

Although in principle absolute, the issues of privacy and confidentiality raise many ethical issues, as most of the psychologist's tasks and challenges cannot be solved through an absolute adherence to the principle. Quite the opposite: assessing and passing on information to others about persons might be central for the psychologist's task, and in some situations deliberate breaking of this principle of confidentiality might also be the best ethical solution.

An assignment often requires assessing information, interpreting and passing information to others in addition to the person who is assessed. In working with children's problems, in forensic work and in industrial consulting this is often the frame. Information assessed by the psychologist about persons is passed on to others, for their problem-solving and decision-making. In most instances the best interests of the persons assessed are the goal, but this is not always the case. Sometimes it is the interests of others; for example societal protective measures will guide the forensic psychologist, the economical goals of the owners may guide an industrial psychologist's assessments of a work-place, and the child's best interests guide the psychologist who is assessing the competences of the parents in a child protection case.

At times it is not only the interests and decisions concerning the clients and their context that are involved. The government will need to register phenomena assessed by psychologists, for planning and political interventions. The more psychologists are seen as important contributors to public services, the more it is of interest to manage these services for the clients. This must be based of information given by psychologists. Governmental requirements for registering, and what issues are seen as important for planning and implementing interventions, are at the next stage contributing to how psychologist's services are formed. This will again depend on the quality of the information psychologists pass on about their clients.

For the purpose of scientific and professional development, psychologists themselves also have interest in the information revealed by the clients. It will be of interest for the psychologist to use the information for scientific studies, methodological development and for training, educational purposes and career advancement. An important part of professional development is that practical, in vivo, experience can be part of training and teaching. Without an active critical relationship to one's own professional experience and the information given by clients, professional development will fail and theories and procedures can be ritualized and detached from reality.

It is possible that in cases where a psychologist for limited purposes uses client information for professional development the clients need not be asked or bothered with this issue. However, at other times it will be necessary to have the client's consent and to see to that the information is made anonymous as to what persons are involved. This is especially important if the information will be part of written and given at public presentations.

The following specifications give some further guidance for handling client information.

i) Restriction of seeking and giving out information to only that required for the professional purpose.

Behavioural assessment and the study of human interactions and mental processes are core issues in psychologists' work. This is also what the persons studied and assessed by the psychologist might see as the central parts of their privacy and personal integrity. As such, psychologists, more than other professionals have to be aware of how information is gathered, passed on and disclosed in written statements, meetings and otherwise about the person assessed and discussed. It can be expected that all information that is not relevant for the psychologist's assignment has the potential of offending the person's integrity; not only giving information, but also seeking information that is not relevant.

Example 4.7

A woman of 35 is having a custody dispute in court. The appointed expert witness, a psychologist, has confronted her during interviewing with a fact, told by her former husband, that she had a two year prostitution career during her early years of studying. Nobody but her ex husband knew about this, and she regretted very much that she ever had told him. This was a period in her life which was very different from how she had lived both before and later. She had no contact with the persons she used to hang out with then, more than ten years before she had her first child. In his report to the court the psychologist disclosed this information including a lengthy paragraph on this issue, concluding that it was of no relevance for the custody issue.

The woman felt very offended by this information coming into the written report and thus being exposed to her social network. The psychologist could have excluded the information from his report, and if the issue was brought up in court, he could have orally stated that he had reviewed the information without finding it relevant for the issue at stake.

If it is not obvious for the client why the psychologist is asking for, or passing on the information, or not asking for or passing on information, it will be necessary to explain the relevance, or irrelevance, and the ethical considerations. Otherwise the requirements for confidentiality and informed consent will not be met. In this example the psychologist seems to have exposed information about the client which was not necessary for the professional purpose. If however, the information should come to be exposed in court by the ex husband, the psychologist could orally have argued his point that this information was of no relevance for the question. Now the psychologist was responsible for the exposure. If not as grave as in this example, it is rather common in expert witness reports, health statements and the like that much information that is of little relevance for the professional purpose of the report in included. The above specification is very useful to have in mind when teaching students and in supervising colleagues in reporting from assessments. Passing on information by third parties might be especially sensitive. Such information might be experienced by the client as "gossip" if it is disclosed without the person's consent, or without being informed that this is necessary for professional purposes.

ii) *Adequate storage and handling of information and records, in any form, to ensure confidentiality, including taking reasonable safeguards to make data anonymous when appropriate, and restricting access to reports and records to those who have a legitimate need to know.*

There is an important practical and technical side of guaranteeing confidentiality. To keep adequate records is a central part of professional practice. In many roles, such as when working in school and health services, the keeping of records will be statutorily regulated and the institution where the psychologist is working will usually take care of the practical issues in protecting the records. In other roles, for example in a private practice, in consulting athletes on their achievements, etc. psychologists must find their own ways for keeping and protecting the records. But for all handling and having access to the records, there will be situations where the responsibility for the practical protection will reside with the psychologist alone. For example, no firewalls in the system are of any use if you leave the office, going to the toilet without closing the window of the computer and exposing information about your patients open to others passing by.

The practical precautions to be taken can be said to have two main purposes. First, the records are necessary for giving the best possible professional service. Not keeping records could be the easy solution, but this would be a deficiency in competence. Professional practice is expected to be a systematic and accountable. Keeping records is thus a basic tool for meeting a minimum of professional competence. Being able to reconstruct what has been done is necessary for evaluations and for addressing challenges and questions at later stages in the work process. Neglecting adequate storage and losing records can be detrimental for the practice, and negligent record-keeping will not guarantee the rights and interests of the client in getting a professional service.

Example 4.8

A psychologist kept his records on a computer, well protected with passwords, locked up when not in use, and never connected to the Internet. One day the hard-disk broke and no backup-system had been established. Five years of information about a flour-ishing practice seemed to be gone. For the first time the psychologist realized that his own memory was of very little help. It was shocking to experience how much the re-cords were an integral part of structuring his daily work. Even for clients he had seen only a week ago, the few words he used to note on the last consultation were decisive for activating his memory of the work process in the case.

Luckily firms specializing in data-recovery exist; firms which have official certificates to guarantee confidentiality and safeguards for electronically theft when handling the information. A few weeks later he was set up with all his data on a new computer, and now with a double backup-system. The recovery bill was huge, and the insurance com-pany refused to contribute as there were no burglary, no fire, no broken water pipe etc. – only the psychologist's naïve trust in technology (sic!).

Problems occur. The second and the most important issue related to guarantying confidentiality, is that practical safeguards and responsible handling of the records are necessary to protect them from deliberate intrusion, or accidental exposure of confidential information.

Example 4.9

A clever and effective colleague had made it a habit, contrary to what was good prac-tice for handling client files in the psychiatric clinic, to take files home for the weekend for preparing written statements when terminating his cases. Going to the grocery store on the way home, his 10-year-old child was left to wait for him in the car. A friend of the child showed up and, happy to see her companion, the girl left the car and showed up in the store asking the father for ice-cream for the two of them. Coming back to the car the door was open and his briefcase was gone! What to do?

After consulting a colleague, mortified he called the director of his clinic, informing him about what had happened. The next stop was the police station to report the theft and plead for high priority, due to the sensitivity of the material. Finally came the most embarrassing part of the chore, to call the client about what had happened and what he had done so far to restore the damage.

A meeting with the client, the director, and the psychologist was set up on Monday morning. Luckily the psychologist was happy to report that the police had called Sunday evening informing him that the briefcase was found by the road not far from the store. The papers seemed intact but the mobile phone and his precious Mont Blanc pen were gone.

iii) Obligation that clients and others that have a professional relationship are aware of the limitations under the law of the maintenance of confidentiality.

The wording in this specification might be a little ambiguous. Of course, it is not specifying any obligation for clients or others. The obligation is for the psychologists to make clients and others in the professional relationship aware of relevant legal limitations to the psychologist's responsibility and right to keep information confidential.

In all countries where psychologists are licensed, registered or otherwise under governmental regulations, there will also be legal demands on confidentiality, as well as exemptions. In most European countries psychologists, in some instances when holding relevant information, are obliged by law to inform authorities who have legitimate power to intervene and decide to protect persons in possible danger. When working on forensic issues, in child protection, or when the information from the client exposes vital threats to persons' health and their lives, psychologists will have such legal obligation, as well as on an ethical evaluation of the situation. Protecting life and avoiding serious damage to a person's health have the highest value.

The specification above, and also the following two, advise the psychologist to take care to inform the client or other relevant parties about the legal the rights and duties of the psychologist, as well as the limitations to the client's rights that apply to the role and professional task at hand (see www.efpa.eu: *Recommendations for working as expert witness*). Therefore it is important for the psychologist to know under what conditions the exemptions to confidentiality, as well as to self-determination apply.

When the role is clear, such as when being appointed as an expert witness to evaluate a case of grave family violence, it seems obvious, but still necessary to inform the clients assessed, how the information will be passed on to the legal authorities. In other roles and situations it will be more complex and the stage and process of the relationship will determine when it is proper and relevant to provide information about what legal issues that are relevant (See chapter 3 for a further discussion of how the responsibility will vary with the stage and development of the professional relationship).

Consider the two versions of the following case. Which version can be said to have the best ethical process?

Example 4.10

A depressed woman in her thirties, a mother of two, came to her first session with the psychologist.

1) Among other issues the psychologist informs her carefully about confidentiality and the legal limitations to this, including her obligation to inform the child protection authorities if any information should come up about her children living under adverse conditions. The therapy proceeds, but the woman doesn't raise any issues or worries about her children. When the psychologist tries to raise this as an issue, it never comes to more than "it is ok", and "you know it"s not easy, but I manage".

2) Among other issues, the psychologist informs the client about her general obligation to confidentiality. One of the first issues the client wants to address is her worry about how her depressed condition affects her children, and that she is worried about her temper, especially as one of her children is frustrating for her to handle. In the third session the mother tells about her remorse and bad feelings for having hit her child, not only this once, but admits to having done so several times earlier too.

Now the psychologist informs the woman about her legal obligation when there is a child protection issue. First the mother gets upset and worried that she might lose her children. A meeting is arranged with the mother, the psychologist and a child protection officer. A plan for protecting the children is worked out. The mother receives consultation on how to manage her children and a weekend-family for the children is organized. The therapy continues and one of the themes is on how the mother can manage her temper and how this is related to her shifting moods. She declares that it has been a relief for her to disclose and talk about her abusive behaviour against her child, and that she is glad for the help the family now gets.

This example shows that giving information about all possible outcomes might hinder the development of trust and confidence in the professional as having a supportive and non-judgemental relationship. The non-judgemental stand is part of the confidentiality issue. In the first version of the example, giving information seems to have affected and reduced the trust in the relationship. Informing about possible outcomes, when there is no information about the relevance of the exemption, seems to be experienced by the client as the psychologist having an initial distrust in the client.

What if the children had been put into a foster home and the mother had terminated the therapy? Would that change the ethical evaluation of the case? Who is in the weaker position – mother or child? What about the psychologist's responsibility? Remember the definition of who is the client – *"including indirect relationships"* and the issue of responsibility and power, also in the client's relations. Can it be said that in this case the child is in an indirect relationship to the psychologist when the psychologist is working on the role and behaviour of the woman as a mother? The psychologist seems to have given priority to the child in his ethical evaluation of the dilemma. It so happened that the child was protected and the professional relationship with the mother survived. This was however not obvious when the psychologist acted. An important point – acting on the base of an ethical evaluation is not a guarantee for being able to care for all interests and needs – a priority must be made.

iv) Obligation when the legal system requires disclosure to provide only that information relevant to the issue in question, and otherwise to maintain confidentiality.

This specification seems obvious, but is trickier than it looks at first glance. The general principle is absolute professional confidentiality. It is not even the right of the psychologist to disclose that a professional relationship with the client exists. On the other hand, in most instances part of the professional contract will require exceptions and limitations to the absolute demand. There will often be a referral process by another profession, a funding body that will register the relationship; a reporting obligation etc. and therefore some information about the relationship will stay with others, according to statutory regulations in many countries. In all such instances only that information necessary for the task should be given. Usually these limitations will be contextually clear and therefore easy to negotiate, handle and to inform the client about when starting the relationship.

One of the tricky issues is for the psychologist to be aware that the legal obligation to confidentiality in many instances will override the legal system's need for an interest in getting psychological information and expert evaluations. Professional secrecy has high legal priority. In many instances where there are legal needs for the assistance of a psychologist's expertise, it is with the client to decide if information should be disclosed. However, it is important to be aware of what might happen when giving statements as an expert witness or as a simple witness, either it is by legal obligation or by the client's consent. The law will vary from one country to another, but typically neither the client nor the psychologist alone can limit what information is to be given, when it is asked for and the professional confidentiality is discharged. Then it will be the judge or deciding body that will set the limits for what information is needed.

The psychologist can of course ask if the information requested really is necessary, but if the request is turned down, the psychologist will have to pass on that information. It is however, imperative to be aware that psychologists who are asked for professional evaluations must decide themselves if they have the information needed or the competence to make such an evaluation. If the answer is yes the psychologist cannot refuse to do so; if the answer is no, the psychologist should explain their limitations and decline.

In order not to behave disrespectfully the psychologists should inform clients that it is their duty not to disclose more than necessary, but in some instances, including mandatory legal situations and when the client has consented to release information, it will not be the psychologist who will decide what questions will be relevant to answer and what information that must pass on. If the obligation or consent exists, the psychologist cannot filter or hold back information asked for if he is summoned as a common witness or as an expert witness. However, the psychologist should ensure that there is a close relationship between the information asked for and the information given, so that redundant and irrelevant information is not disclosed. This is what the above specification underlines.

v) Recognition of the tension that can arise between confidentiality and the protection of a client or other significant third parties.

In example 4.10 there was a tension between the mother's right to confidentiality and the child's need for protection. As discussed, the psychologist decided to give priority to the protection of child, but sought cooperation with the mother and succeeded. The above specification reminds us of this kind of dilemma. In that example the tension was obvious and there was a legal obligation also for the psychologist to act on. At other times this dilemma must be handled in communication with the client – *Who should I inform? How can we handle this situation? What may happen if we don't inform --?-* etc. may be questions to ask when the right to confidentiality is contradictory to other vital needs of the client or others. At times it is the needs of client him or herself that may be at stake.

The most dramatic dilemma is when the psychologist is confronted with the suicidal thoughts and plans of a client. Then the most classic moral dilemma arises – respecting the client's right to self-determination vs. protecting the client from self-destruction. Sometimes this may be acute, and then the legal obligation to lifesaving action helps in decision-making. At other times such assessments will be more difficult, where protecting the right to self-determination should be given higher priority, while still accepting the risk of suicide being active. When in such a difficult dilemma, consulting a colleague might be very important. Psychologists, who have experienced a client who commits suicide, also become victims of the effects of suicide. Self-protecting actions for the psychologist are therefore important for finding the best ways to balance the dilemma, and hopefully to help the clients through their crisis.

vi) Recognition of the rights of clients to have access to records and reports about themselves, and to get necessary assistance and consultation, thus providing adequate and comprehensive information and serving their best interests and that this right to appropriate information be extended to those engaged in other professional relationships, e.g., research participants.

As a rule of the thumb, all information and evaluations about a client are the client's "property", taken care of by the psychologist for professional use. As such it is the client's right to know about and to decide on how this information should be protected and distributed. Thus only contracts with the client and legal obligations protecting the client's rights will regulate how the psychologist can handle this information. With this point of departure, the psychologist's recordkeeping can be seen as administering the information produced by the psychologist, for the client, and in the best interest of the client. This implies the client's right to see and control their "assets", and to get necessary assistance to understand and monitor the information.

It is also important to note that research participants, giving information about themselves for scientific use, will have the same right of access to the information and to know how it is to be used and protected. Collaborating colleagues and institutions are also entitled to be respected and know how and what information they have given to the psychologist is recorded.

vii) Maintenance of records, and writing of reports, to enable access by a client which safeguards the confidentiality of information relating to others.

As noted earlier, record keeping is an important tool for structuring and being systematic in the work process. It is necessary for communicating with others on the basis of facts and actions without relying on the often failing human memory. A minimum amount of record keeping is necessary for being able to reconstruct and explicate contracts, actions, assessments and evaluations, and, to be able to provide information, with integrity, on demand.

One of the challenges in protecting records is that in many instances more than one person is involved in the client's system, as well as at the work place of the psychologist. Information about more than one person might then come into the same files: for example in workplace assessments and child custody cases. There should therefore be a clear distinction between information given *by* the person, and information by a third party *about* the person. Any persons who might want and have the right to review their records, should not be exposed to information about third persons who themselves should be protected by the psychologist's obligation to confidentiality. The following example should illustrate this distinction:

Example 4.11

A psychiatric nurse was cooperating in a team with a psychologist and others in an ambulant home-based treatment program for young schizophrenic patients. The nurse sought the psychologist for consultation after a frightening episode when working with one of the clients. She reported how she felt re-traumatised when the paranoid youngster had locked the door and kept the key. It had taken her more than half an hour to calm him down and let her out again. The feeling of re-traumatisation was connected to an episode she had as a teenager. When hitch-hiking, she and a friend had been locked up in a car by two men who sexually abused them. She was now completely caught off guard, as she had thought that this was a well integrated experience in her life. The psychologist wrote all this information in the record of the young client. The social worker, who also worked in the team and had access to the team's records, was very upset by reading about her colleague in this way. The incident came to a crisis for the team and endangered the whole treatment program. A lot of effort had to be used to rebuild trust in the team, and one of the measures was to discuss the ethical issues connected with recordkeeping, and how this should be done.

In this case one of the psychologist's work colleagues confided in the psychologist so that a new professional relationship was established when the psychologist accepted to consult on the episode. This new relationship, however how limited it might be, had the quality of being a client relationship. However, the psychologist did not seem to have been aware of how this changed his set of obligations, for example in how information about this private issue of his colleague should be recorded and protected. And how should this information about his colleague be handled if the client later in life wanted access to the psychologist's records, and the information about the nurse's re-traumatisation was in the file? Neither the psychologist nor the social worker might then be working in the clinic. It is important to have in mind that records mostly will stay with the institution's files and therefore often outlive the recording psychologist's time in the institution.

When the records belong to the institution, the recording should also reflect this condition – being understandable for other professionals, giving respect to the client by avoiding descriptions that may be experienced as degrading and abusive, and not including information that is not necessary for the professional issues worked on. For example, in many school psychology files, as well as in clinical records, you may find a lot of redundant information left over by colleagues who never took their time to clean up the files before they changed jobs. The best way of avoiding this is of course by being aware when recording, that the files will dwell with the institution after you have left the position.

Being proactive in recording is always the best solution, but a useful precaution can be that before giving the client or colleagues their rightful access to records, you should always read through the records. This can allow you to safeguard that information about other persons, who have their individual rights to confidentiality, are protected from accidental exposure. The following example illustrates this point.

Example 4.12

A former client, asked the psychologist to return copies of some correspondence he had had with the psychologist; he also wanted a copy of his records. The relationship had been a brief one. The psychologist read through the file, and had no problems with copying and giving the client what he wanted and had the right to. A week later he got a note from the client together with a copy of a sensitive letter concerning another of the psychologist's clients. There was a not so subtle threat in the following note: "I will keep the original, just as "capital" that might be useful at another occasion". In a moment of distraction the psychologist had included this extra sheet of paper which he copied at the same time in the copy- room, and this had been included in the copies he had sent to the first client.

What to do? After consulting a colleague (always a good thing to do when what should not happen, happens!) he wrote back that he expected the misplaced original letter returned within a week. If not it would be regarded as a theft and as such handed over to the police to handle. The letter came back after three days. Then there was the more embarrassing part of informing the second client that confidential information had been exposed to a stranger.

As we have seen in other examples, problems happen, but more problems happen if record keeping and handling of the records are sloppy.

Informed Consent and Freedom of Content

The simple and basic idea under this heading is that before entering a professional relationship, the client should be informed about what will happen and that on the basis of this information the client is free to enter or decline the relationship, and also to continue or terminate at any time in the process. However, in practice, as we have seen on confidentiality, there are also many challenges to this straight forward principle of informed and freedom of consent. The following specifications are useful for coping with these challenges

i)   *Clarification and continued discussion of the professional actions, procedures and probable consequences of the psychologist's actions to ensure that a client provides informed consent before and during psychological intervention.*

At any stage of the development of the professional relationship, proper information should be given, so that the client understands the premises, limitations and elements of what is going to happen. In many cases the stages are not always clear in the beginning. A sorting together with the client, and maybe others, is needed for the decisions to be taken both by the psychologist and the client at different stages of the work process.

As we have discussed on confidentiality, there may often be limitations of the client's actual freedom to choose the relationship to the psychologist. However, information is always essential, even when the client's options are limited or non-existent. For example, a patient committed to psychiatric ward, will have very limited options with whom and how he wants to cooperate within the clinic. However, within the restrained conditions of the client there will always some leeway for self-determination, consent and cooperation. These options should always be optimized so that consent and cooperation can be enhanced as far as possible. On the other hand, it is important to be open and clear about the restraining conditions and their legitimacy.

Example 4.13

A forensic psychologist is approaching a woman in jail who had murdered her husband and their 5-year-old child, before trying to commit suicide. The psychological assessment is decided by the court. She is reluctant, but her solicitor had informed her and pleaded that it would be in her best interests to cooperate with the psychologist. Not cooperating might reduce her possibility to be sentenced to psychiatric treatment, which would be far better than being sentenced for life to prison. When contracting with the woman, the psychologist informs her clearly about the court's decision, the procedures and methods he will use, and roughly how he will present his report at the end. Although the woman says she does not feel she has any choice, he asks her still to think through the information for a few days before she gives him her reaction and her final decision to go on. In the next meeting the woman agrees to cooperate, they jointly decide on some practical issues and the psychologist decides on some minor changes in the procedures after getting her reactions. Among other things, he decides to interview a friend of the woman on her proposal and wishes. This idea turns out to be an important source of information.

In this example the psychologist takes care to present both what is going to happen and the contextual limitations, and also tries to optimize the client's self-determination, within the restrained context of the relationship. This also happens to bring in a resource for the assessment and clearly seems to foster cooperation. Somewhat paradoxically, taking care to inform and to explicate the limitations and degrees of possible consent, might be especially important when the capacity and freedom to consent are restrained.

When approaching the issue of consent, there will always remain a discrepancy between the psychologist's privileged information and what information the client can be expected to understand. Clients' capacity to understand and reflect on consequences will also have wide variations. Consent will in the end also have to be based on the client's trust in the psychologist's integrity and his/her ability to behave with professional responsibility. Thus, how psychologists present themselves and the relevant information that the psychologist gives about the actual relationship and situation, as in the case above, as well as the general trust in psychology as a profession, will be important bases for consent and cooperation.

ii) Clarification for clients of procedures on record-keeping and reporting.

The requirement to clarify and inform about reporting and record keeping discussed here is linked to the issue of consent. The general duty is to give all information that might be relevant to allow the client to give consent to the question at hand. Recording and reporting what and to who can often be of special interest for the client, as this will affect motivation and willingness to cooperate. Consent is not only an issue of entering or not entering a relationship. Most importantly it is also a question of how to optimize the cooperation and reliability, and is thus fundamental for the quality of service and producing results. The question of consent is thus a relational issue that should be addressed during the whole work process, not only when establishing or contracting the professional relationship. As well as being a right for the client, continued consent can be seen as a tool for keeping up cooperation and motivation for solving the relationship's assignment. As such it is of outmost importance for the psychologist's work.

On the other hand, clients should not be bothered with all kinds of information that would not be relevant for consent. An overload of information could, as we pointed out in discussing example 4.10, reduce the confidence and trust in the relationship.

Example 4.14

A school psychologist often conducts her assessments in the school buildings in rural areas, rather than bringing the children to her office in town. Before starting to interview the children and their parents, she takes care to inform them that all records from the tests and interviews will be kept at the school psychology office in town, and that nothing will remain at the school. She also informs them that before she sends her reports and gives her recommendations, written as well as in oral consultation, she will inform the children and their parents and discuss what information should be given to the teachers.

When assessing the children at her town office, she does not bother giving special information about how the records are kept at the office, only about the procedures for her reporting.

In informing about how records are kept and how information is passed on, the psychologist takes care to see what may be the position of her clients when informing. She understands that the changing contexts for her work will require different types and amounts of information; although what she is actually doing might be the same whether she works in town or in the rural district.

iii) Recognition that there may be more than one client, and that these may be first and second order clients having differing professional relationships with the psychologist, who consequently has a range of responsibilities.

As discussed earlier in this chapter, many work assignments for psychologists involve several persons. They will often have varied expectations and are affected in different ways, directly or indirectly by the psychologist's actions. This point is highlighted in this specification. Sometimes this can involve conflicting interests in the client system. This requires the psychologist to sort out and weigh the different responsibilities. Using the guidance from the qualifying formulations outlined in chapter 3 will be useful; the stage and degree of involvement, the difference in dependency and power etc. will decide both the width of responsibilities, as well as priorities. (Examples 3.01, 3.04)

Self-determination

i) Maximisation of the autonomy of and self-determination by a client, including the general right to engage in, and to end the professional relationship with a psychologist while recognising the need to balance autonomy with dependency and collective actions.

Self-determination is a broader issue than just being a question of giving consent to the psychologist's work-plans and actions. The above formulation highlights the tension between individual and collective interests, autonomy and dependency, a tension that is often at the core of ethical dilemmas. Dependency and autonomy are seldom completely independent entities, but describe different aspects and stages of balance in the human relationship. "Two against the one" can be seen as the basic problem, where the individual can come to be repressed, rejected or isolated by the overwhelming "Two". A higher social status can be said to be established by "the two". This creates a triadic system of imbalance in power also in the single, dyadic relation, as one of the two is connected to a higher status. Thus, relationships where there is difference in social status will have the characteristics of "two against one" processes.

As we discussed in chapter 3, and earlier in this chapter, the complementary nature of a professional relationship and difference in power based on status and privileged information can foster compliance. This can happen to the degree that self-determination is affected, even in situations where there should be no other obvious external restrictions. In some complaints to ethical boards, such as in the following example, this phenomenon becomes evident.

Example 4.15

After a few sessions, the client of a psychologist reported that he had been hesitant to have a new referral for psychotherapeutic treatment by his doctor. His former experience with a psychologist had been not so good. From time to time it happened that this psychologist fell asleep during the therapeutic sessions. The client felt it embarrassing, as he had to wake the therapist up by coughing etc. Then the psychologist carried on as if nothing had happened, but often on a very different track than before he fell asleep. The psychologist could also suddenly leave the room saying he had to make a phone call. The client felt strongly he was being rejected, but never confronted the psychologist. After a while he started to cancel his appointments and finally dropped out. He did not even tell his doctor when asked why he had quitted the therapy, but blamed himself for not being able to come regularly and gave some excuse about traffic problems in the direction of the therapist's office. He had consented to a new referral without really wanting this himself.

With the permission of his client, the new psychologist confronted his colleague with the experience of the client. This psychologist refused to discuss the case with his colleague and blamed the client for being an unreliable person having serious personality problems. Finally the case came up as a complaint for the ethical board that found that the first psychologist had practised in conflict with several formulations of the principle of respect, both in the relationship with the client, as well as in relation to his colleague.

This specification can also be seen as having an aspirational aim: to promote the self-determination and autonomy of clients. This obligation is an important reminder for balancing power and thus to prevent repressive effects both in relation to the psychologist, as well as in the client's other relationships. The formulation can be seen as an implicit goal in all psychological practice, at least in the West where individual autonomy is generally considered an important characteristic. In other cultures, however, the collective might be regarded as more important, where for example the collective values of the family or the village have higher priorities. In immigration and in integration of cultures, this contradiction of values is often at the core of conflicts. This incongruity of values will also enter the psychologist's relationships when working with varied cultural issues.

The formulation of the above specification also points to the *right to* have one's need for *dependency* respected. Dependency is also a worthy social position. Without the right to be dependent, and to appeal for dependency, developmental support and proper care when needed would not be achieved. Psychologists promoting and insisting on autonomy when the resources for clients taking care of themselves are limited, can be seen as denying a social responsibility and rejecting a person's needs and interests, when caring and collective actions are needed. Accepting dependency and proper caring is often the first step in fostering later autonomy.

Again, it is important to be aware of the tendency to over-compliance in complementary relations, due to dependency. Promoting autonomy and self-determination can become expectations that mask dependency and needs for caring. The client complying, and the psychologist being unaware of the power issues in the background, can come to enhance autonomy in a situation when accepting dependency and the support of others is needed.

Quite another thing is to see dependency as a step towards greater autonomy. The expectations towards autonomy must always be matched with the client's actual competences and need for support. The balancing between autonomy and dependency is best captured in a developmental frame which can enhance autonomy in the process: *"How can I support you to your comfortable level of autonomy, and relatedness?"*

Promoting autonomy in one relationship must not result in isolating the person in other important relationships. In our ethical discourse, autonomy should always imply a relational position, where autonomy is enhanced according to needs and responsibilities within the client's system of relationships, a system of which the person's relationship to the psychologist is but one. The definition of the term "client" is important to bear in mind for weighing and finding the best balance between autonomy and dependency.

ii) Specification of the limits of such self-determination taking into account such factors as the client's developmental age, mental health and restrictions set by the legal process.

In many of the psychologist's relationships with clients there will be legal and other contextual restrictions and limitations. For working with children it is obvious that both parents have responsibilities with respect to decision-making, while the child's rights and capacities for consent will grow with age and development. For a suicidal 15-year-old it will be important for the psychologist to seek cooperation with the parents who have the obligation to protect and support their child. This is so even if the parents" handling of their youngster has contributed to the problems. When there are clear differences in responsibility for initiating the relationship, such as when working with children, one might say that parents or others with a legitimate responsibility are to define the need and main goal for the relationship to be established and to proceed. However, the child, or the dependent person must be met, respected and motivated during the process.

When there are clear legal limitations, such as in forensic work, it is rather easy to specify the limitations to self-determination, as in example 4.13. In other instances there can be more implicit limitations, where not complying to enter the relationship with the psychologist might have more or less clear consequences for the person:

Example 4.16

She might leave me if I don't join in couple's therapy? If I don't undergo a vocational assessment they can take away my social security checks? I might lose my career opportunities within my work-organisation if I don't cooperate with this psychologist coaching me (my leader's stupid idea!)?

Such more or less well-founded ideas, embedded in contextual expectations and power-structures, might limit self-determination. The client's actual experience of relating to the psychologist can thus be a humiliating event, even if he or she is consenting to be in the relationship. Once again it is worth underlining that communicating about, and specifying the contextual conditions and possible costs and outcomes, are important when the psychologist is about to enter a new relationship with a client. And entering a relationship also obliges the psychologist to continue to foster the relationship in an active, informing and discursive process with the client. Then the client can uphold optimal consent and self-determination in an often changing context where the possible restraints and power issues become clear and have a legitimate base. Dialogue and taking responsibility for the relevant outcomes of these communications is the only way to fulfil *the Principle of Respect.*

Conclusions

This chapter has explored the Principle of Respect. As set out in the definition of the Principle, this covers a good deal of ground. Fundamental is a respect for all people, their dignity and worth and a recognition of their fundamental rights. Operationalising this respect takes various forms. Psychologists respect confidentiality but also recognise that this can be problematic, when there is a risk to the rights and/or safety of a third party, to give just one example. As will become evident throughout these chapters discussing the Principles, there may often be tensions for the psychologist in reconciling *competing* principles. This issue will be addressed more fully in chapter 8.

Chapter 5

The Principle of Competence

Geoff Lindsay

Psychologists strive to ensure and maintain high standards of competence in their work. They recognize the boundaries of their particular competencies and the limitations of their expertise. They provide only those services and use only those techniques for which they are qualified by education, training or experience.

This Principle is elaborated in the following specifications:

- Ethical Awareness
- Limits of Competence
- Limits of Procedures
- Continuing Development
- Incapability

This principle addresses the more technical aspects of a psychologist's practice. It is concerned with how a psychologist makes use of the knowledge and skills that have been developed as a result of initial training, subsequent practice and further training as part of continuing professional development. Sometimes the issues addressed in this chapter may not be recognized immediately as concerning ethics as such. For example, the development of a research project will require consideration of appropriate measures. This consideration will take into account the technical qualities of the instruments to be used but, in addition, the process of ensuring that the measures are appropriate brings the psychologist firmly into the domain of ethics. Furthermore, even if the instruments are appropriate, does the psychologist have the necessary knowledge, skill and ethical awareness to use them competently.

Example 5.1

Mr Brown has just been awarded a research grant to investigate the reading ability of 8-year-old children. He will compare their performance on reading tests and reading material readily available in the classroom under different conditions of noise. The aim is to investigate how the children's performance varies and so identify the benefits of different forms of sound reduction furnishings and materials, as well as the implications for there to locate schools. Unfortunately, although Mr Brown has extensive experience of acoustics and the laboratory study of university students, he has never before tested, or even spent time with, 8-year-olds – as individuals or in classrooms. Mr Brown has, however, read the test manuals and is confident this will suffice.

In this example, can we say that Mr Brown strives to ensure and maintain high standards in his work? Certainly he is an expert in some aspects of the study he proposes. Does he recognize the boundaries of his competence? Well, yes he does. He distinguishes the skills he has from those he does not. However, this is only a partial assessment. Because of his inexperience with 8-year-old children, and with the classroom setting, he has no sound basis for his judgement. Consequently he cannot reasonably judge the limitation of his expertise. The third part of the Principle captures this when it highlights the need to use only those techniques for which he is qualified by education, training or experience.

This example is not an unfamiliar situation in which psychologists may find themselves. Science is constantly progressing and psychological knowledge is increasing all the time. New techniques arise and are promoted. All of us, however experienced, may be faced with the possibility of practising at the very limits of our competence. This may pose dilemmas for our practice and we will return to this later. First, let us consider each of the specific elements that the Meta-code sets out under the Principle of Competence.

Ethical Awareness

Obligation to have a good knowledge of ethics, including the Ethical Code, and the integration of ethical issues with professional practice.

Knowledge of ethics is the base for professional competence. It is necessary first to distinguish knowledge of ethics from knowledge of an ethical code. The former is a general awareness and understanding of the basic ethical principles and how they might be implemented. The latter concerns the specific determination of these principles by an organization into a written statement. This distinction is particularly important across Europe as the situation varies in different countries. Some countries have very well established psychological associations whereas others have relatively new associations (see chapter 1).

The situation facing an individual psychologist, therefore, will differ depending on the state of development of the psychological association. Put simply, if there is no agreed ethical code the psychologist has no formal statement to guide practice. In such instances the psychologist must use other means, for example the Meta-code.

It is implicit in this discussion that the presence of an ethical code should be helpful to individual psychologists. After all, it is much easier to look up a relatively brief document than to think about ethical principles in the abstract. It may be surprising, therefore, that the development of ethical codes has not always been considered to be a positive action (See chapter 1).

The current reality is that the EFPA Meta-code provides guidance which any psychologist may use if there is no national code. Let us consider an example of how knowledge of ethical principles is important.

Example 5.2

Ms Castilla is a final year student who is about to undertake her research project. Her department does not have a very well developed programme of ethical training. In fact, the academic staff are rather dismissive of ethics arguing that gaining ethical approval for their research is simply a hurdle that must be jumped – it gets in the way. Ms Castilla slept late on the morning that the single ethics lecture was given and she had not followed up the references given out by the lecturer. In the coffee bar she did mention to her personal tutor, informally, that she had missed the lecture. He told her not to worry and to be sensible – it was all very straightforward. Ms Castilla then developed her research proposal to ask adolescent school students about their sexual identity as she thought this would be a "cool" topic and she could perhaps write an article in the student newspaper.

1. What are Ms Castilla's responsibilities in terms of ethical knowledge?
2. What are the responsibilities of her psychology department to develop ethical knowledge?
3. What should she do in this situation?
4. Is it relevant that Ms Castilla is a student?

In this case, the student wanted to undertake a study that raises a number of ethical issues, for example the sensitivity of the topic and her plans for dissemination. Missing lectures is not unknown among students – how many of us can claim never to have missed a lecture? But in this case Ms Castilla lacked the basic knowledge necessary to plan her research project in accordance with ethical principles.

The role of the academic staff, however, was also important. Did they inculcate in students a respect for ethical practice? Would students have seen ethical guidelines as essential to check? In fact the staff have a heavier responsibility in this situation. It is not enough to take a laissez-faire approach, still less one that is dismissive of ethics. Students are expected to do a lot for themselves but, as students, they have a right to expect positive support and guidance. So, in addition to Ms Castilla's responsibilities this example highlights the responsibilities of lecturers and tutors.

Furthermore, a point to stress here, as elsewhere in this book: thinking about ethics need not – should not – simply be a solitary practice. The working environment may provide a positive setting (for example, good role models, others willing to discuss issues) or a negative setting (colleagues or superiors who are actively dismissive of ethical issues). *Each* of us has ethical responsibilities, and these are greater with more status (e.g., lecturer v student).

Example 5.3

Mr Oldtimer is a highly experienced psychologist working in a small town in independent practice. He trained in clinical psychology 40 years ago. At that time his course did not include any training in ethics. Rather, students were expected to bring any issue to their supervisor for discussion. Dr Oldtimer was a good student and brought issues to his tutor regularly but these focused on technical issues as he learned the use of instruments and the interpretation of results. Dr Oldtimer's practice has been with adults and he has been successful. He has been a thoughtful practitioner. Over his long career he has been faced with many and varied presenting problems in his work with individual clients and couples. He has never read his psychological association's ethical code. However, he has a colleague in a nearby town and they meet, informally, on a regular basis, but at these sessions they invariably also discuss difficult cases. Both find these discussions intellectually challenging and helpful to their practice.

1. Does it matter that Mr Oldtimer has not read the ethical code?
2. Is this informal and primarily social arrangement sufficient to support ethical practices?
3. What risks are there?

This is an example of a senior practitioner with no formal training in ethics. Neither has he taken steps to check the ethical code that would be relevant to his practice. On the other hand, it appears that his practice has been successful for 40 years. If that is the case, what might be the reason?

The first factor concerns Mr Oldtimer himself. He is a thoughtful and careful psychologist who reflects in his work and takes pride in his practice. Consequently he is disposed to act in a "good" way. Secondly he has developed a form of peer support. As a result he can raise issues with his friend and colleague, albeit that the main purpose of the events is social. Furthermore, it is important to stress that in addition to "professional ethics", that is those ethics that are specific to each profession, there are "common ethics". Even if a person is not very aware of the former, the latter can provide useful guidance.

If his practice has developed well then he has managed this by considering the *principles* rather than the content of a *code*. Perhaps this has not been a deliberate decision: it appears that it has happened as a result of circumstances regarding his initial training and relatively isolated work situation. Nevertheless, this is an example of where a code *may* not be essential.

However, are there risks? In the case of Mr Oldtimer there are two types of risk. The first concerns the lack of formal training and keeping up to date with respect to the code. If a complaint were made about his practice he would need to defend his lack of awareness.

Secondly there is a risk associated with a single colleague and a social rather than formal setting. There can be a tendency for close colleagues to develop similar ways of thinking – that may be an important part of the reason they are friends and colleagues. This can lead to unconscious collusion, a tendency to agree with the other's actions rather than to challenge. This general style will depend on the personality of each and the basis of their friendship – some actively seek out challenging conversation.

The third risk concerns keeping up to date. Even if each psychologist is challenging perhaps they do not know the latest thinking that affects their practice. Recent examples include the use of the internet and responsibilities regarding the reporting of suspected child abuse. In each case many associations have set up groups to consider the need for new guidelines and/or modifications to their ethical code. The EFPA Standing Committee on Ethics, for example, reviewed the use of the internet and produced a set of guidelines (www.efpa.eu).

The Standing Committee on Ethics considered whether the EFPA Meta-code needed to be changed, but decided that this was not necessary as the ethical issues raised by practice with the internet were judged to be covered in the Meta-code. However, the Standing Committee felt that guidelines to assist psychologists would be a useful addition. Hence, although there may not be a substantial impact on the basic principles considered by Mr Oldtimer, he will not have easy access to the thinking of others. Limiting his thinking about ethics to his own reflections and discussions with one colleague, therefore presents a risk.

Limits of Competence

Obligation to practise within the limits of competence derived from education, training and experience.

The implications for ethical practice include the need to recognize the different routes for gaining levels of competence appropriate to the activities in question. The clause in the Meta-code that is addressed here concerns the obligation to practise within "limits of competence" but note that these may be derived from "education, training or practice".

The role of psychologists varies across many fields of practice but in all jobs the psychologist is required to have developed an appropriate level of competence in the work that is likely to be required. Competence may be achieved by one or more of several different methods. In the early period of a profession it is not uncommon for practitioners to learn their role by relatively informal means. The universities and colleges developed, in part, to formalize the education of professions such as law and medicine. While it is possible to try to distinguish professions from trades (for example, plumbers, carpenters) this is not straightforward. For our current purposes it is also of importance to note that the education and training of psychologists has been undertaken not only in higher education settings but also in apprenticeships and even individual practice.

These variations reflect the status of the development of psychology at the time. For example, in the UK in the 1950s it was not uncommon for many senior psychologists to have trained initially in another discipline such as mathematics or the natural sciences. If training opportunities are limited then we must use what is available. This state of affairs has been found in other countries more recently. In the 1970s, for example, I contributed to a programme in Lisbon, Portugal to aid the development of applied psychology. At that time, a sizeable number of the students on the programme, which was led by UK psychologists, included academic staff of the institutions who were themselves also teaching other components of the programme.

In short, the methods of gaining competence are many and varied and we cannot assume that they are limited to formal degrees in specified institutions of higher education. This continues to be the direction of travel, however, EFPA's development of a certificate (the EuroPsy) to provide recognition of a psychologist's qualification to practise across Europe is an important strategy to formalize the recognition of qualifications.

Example 5.4

Ms Petite was trained as a clinical psychologist to work with adults but was unable to secure an appropriate appointment. There was a serious lack of psychologists in her town for working with children and the authorities were pleased to have any psychologist who had a recognition that allowed them to practice. Although they had some doubts, these were quickly overcome when Ms Petite impressed the interview panel with her charm. She was keen to move on as quickly as possible from this new post and was not keen to undertake further training of any kind to develop relevant expertise for the post.

In responding to a general practitioner's request for an assessment of an 8-year-old girl who was not reading very well she used a reading test that was no longer current and for which there were no appropriate norms. She was skilled in cognitive assessment of adults but had never assessed a child. However, she noticed that there were similarities between Wechsler scales designed for different ages of client and decided she could easily implement the test needed. However Ms Petite failed to note all the requirements for using the instrument and also misread the scoring instructions. As the mother was waiting to hear the girl's results she scored the tests quickly and produced a substantial over-estimate of reading ability, suggesting that the girl had no major problem with literacy but under-estimated her cognitive ability. She told the mother that her daughter was not very intelligent and developing as well as could be expected. The mother (and the teachers when they heard the report) were annoyed and sought a second opinion.

1. Should a psychologist trained to work with adults take a job as a psychologist with children?
2. What would be necessary to ensure competent practice?
3. In what way did Ms Petite act in an unethical manner?

Staff shortages exist. If nobody fully qualified is available then it is not unreasonable to consider employing a part-qualified psychologist. However, in this case the appointment panel bear some responsibility. They had concerns but were swayed by charm. They could have asked more searching questions to satisfy themselves or reveal unacceptable deficiencies in Ms Petite's experience. Even if her competence were recognized as insufficient they could have employed her with a requirement for specified supervision and training. In the last instance, however, the final responsibility always rests with the psychologist.

Ms Petite also had responsibilities herself. She knew she lacked competence yet she was not prepared to develop necessary skills. Furthermore she placed herself in an unacceptable position in at least two respects. Firstly she was insufficiently prepared. Her understanding of the similarities between Wechsler tests was superficial and she should have researched the instrument more thoroughly. Secondly, she should have acquired *fluency* in giving the test so that her results would be likely to be comparable to those of other qualified psychologists. She could have practised on one or more willing volunteer children. Thirdly, she left insufficient time to interpret her results and check their accuracy before reporting to the mother.

The underlying problem in this example was a lack of competence in the areas necessary to respond to the referral issue. The *ethical* issue was Ms Petite's failure to practise within the limits of her competence.

Example 5.5

Mr Brod is an educational (school) psychologist working for the psychology service in a large town. He has been in practice for 15 years and is known to hold strong views on certain contentious issues. The psychological service is organized so that every psychologist covers an area and is responsible for all referrals from the schools, parents and other professionals originating from their part of the town. Some psychologists hold that this arrangement has limitations. They do not feel expert in all areas and the service now has a system for passing a referral to a colleague who has greater specialist experience and knowledge. Nevertheless, the initial point of referral is with the local psychologist.

A mother is very concerned that Peter, 10 years, is reading at a very limited level. She has seen television programmes about dyslexia and believes her son could be dyslexic. Mr Brod does not agree that there is such a condition. He thinks that all children can be taught to read – if they do not learn it is because of poor teaching or perhaps lack of attendance at school or other matters. He assesses Peter's literacy abilities but declines to assess his cognitive abilities. Peter's mother is confused and becomes angry when Mr Brod tells her that Peter is not dyslexic.

1. Is this an issue of competence?
2. What competencies should Mr Brod have in order to respond appropriately in this case?
3. Is Mr Brod acting unethically and, if so, in what way?

This case is not one of competence in a simple sense, as in the previous example. Rather, it concerns both the psychologist's competence in a more complex sense, and his lack of willingness to consider others" perspectives.

It is not clear whether Mr Brod had the competence necessary to give the assessments other psychologists might give. However, his assessment of what was required was deficient. Dyslexia is a contentious issue but the reasons for children's difficulties in learning to read are many and varied. Consequently, whatever his view of dyslexia there was a responsibility to assess the nature of *Peter's* difficulties and not simply impose a dogmatic rejection. At that point various courses of action could be justified but he failed to get that far. By focusing only on literacy Mr Brod chose not to explore relevant cognitive abilities.

Limits of Procedures

Psychologists use a wide range of methods for assessment and interventions. The former include standardized tests (e.g., of cognition, memory and attainment), rating scales (e.g., of behaviour) and direct observation methods. Some are norm-referenced allowing a person's performance to be compared with the performance of a sample or population. Others are criterion-referenced, allowing the performance to be judged against a specific level of performance such as mastery other methods are exploratory. Some focus on overt behaviour others comprise methods designed to access non-observable wishes, projections and feelings. Psychologists also use a wide range of interventions depending on client (e.g., child, adult), nature of presenting problems, context and whether the intervention will be implemented by the psychologist (direct) or through another person such as a teacher, parent or nurse (indirect). This list is not exhaustive; for any psychologist the range of procedures that could be used will be substantial.

The focus of this section of the Meta-code is the ethical use of alternative procedures a psychologist chooses to use. However, as a *scientific* discipline the primary starting point is that any approach used will be *evidence-based.* Special considerations apply when a new method is being developed (see below).

i) *Obligation to be aware of the limits of procedures for particular tasks, and the limits of conclusions that can be derived in different circumstances and for different purposes.*

Example 5.6

Miss Bardot had practiced for 10 years in the part of central France where she had been born but decided to move to a city. The clients she now received were substantially more diverse, with many different languages and cultures. She was asked to assess the cognitive ability of an 8-year-old child whose parents were from Mauritius where French has historically been a dominant language. She administered the tests she had previously used but was unsure if this was appropriate.

1. What is the significance of working with a client from another country?
2. Does it matter whether the same language is used in both countries?
3. What questions should Miss Bardot ask?

We live in an increasingly diverse world. Countries are now increasing in their range of ethnic groups and cultures. In London schools, for example, there are well over 100 different languages among the families of pupils. This provides a major challenge to the validity of psychological assessment.

A method of assessment is typically validated against the population with whom it will be used. There are several relevant factors taken into account. The age of the person being assessed is one factor. In addition to the development issue, whereby older children may be expected to perform to a higher level than younger children on a range of material, there is also a question of salience of the material. For example, the interests of a 5-year-old will differ from those of a 10-year-old, and from an adult. Vocabulary knowledge will therefore be partly dependent on material but also on relevance of the vocabulary to the person.

In the current example, language and culture would be relevant. Even though Mauritius has a strong French history, and the language used by most Mauritians is "French" it cannot be assumed that it is directly equivalent to the language spoken in France. Furthermore, even within a country there may be subtle, but important differences between the language spoken by different sub-populations. Misunderstanding resulting from such subtle differences can have major implications. In the UK applied psychologists are not yet regulated by law but this is close. In discussions about standards of proficiency we have had to make strong arguments that psychologists must have the highest level of language competence in order to understand such subtleties: for example, whether in a therapeutic intervention, an analysis of a child with developmental language difficulties or an adult following a stroke. Other cultural differences are also important. For example, tests of reading comprehension or of verbal understanding often use "real" situations to test understanding. These may be unfair if such cultural differences are outside the experience of a person being given the assessment.

Ms Bardot is right to have concerns. She will need to consider the degree to which her measures are appropriate for this child – any others – and hence the limits of the conclusions she can derive. The danger is to under-estimate abilities by unfair assessment.

Example 5.7

Dr Gonzales is a psychotherapist who is finding it difficult to earn the amount of money he believes is appropriate for his expertise. He decides to increase his productivity by changing from individual to group therapy. He tries this initially by bringing two clients together. He then decides to increase group size to increase his income even more. He was very experienced as a therapist and believes this change is simply one of scale.

1. Are there any risks in Gonzales's actions?
2. What questions should he ask himself?

There is a strong tradition of individual therapy but group methods were also developed by practitioners. In some cases, at least, these were a response to economic pressures. For example, in the UK the National Health Service provided free treatment but limited resources led some therapists to develop methods so that more clients could be helped. Group versus individual therapy is not the main issue.

In this example, Dr Gonzales's motivation is to increase his income rather than help more clients (although that could be the outcome). We may well have views on his motivation but it is not specifically an ethical issue. More central is the question of the *appropriateness* of the implementation of a successful method in a *different way*. Dr Gonzales is using the same method with a group. He cannot be sure that its effectiveness with individuals will be replicated. His actions pose the risk that his practice will be less effective.

Dr Gonzales should therefore ask himself firstly, what evidence is there to support his groupwork? Assuming evidence is supportive it may indicate important considerations. Dr Gonzales should consider these: for example, is effectiveness less than in individual therapy? Is it differentially effective for different clients? Are more sessions required to reach equivalent effectiveness?

Such questions will allow Dr Gonzales to consider whether this form of therapy is appropriate if he is to maintain his standards. If impact is less or range of clients helped is smaller then he would need to consider how his practice should take these into account.

ii) *Obligation to practise within, and to be aware of the psychological community's critical development of theories and methods.*

Science is typically theory-driven, but there is a developmental process. Initially, ideas and hypotheses may be considered and examined. As evidence accumulates a theory may start to be developed. With more evidence a stronger theory may be formulated. This may then lead to a sustained period of research to examine its strengths. Theories are generally regarded as not being capable of proof. Rather, scientific endeavour seeks to *disprove* theories. By doing so, a theory becomes supported by failures to disprove it. Or, modifications to elements of the theory may be proposed on the basis of accumulated evidence.

This position is evident in psychology as a scientific discipline but is more complex. Training in psychological science and practice requires critical engagement with theories relevant to the area of practice. At any particular time there will be dominant theories that command general support on the basis of the evidence in their favour – and there will be some evidence in favour of competing theories.

Example 5.8

Ms Crystal is an experienced and creative psychologist. She is an avid reader of a wide and disparate literature related to psychology and human behaviour. She does not believe in limiting herself to formal research. She is very wary of what she sees as an over-reliance on positivistic research methods. She believes much can be learned from evidence that is experiential. Having been engaged herself in a number of experiential groups and New Age activities she decides to make use of an exciting new therapy promoted by the charismatic leader of the group she has joined. This involves a combination of meditation and extreme exercise. She believes this combination reduces depression and improves self-esteem.

1. Is Ms Crystal right to offer such therapy as a psychologist?
2. Are any safeguards necessary?

It is very difficult, if not impossible, in psychology to argue that any form of therapy is "proven". In the 1950s, for example, there was much criticism by Eysenck and others of the benefits of psychoanalysis. The demonstrable benefits of theories based on behavioural psychology (e.g., systematic desensitisation) allows judgements to be made of the likelihood of improvement for particular clients with particular conditions. More recently, cognitive behavioural therapy has become a well regarded method which has also been subject to much study. However, as research has increased our knowledge so the limitations of the approach have also become more evident.

Ms Crystal appears to be a psychologist willing and keen to explore new options. This is, in many respects, an admirable characteristic. Having this orientation leads psychologists to challenge the status quo and move the discipline forward (see also chapter 6, Integrity). However, at any particular point in time it is necessary to ask how secure is the evidence for this method? If the evidence base is limited there is an obligation on the psychologist to be cautious. This might result in a deliberately reflective approach, reflecting on and examining the outcomes of each therapeutic intervention. Any clients should also be made aware of the scientific status of the therapy to be offered.

Example 5.9

Mr Schmidt is a colleague of Ms Crystal. He is also convinced of the benefits of this therapy. He is much more sceptical about the generally recognized therapies and does not accept the need for evidence. He argues that it is belief that is necessary. He has this and he insists that it would be wrong for any client to be told about the lack of evidence for the therapy – not only is evidence irrelevant, in his view; a client could be "confused" by being told about the lack of evidence. Instead, he requires all clients to believe in him and his therapy, assuring them that this therapy will work if they believe.

1. Is there any ethical difference in the positions of Ms Crystal and Mr Schmidt?
2. What are the ethical questions about Dr Schmidt's approach?

Dr Schmidt shares Ms Crystal's enthusiasm for this new therapy. His commitment is also affected by his rejection of a central element of psychological practice; namely the need for evidence. Psychology was once very heavily characterized by positivism but this has changed substantially over recent years. The benefits of evidence derived from different sources have been recognized. Quantitative and qualitative methods are both recognized as having an important role, albeit for addressing different questions. Large samples, small groups and even studies of single cases ($n = 1$) are all now recognised as valid approaches. However, this is different from adopting a position where the only worthwhile evidence is judged to be the psychologist's own opinion based on their own experience.

If challenged, Dr Stardust would need to justify his approach to therapy. If this is limited to his own opinion then his position would be difficult to sustain. If on the other hand he could show evidence of benefits among a number of his clients then his position could be considered viable – even if he did not himself wish to take note of such evidence.

Furthermore, this example raises the issue of *professional consensus*. At any point there will typically develop a consensus about major methods used in psychology based on research and professional experience. The profession, particularly through psychological associations and related organizations has its own responsibility to facilitate this consensus by supporting by bringing together and dissemination of these two types of evidence. However, in each case we are talking about *evidence-based* practice but recognizing that the quality of evidence may vary. What is not acceptable is the *Collusion of the prejudiced and/or uninformed*. In such instances people convince themselves and other by considering only *part* of the evidence, perhaps that which supports their prior views.

All methods have limitations as well as benefits and an important role for a psychologist is to be able to assess the relative status of these factors. In this context assessing the status of a new, under-researched approach is simply a difference in emphasis: the purpose is the same. Hence it is important to stress that ethical codes do not prohibit new methods – that is the death knell of the development of a profession and not in the interest of clients. Rather, all psychologists have a responsibility to ground their practice in approaches with good evidence but also to be open-minded to new methods and their developing evidence-base. Each psychologist may then feed back intelligence into the profession as a whole to enhance the development of the profession's undertaking.

The general position within the community of psychology is therefore an important factor when judging practice. There is a danger with this if the community is very conservative and refuses to consider any new developments unless there is overwhelming support for its validity and benefit (see below). Nevertheless, it is important to balance this risk against those arising from a lack of evidence.

Example 5.10

Mr Strong worked with clients who typically had multiple difficulties. They had many mental health problems and problematic lifestyles. He had attended a course designed to improve his efficacy as a professional. He was attracted by the theoretical and evidence base for this approach and decided to implement it with certain clients whom he judged to be likely to benefit. One element of the course had been to challenge the professionals by strong confrontations, using forceful language and judgements. He used this approach with one client, Mr Down, who was very upset at this method and felt his self esteem had been seriously undermined and his development adversely affected. He made a complaint to the ethical committee. Mr Strong was affronted by this ingratitude and defended himself vigorously.

1. Was this approach reasonable?
2. Did Mr Strong make any errors?

This example touches upon the generalisability of methods from one domain to another and the necessity for the psychologist to consider whether it is appropriate to do this. A strength of psychology is that it has applicability across many areas of life. George Miller's famous phrase to give psychology away has been a mantra for many of us who want more people to benefit than could be the case if the delivery of psychology is restricted to a necessarily small number of practitioners. A similar view concerns the application of psychological practice shown to be appropriate in one setting to a new setting.

There has been much interest in using psychology to assist the personal development of well people, not just those who have problems. This can be found extensively in educational and work/organizational psychology where the aims are to improve satisfactory or good performance and to make it even better. Mr Strong appears to have been motivated by a positive wish to apply the lessons he learned himself, and for which there was evidence, into his own work. The main question concerns the transfer and the ethical issues Mr Strong should address.

Firstly, and unlike the course Mr Strong attended, he intends to apply the method to clients who are not functioning adequately. Secondly, he adapted an element of the method that is high risk, not least because it is likely to cause upset even in strong personalities. Thirdly, there is a question of Mr Down's understanding and his giving informed consent. Whereas Mr Strong may have known he would face confrontation on his course, did his client, Mr Down? Even if he did warn him, could he be sure that this awareness was comparable to that which he had, given that Mr Down's status was a man with mental health problems?

What should Mr Strong have done when Mr Down complained? His reaction was to be defensive. He might have put himself in Mr Down's position and realized that this was very different from the position he had been in when he was on his course. He might have chosen to apologise and to try to explain further, debriefing Mr Down and offering further therapy from himself or another psychologist.

iii) *Obligation to balance the need for caution when using new methods with a recognition that new areas of practice and methods will continue to emerge and that this is a positive development.*

Example 5.11

Dr O'Malley was asked to advise a company on the employment of staff. The Green-R-Ss company was expanding and sought staff who would be high quality managers with strategic vision, sensitive interpersonal skills and a strong commitment to the company's values associated with "green" issues. Dr O'Malley administered a set

of psychological assessment instruments based on the Theory of Green Motiva-
tion". He had developed the theory himself and was very keen to have validation
results from a study in a "real" setting. He was pleased to find the measures dis-
criminated between applicants and he advised the company accordingly of who
would be suitable managers for the posts.

1. Is it ethical to use your own theory and measures you have devised?
2. What information should Dr O'Malley provide to the company?

A number of measures and groups of measures are well established in psychology, for example the Wechsler scales of general cognitive ability. However, the
discipline continues to grow and show creativity. New perspectives on theoretical positions may lead to different types of measures whose construct validity is
related to the new theoretical position. In other cases measures are designed because they seek to be improvements on current measures of a well established
theoretical position. For example, vocabulary scales are well established as useful measures but must be revised to reflect the current range of vocabulary in a
population.

Dr O'Malley's own research has led to the development of a theory and to associated measures which could be relevant to the tasks set by Green-R-Us. The first
issue concerns the evidence for the theory – is it well established? Have others examined and supported the validity and usefulness or is it just Dr O'Malley's work?
Have the measures been shown to be reliable and valid? Have they been used in
field trials? With other companies? By different psychologists?

These stages in the development of measures are important in order to provide
the basis for this element of the Meta-code: what are their *limits?* At the most basic,
is the theory supported and, if so, do the instruments adequately measure the factors
identified by the theory as important? In this example it does not appear as though
there is the weight of evidence necessary. However much Dr O'Malley believes in
his theory, this is not sufficient: Evidence is required.

Does this mean that the instruments Dr O'Malley developed cannot be used? No,
but Dr O'Malley must exercise caution. If his instruments are essentially still in a developmental phase then he is obligated to make this clear to the client. He might
choose to use a well established instrument alongside his own to provide additional
information on which to base his advice – this would also allow further evidence on
validity to be gained.

Dr O'Malley should also inform any potential client of the nature and status of
measures he proposes to use and the limitations that may exist. In this case the relevant
factors are:

- These are new instruments and evidence on technical quality appears supportive
  but more is required.
- As *he* developed the instruments, this should be made clear to provide transparency.

If Dr O'Malley is adopting an ethical position, is researching his theory and measures objectively, and is open with clients, he will be able to respond to clients like Green-R-Us ethically. However, he still has a further obligation:

- He should critically examine his evidence and include in his advice a judgement of the impact of his own measures.

This is important as, however open he has been, Dr O'Malley should still make a judgement of his evidence. If, for example, his measure provides very different results compared with other, established measures he should weigh this up and include this in his advice as there may be *limits to the conclusions* that can be derived at this stage.

Example 5.12

Miss Smart worked as a forensic psychologist in an institution for young male offenders. She had found clear evidence to support research findings that a very high proportion of the young offenders had low literacy ability. She had read of a new technique for helping develop literacy based upon the use of coloured lenses or acetate overlaps from the printed material. She had researched this approach and was aware that it was controversial. However, the method currently in use did not seem successful and she decided to trial this method. She asked a professor from the local university to work with her to supervise a research study. She discussed the proposal with education staff and the young people themselves. She was told that only one teacher could be allowed to teach a group to try out this method. She set up a 2 month trial with one group followed by a further trial for a second group of young offenders.

1. Was the use of a contentious method with an incarcerated population justified?
2. How appropriate were the safeguards taken by Miss Smart?

Particular challenges are presented when working with persons who have limited ability to choose to be the recipient of a psychologist's service is. When the evidence for the method used is partial there is an added responsibility to be careful. Those who are incarcerated may be open to abuse from researchers who know their ability to refuse to participate is limited. In this case Miss Smart did consult and offered the method, she did not insist that it be used.

All new methods used by psychologists, by definition, have limited evidence for their validity and usefulness at the beginning of their use. Evidence must be developed and replication of findings is a powerful approach to validity. Miss Smart was aware that she may lack the research knowledge to run this programme. She also realized that the sensitivity of the situation required an adviser, more senior and experienced that herself. Furthermore, her chance of an *outsider* provided access to advice from someone who was not employed in the service which had incarcerated these young offenders.

Miss Smart adopted a reasonable method – the "waiting list control group". This ensured that the benefits, if any, of the method were made available to all the young people, not only those in the experimental group.

Miss Smart's actions, therefore, showed sensitivity to a number of relevant factors. This example also stresses the inter-relationship of ethical principles in practice. While the focus here is on an issue of competence, the ethical challenges were broader.

Continuing Development

i)   Obligation to continue professional development.

A characteristic of a profession is that there is a formalized and consistent initial training programme. This may take various forms. In psychology there will be strong research and theoretical elements plus supervised practices. This is a model used in other professions (e.g., medicine). The completion of initial training was seen as the only necessary formal training in the past. Increasingly, and across many professions, it has been recognized that the practitioner must continue to undertake continuing professional development (CPD).

However, the formal approach to CPD is very varied. Even in those countries with very well established initial training of psychologists formal requirements for CPD are relatively recent. Also, the monitoring of CPD by a professional or regulatory body is quite complex. Unless particular training courses are specified the psychologist may be required to undertake a range of CPD activities. These may be very varied and broad in range to allow for many different needs. Initial qualifications will seek to produce high levels of common training, so optimizing consistent practice. Once a psychologist is in practice, however, there will be different populations, challenges and opportunities to learn. Typically, where requirements for CPD have been developed these allow a mixture of some core experiences plus individually specific elements. The British Psychological Society, for example, requires all chartered psychologists to demonstrate they have undertaken CPD in core domains which does not specify *what* the training should be or *how* it should be developed. Instead, a portfolio of CPD is maintained and presented for inspection. Other countries have similar requirements.

However, not all Associations have such a system. The requirement for CPD in the Meta-code is a stimulus to ensure that CPD is required and undertaken by psychologists in every country. It is an obligation to maintain and develop competence.

Example 5.13

Dr Methusalah is at the end of his career. Very experienced, he has generally been unremarkable in his practice. He has never had a complaint made about him, but neither has his work been innovative. Rather, he has kept to the approaches he learned in his initial training, adding to these very sparingly over the years.

Dr Methusalah was asked to assess three young children in a family, where there was an acrimonious dispute about custody. He decided to take the children with their mother and her social worker to the local bowling alley to observe their interactions. He offered to take two of the children in his car while the mother drove the others. He absented himself when they arrived, so requiring the mother to pay for them all. However, he did offer to take the young boy to the toilet. He also became friendly with a female assistant and offered his visiting card. The mother had been confused by this method of assessment and then annoyed by the interaction with the assistant. She became rather emotional and accused Dr Methusalah of "chatting up" this young lady. In his report he claimed that the mother was not a good parent, was emotional and irrational, lacked caring skills and that the father should have custody. The mother complained to the Ethics Committee. At the Tribunal Dr Methusalah claimed that his actions were all appropriate. When asked to justify why he took the family to the bowling alley he claimed that it was based on sound psychological principles he had always practised.

1. Was Dr Methusalah's approach to assessment appropriate?
2. What are the issues regarding competence?
3. Was the mother right to complain?

This case has a number of worrying features but our present concern is about competence. The basic issue, from which all other questionable actions followed, concerns Dr Methusalah's decision to take the family to a public place in order to assess the children's interactions with their mother. The use of naturalistic settings can offer helpful information in an assessment but only as *part* of an assessment. Dr Methusalah limited his assessment and never interviewed any child, individually or in a group. He never observed in the home. He was unaware of the child protection requirements which were relevant to several of his actions, including driving the children with no other supervising appropriate adult; and taking a young child to a public toilet.

Child protection has been of increasing importance in professional training. The evidence of inappropriate behaviour by adults and of abuse has been revealed across Europe and beyond to be of a scale previously unimagined. It is a fundamental requirement of training to work with children and young people that a psychologist is aware of the issues, and of guidelines and the requirements, whether by law or professional practice guidance. Dr Methusalah was quite unaware of these issues. Even if his actions were well meaning in intent they were unwise and revealed a serious lack of understanding of current practice.

His approach to assessment was also very limited. He had not received any specific training in child custody cases. Neither had he sought advice from colleagues or received supervision. Instead, he decided on an action which was highly risky and would not typically be the *initial* assessment procedure even if some form of naturalistic assessment were to be used at some stage. He had no way of assessing risk (for example, of one child running away, of the mother's competence to control her children). Neither did he include any other form of assessment, so resulting in a very limited evidence base.

Dr Methusalah also wrote a report where he made, in effect, a judgement of the relative competence of mother and father – yet he had never met the father, let alone assessed his capabilities.

Dr Methusalah was not inherently a malicious person. However, his lack of awareness of what was appropriate in the case he took on revealed a serious lack of professional development. If he had undertaken CPD on child custody he would probably have had the opportunity to address all the key issues where he acted inappropriately.

Example 5.14

Mr Binet had practised as a child psychologist for nearly 40 years. Whatever referral he received he always administered the first edition of the Wechsler Intelligence Scale for Children he had learned this in his training. He had used it several thousand times and claimed he had an excellent understanding of the results and their relationship to school-related problems. For example, he would associate subtext profiles with types of difficulty and use these when advising teachers and parents.

1. Is it appropriate to use instruments superseded by more modern editions?
2. Are there any benefits in Mr Binet's actions.

Over the past 40 years there have been revisions of major psychological instruments such as the Weschler scales. These have included relatively minor changes to items; new norms from restandardizations in the US; new standardizations in many other countries; and new theoretically driven structures of the way elements in the tests relate to each other. These changes reflect the evidence that has accumulated plus the requirements of good test design, including restandardization to reflect current norms.

Unless a psychologist keeps up with changes and considers using new versions of a test (or a different test entirely) there is a danger of inappropriate assessment taking place. For example, the mean IQ in many countries has risen over the past 40 years. A child assessed on an earlier edition of a test is likely to have an *inflated* score suggesting they are more able relative to others of their age than is the case at this time. Mr Binet is laying himself open to this risk.

However, it is worth noting also Mr Binet's practice does have positive elements. A feature of multiple assessments using the same instrument is that the psychologist can develop potentially useful awareness of children's patterns of performance. The difficulty that must be faced, however, is distinguishing clinical awareness from objective evidence. It may be that certain patterns are noted but others are not, for example.

It is also reasonable to argue that a new test is not necessarily better than one it is designed to replace. This will depend partly on the construct validity of the instrument and also on empirical evidence collected on those assessed, children in this case.

Mr Binet, therefore, could argue to support his actions up to a point. Nevertheless, he cannot reasonably ignore developments that challenge a simple adherence to the past. Mr Binet should be reviewing his practice continuously. When new instruments are produced he has a responsibility to consider their relative strengths against those he currently uses and make a decision based upon that assessment.

The practice of psychology has changed so much, and continues to change at such a fast rate that initial training can only be realistically conceptualized as a starting point for a person's career not the knowledge and skill base for a whole career. Psychologists are not alone: medicine is another clear example of this phenomenon. Consequently, CPD is becoming recognized as essential. Not only is there more to know and be able to practise competently, we may also feel less sure about what we know and, perhaps more importantly, are in that uncomfortable position where *we don't know what we don't know*.

Finally, it is worth noting societal changes of expectation. As a relatively newly qualified educational psychologist I noticed a plea from a journalist in the education section of a serious newspaper. She wanted to write a series of articles "A day in the life of" different educational professionals. She reported that she was having great problems. Either professionals that she approached simply declined or agreement would be broken. Being enthusiastic to disseminate our work I offered her a day.

As part of the day's work I visited the nursery unit of a school. This was a new venture: a "special" nursery where children with significant special educational needs were integrated into a mainstream nursery. Inclusion was aided by enhanced staffing. During the visit I worked with one little boy I knew well on a table top activity, using available toys to explore his conceptual and linguistic development. This boy had significant language delay plus high levels of activity and distractability. As usual with small children (he was 4) I sat on my haunches to bring myself to his level at the table. During the session he gradually left his chair and moved onto my knee. The journalist took a very good photograph of this little boy carrying out his tasks. Her article (a rather positive report) was published in a very popular magazine for early years teachers, illustrated by the photograph. Several teachers commented as I visited their schools that they recognized me and were very interested to see the range of work I did.

The point of this anecdote is that many psychologists working with young children in the UK would be very reluctant to allow a child to come and sit on their knee. Our concern for child protection has altered what many regard as "safe" behaviour. In addition to a child's safety, professionals must consider their own "safety", especially when many teachers have been accused unfairly of abuse, with serious negative consequences for their careers.

The issue this raises concerns boundaries, of course, and safe practice but also the way that societal expectations affect our *interpretation* of these factors. Many charges resulting from such expectations are for the better, but perhaps not all. You might like to consider the following questions:

-   If you work with young children, would you allow a child to sit on your knee in a classroom to carry out a table top activity?
-   If not, why not?

Incapability

Obligation not to practise when ability or judgement is adversely affected, including temporary problems.

Example 5.15

Mr Carlsberg has gradually become dependent on drinking alcohol. Initially he was a social drinker, including a little wine or beer with his lunch. Now he drinks spirits before work and even during the day – he keeps a drinks cabinet in his office. One client complained that he fell asleep during a consultation and his breath smelt of alcohol.

This sad example is probably a clear case of unethical behaviour. The intake of alcohol itself appears to be adversely affecting Mr Carlsberg's ability to perform his practice. As such it would clearly be seen as unethical.

But what if his ability to perform his duties were not adversely affected? Many people with addictions to alcohol (and indeed to hard drugs such as heroin) remain capable of performing their jobs. Traditionally medical practitioners have been regarded as particularly at risk of developing certain addictions because of the easy access to a range of drugs.

The primary focus of this clause is that either (or both) ability or judgement are adversely affected. But what about social expectations? Many employers forbid alcohol on the premises and now, in many countries, smoking is also forbidden. Each may have an impact on ability and judgement (a frustrated smoker may become irritable or make less good judgements). But, in addition, each may be offensive to different degrees to others including clients. Many find a smoking atmosphere very problematic apart from any health risk. Consequently, many employers, or psychologists themselves, would choose not to smoke or drink alcohol, for example, because they regard this as an unreasonable intrusion on their clients (and possibly colleagues).

However, some professionals might argue that there is a positive benefit in engaging in some of these behaviours. For example, a client who smokes may be more at ease if they have shared a cigarette with the psychologist. It may be part of a ritual for developing rapport. Some social workers, for example, who visit clients with alcohol problems argue similarly that to take a couple of beers with the client has a similarly beneficial effect.

These matters, however, are not central to this specification. They may relate to any of the other three sections of the Meta-code. Nevertheless, although not central, they are also relevant here. Although small amounts of alcohol and tobacco may not adversely affected judgement, the psychologist's ability to act as a professional may be adversely affect if the client's trust and respect are undermined. Nevertheless, the basis of this clause is not a disagreement about social expectations of appropriate behaviour but rather an *impairment* to the psychologist's ability or judgement.

Example 5.16

Ms Dynamic is a hard-working highly committed psychologist. She is always prepared to work long hours and to take other clients if a colleague is ill. She has a very strong sense of responsibility and sees such actions as a way to prevent clients being let down or going without the necessary help they were expecting.

One morning Ms Dynamic woke up with a very heavy cold. Is it flu? Will it pass quickly? Although she felt awful she had a full day's work with many clients, some of whom will have travelled a long way. So, after a hot shower and light breakfast she set off for work believing her walk (instead of a bus) would "clear her head".

At first this seemed to work but as the day progressed she felt increasingly tired, her muscles ached, she developed a cough, a headache and other symptoms. Nevertheless, she carried on and saw all her clients. As this was a Friday, she had a weekend to come. She spent this at home, mostly in bed, and by Monday she was generally OK, perhaps at 90% efficiency. She went back to work.

Note that this specification makes it clear that *temporary* problems are also covered. In this case, perhaps Ms Dynamic's problems were temporary, in practice she had a "bad day", and perhaps from the Monday she is pretty well back to normal. But what of the Friday? What kind of service did her Friday clients receive? Was her ability and/or judgement affected that day?

This is a very familiar scenario for most if not all psychologists, the more so if they are committed. Whereas some people take time off work (in all kinds of jobs) at the first sign of a problem such as a cold, at the other extreme we have those like Ms Dynamic. Let us not forget the first group, however. By their actions such psychologists will not offend this specification. But they will limit client's positive input by their absence if this cannot be adequately covered. Hence, questions of Responsibility and Integrity arise here.

Those that try to work unless totally incapable (or refused or permission) are driven by positive intentions but their actions may have negative consequences. There is a real dilemma: how to balance the two? The first point is that all psychologists should *consider* this specification. Ms Dynamic did not: she had a very clear view of professional duty which did not have this issue on the agenda. That was her mistake. Many of us who are committed are similar. All the more reason, therefore, for committed psychologists to reflect on this clause and make a decision that balances the benefits to be gained or lost by clients. In addition, they should apply this reflection to themselves also, not least because an illness may be aggravated by not taking it seriously. This may have serious consequences for the psychologist – and also for clients who may be deprived by a longer period of absence.

Example 5.17

Mr Nord is approaching the end of his career. He has been a highly competent psychologist, keeping up to date and working diligently. He is highly respected in his small town. However, recently he has become forgetful. Not only has he "lost" a number of things that he misplaced he now finds it necessary to have test manuals to hand when carrying out an assessment to be sure to read instructions accurately. He wonders if he should retire, but there is a shortage of psychologists and this is not a popular town to move into.

Here we have a psychologist who has worked competently and ethically but he has a dilemma. Unlike Ms Dynamic, he is sensitive to the dilemma and works to resolve it. If he retires he may deprive the town of a most important resource. If he continues, will he start to practise without the necessary level of competence. Which should he do?

This is not likely to be a temporary problem but this possibility should be considered. Some event or medication can adversely affect memory but this can be overcome. So, initially he should consult his physician for advice, perhaps an examination. If it seems that he has the beginnings of some of the characteristics of older age then there are still actions that can be taken without the necessity to retire. In fact he has already started to implement useful strategies – using manuals rather than memory. There are a number of strategies that could be adopted and the support of other staff and colleagues will be useful. For example, a good secretary will be a huge benefit in not only organizing his diary but ensuring he is informed specifically of his appointments and obligations.

This specification is important not so much for the obvious but more for the less clear situations. Furthermore, it is a clause that, may be particularly relevant to the most ethical psychologists who are so driven by the desire to "do good" that they are blind to limitations on them.

Conclusions

This section of the Meta-code addresses the core issue of Competence. However, as can be seen from the examples, competence has many facets. It covers initial acquisition of knowledge and skills, maintaining and developing these, and finally recognizing when such abilities are in some way less optimal or even impaired. Competence is also driven by the scientific nature of psychology as our practice should be evidence-based. Competence, therefore, requires reflection throughout a psychologist's career, to check that performance is still optimal and that our clients are receiving the best possible service.

Chapter 6

The Principle of Responsibility

Fredi Lang

Psychologists are aware of the professional and scientific responsibilities to their clients, to the community, and to the society in which they work and live. Psychologists avoid doing harm and are responsible for their own actions, and assure themselves, as far as possible that their services are not misused.

This Principle is elaborated in the following specifications:

- General Responsibility
- Promotion of High Standards
- Avoidance of Harm
- Continuity of Care
- Extended Responsibility
- Resolving Dilemmas

This principle expresses the obligation for psychologists to reflect on their different responsibilities to clients, the community and the society. Therefore a main task for a psychologist is to gain awareness about the responsibilities to the parties involved and to maintain the professional ethical standards of their actions. The client's trust in the psychologist's professional competence, the respect of self-determination, freedom of consent and informed consent, and the maintenance of confidentiality are some constitutive premises of psychological practice. Inequalities of knowledge and power constitute further factors requiring a special responsibility in psychologists' professional practice.

The principle of responsibility is widely and tightly associated with the other principles stated in the Meta-Code. Since responsibility incorporates all areas of professional and ethical competence, a listing of the subsections of respect, integrity and competence as relevant dimensions could appear here. The meshwork of responsibilities towards the primary and other clients, the community and to society as a whole varies with respect to complexity and potential for conflicts. This becomes apparent when comparing the professional roles of psychologists working in schools, health system, psychiatric clinics, prisons or companies, for example, regarding client constellations and relevant legal requirements.

But also within their areas of work psychologists are continuously facing new duties, challenges and responsibilities. As part of their professional development psychologists internalise the principles and orientations as stated in the Meta-Code. They follow them either explicitly in decision making processes or implicitly in decision routines and, probably more often, in a mixture of these. The assumption of responsibility as a psychologist does not only mean being aware of the role as a whole and of the individual parts. There should also be a process of integration of ethical reflection in everyday life as a part of the professional role, while keeping in mind the complexity of responsibilities.

An important aspect of professional practice as a psychologist is the necessity to have a scientific basis of applied theories, methods and appropriate knowledge about, and respecting of, their limitations (especially when dealing with new theories) see Examples 5.8, 5.11 Consequently a part of responsibility consists of continuous education and training and in the disclosure of weaknesses and limitations of applied methods, procedures and treatments as appropriate to the client. Not only are limitations arising from the current state of science and scientific debate of importance for ethical reflections, but also factors affecting one's competence concerning the job including those arising from one's private life such as sickness, or the death of relatives.

The nature of psychologists' ethical responsibility for their professional actions and their consequences is personal. It doesn't matter whether psychologists act in a personal capacity or in cases where they bear responsibility for colleagues or assistants. Also it is not fundamental for the nature of ethical responsibility whether psychologists can act freely or act under the guidance of a supervisor, are following orders of the management or whether others bear even more responsibility. These are important factors that have an influence but ultimately each psychologist has a personal responsibility to act ethically.

Psychologists strive to act in the best interests of their clients, avoid harm wherever possible and minimise unavoidable harm. Nevertheless, respect for the client's rights in case of an ethical dilemma may, even after careful consideration of the different responsibilities, directly or indirectly lead to decisions with consequences of sadness, emotional distress, grief or even harm, either to the primary client or to relevant third persons. The wording "avoiding harm" in the Meta-Code serves as an absolute dictum insofar as psychologists consciously never deliberately contribute to the genesis and/or the maintenance of suffering – neither directly nor indirectly. If a psychologist considers this possibly could be the case, careful checks need to be made before acting; for example, by challenging referral requests or, in some situations, orders.

In case of ethical dilemmas with unavoidable harm for the client or one of the parties, psychologists have to balance carefully the effects and the consequences of their actions seeking the best balanced decision possible at the time. Furthermore the concept of avoiding harm requires a personal commitment to seek a way to minimise harm and to take action where harm is foreseeable and unavoidable. For instance in a case of carrying out an expert witness evaluation of a victim of rape, emotional distress is likely to be caused by the evaluation however carefully the psychologist carries out the task.

Associated with the avoidance of harm, the avoidance of misuse of psychological knowledge and methods is also part of psychologist's responsibility. Misuse may occur in many circumstances, for instance by applying outdated models, going beyond the limits of methods and procedures or using them with groups, settings or for purposes not within their specifications. One can distinguish between violating the principle of competence by using methods and procedures for other purposes and the use of psychological services for the achievement of unethical or ethically questionable ends and by so doing accepting harm or even torture, e.g., in TV-shows or interrogations by national security services. Checking the ethical compatibility between goals and the consequences of psychological services on the one hand and the client's goals and ends on the other is an aspect of responsibility that is important to consider before accepting a referral, commission or order. In the context of the common and increasing delegation of psychological services by senior and fully qualified psychologists, an important aspect of responsibility is to make sure that psychological services delivered by assistants and colleagues are carried out competently and with full consideration of ethical standards.

General Responsibility

i) For the quality and consequences of the psychologist's professional actions.

This first clause states a general responsibility for the quality and consequences of professional actions and in a general way covers all possible areas of work and relationships. Implicit in this general clause is the need to consider complexity and the implications of new situations and ethical dilemmas occurring as part of professional responsibility in daily practice.

Responsibility as a principle of social life is well known but it varies depending upon different roles and their significance, for example between citizens, parents and their children; among liberal professions, like lawyers, psychologists, medical doctors, and their clients.

The responsibility of psychologists as a part of their professional role differs from those related to being a citizen, father etc. or those arising from other social roles. Problems or ethical dilemmas may not only derive from the professional relationship but also from multiple relationships, conflicts between the role as psychologist and secondary professional roles, for example as businessman or consultant for services on national security issues.

There might be the idea that responsibility is implicit by the psychologist aiming for the best interests of the client. However, since responsibility covers the quality of actions undertaken, there is also a close relation to competence i.e., using scientifically based knowledge and the adherence to commonly accepted guidelines. Since psychologists are often in charge of supporting or intervening in processes of human development their responsibility is not only related to the action undertaken but also in a general way to activities *not* conducted and their consequences. Furthermore the combination of the qualities of actions and their consequences leads to the need to include both the goal and the process into ethical reflection and decision making.

Example 6.1

A 14-year-old adolescent breaks down in school. The teacher refers her to a psychiatric outpatient clinic where she is seen by a clinical psychologist on a weekly basis. The parents are informed their daughter is being treated for depression, but – as she asks for strict confidentiality – they do not know any details. The adolescent's secret is that she has been sexually harassed and threatened in serious ways by her brother for several years. She pretends that she can cope with the situation – she wants to manage it herself and definitely does not want her parents or even the police to be informed. The clinical psychologist wishes to respect confidentiality but feels that her patient is not able to make the harassment stop all by herself. She knows she would lose her client's trust and, as a result, would not be able to continue therapy if she notified the parents or the child protection agency.

What ethical principles can help the psychologist in her decision on how to proceed?

In this case many clauses from the Meta-code are of relevance for ethical reflections: confidentiality, self-determination, informed and freedom of consent, avoidance of harm, general responsibility, resolving dilemmas, straightforwardness and openness. Some of them are in conflict.

The respect for confidentiality and of the client's autonomy and self-determination are in conflict with the obligation to avoid foreseeable harm and negative consequences of one's actions. Therapy aims to minimise the consequences of harm that has been experienced and to maximise the client's autonomy and self-determination. Further sexual assaults would compromise this aim while therapy could have a stabilising function. Therefore, first of all it should be considered whether the client could be empowered to stop assaults soon and then may take further steps. If this is not likely to be the case, steps to be taken by the psychologist depend on the particular circumstances of the case as well as the progression of the therapy. In this example several steps could be considered ranging from temporary respect for confidentiality and an agreement with the client to seek to stop assaults in the medium-term, to directly passing information of the child protection agency. A staged approach with temporary respect for confidentiality requires the consideration of the effects and consequences of this strategy regarding the balance of minimisation of harm and maximisation of client's self-determination.

When the psychologist's belief that the client is not able to stop harassment by herself becomes very likely or proved, a new consideration is necessary. In a constellation where sexual assaults are occurring as well as therapy dealing with this is being provided the client's best interests regarding self-determination, autonomy and free development of sexual identity are diminished. The aim of maintaining the therapeutic relationship is related to its consequences and is not an end in itself.

Where therapy might be terminated by the client as a reaction to the breaking of confidentiality, an adequate aftercare by another therapist could be sought as well as other possible steps. When considering the client's competence for self-determination, factors such as developmental age and mental dependency on the brother must be taken into account as they may impair her ability to make judgements (see also chapter 4, self-determination), This must be kept in mind in the psychologist's decision-making process. Furthermore, universal principles, e.g., the UN Charter of Human Rights, the UN Convention on the Rights of the Child and the national regulations on child protection, should be considered.

Despite its important role, in this case the obligation to maintain confidentiality is weakened by the following aspects: Firstly the consequence of respecting confidentiality could be the maintenance of serious harm. Secondly, the client's limited ability to judge as a function of her developmental stage is also a factor with regard to the necessary conditions for her development towards self-determination.

When the decision is in favour of breaking confidentiality a graduated course of action is an option in such a way that, for example, in the first instance, only the parents are informed and the decision to initiate or not therapeutic and other steps is committed to them as the adolescent is still legally a minor. To preserve integrity a decision to break confidentiality and restrict autonomy and freedom of consent should be discussed with the client in advance. Furthermore, the accordance of breaking confidentiality with the national law has to be clarified. For example, German law requires the existence of severe and objective danger as a premise for psychologists having the option of breaking confidentiality. Only very severe crimes likely to be committed in the future constitute the grounds for such an obligation. However, in many countries there are obligations on professionals, including psychologists, to report suspected abuse of vulnerable persons, including children. Legal requirements to inform parents vary. In the UK, for example, the so-called Gillick judgement confirmed that the test to decide whether a young person could require a health worker not to breach confidentiality and inform the parents (in that case about the adolescent girl's wish to have contraception) is not one of age but of competence to make the decision concerned. Consequently, any particular minor could be judged competent to make some but not other decisions. In this formulation, risk is a significant factor that a court would take into account; that is, the court could require a higher level of proof of the minor's competence if the decision is very serious, e.g., as life-threatening, The principle is important as it empowers those judged competent while protecting those who are vulnerable.

In Example 6.1 a complex legal and ethical situation applies with legal differences in different countries. The possible actions and their consequences should be clarified in advance and evaluated for further steps afterwards. Furthermore in constellations of this complexity changes in circumstances may require reconsideration of the previously balanced decision, and often require modification of that decision.

ii) Not to bring the profession into disrepute

Example 6.2

Dr Stevens is an experienced clinical and health psychologist who had worked for 20 years in the areas of crisis and disaster psychology and occupational health inside an international rescue organisation. For family reasons he changed his job three years ago and is now working part-time in a hospital with clients suffering from chronic somatic illness. Referred to him by his former manager, a reporter from a nearby broadcasting company asked Dr Stevens to make a statement on the next television news fifty minutes later. There had been a train accident with many dead and injured persons and they wanted to know how people feel and what psychologists can do... Although he had not been following the scientific discussion in this area as was previously the case, and with no time to prepare himself, he still felt experienced enough to answer. At the end of the interview he stated that in addition to aftercare activities a psychological debriefing should be carried out for all persons who might have been traumatised. After the interview a former colleague discussed with him a meta- analysis of research results published two years earlier showing no evidence to support his advice in general, but some risks for some groups. Dr Stevens became very upset about his error and started to reflect on causes and consequences.

Dr. Stevens may cause harm by inadvertently promoting future false interventions with his advice. Since he had not undertaken Continuing Professional Development (CPD) in the area requested he had implicitly run the risk of not being aware of the actual limits of the procedures and he may thereby cause harm without realising it. As many of the rescue service staff are not psychologists and are not aware that the evidence for the use of debriefing the general public had changed, the interview could have been an opportunity to make this information better known.

The responsibility for both the quality of practice and the consequences of that practice, combined with the obligation to be self reflective on one's limitations, should have led Dr Stevens to exercise special caution when making statements on matters outside his current level of expertise. In the first place it is the task of psychologists themselves to promote high standards supported by the professional association of psychologists.

Although there could be many possible cases where the profession might be brought into disrepute, false or improper public statements are obviously addressed by this clause. On the one hand immediate publicity is not a requirement for unethical behaviour to be exhibited under this clause. A story about a psychologist carrying on working despite personal incapability could damage the image of the profession even if it is published for the first time years after the event. On the other hand it is important to bear in mind that this clause is not aiming to demand political or scientific correctness defined as adherence to the most mainstream theoretical opinion.

Therefore this clause suggests violation of one or more of the other clauses in the Meta-Code. When considering the implications of this clause, the possible damage to the image of the profession in the public consciousness or the scientific community on a national and international level will be an important factor. Violation of this part of responsibility is not strictly linked to measurable negative effects on public reputation. The level of possible damage to the reputation will be a difficult issue for the professional association or others to consider if a complaint addressing this clause should arise.

But how to avoid mistakes in public statements caused by lack of new and relevant knowledge and time pressure? Even or especially in situations with limited time it is important to lean back for a moment and consider the upcoming professional role in terms of ethical and professional dimensions. That means not only reflecting about what one will say but also on what one will not talk about, or will need to express very carefully. A general aspect of responsibility is to handle problems, relations and public statements in a professional way. Consequently carefulness should be at a premium and ethical reflections should be undertaken in advance. Special caution is needed when working in or when giving statements on questions in new and developing areas.

Promotion of High Standards

i) *Promotion and maintenance of high standards of scientific and professional activity, and requirement on psychologists to organise their activities in accord with the Ethical Code.*

This clause shows the close relationship between different principles very clearly. It is obvious that high standards in practice are dependent upon competence, but considering also the responsibility for actions and consequences, it is necessary to take care about and to promote a high level of quality. This leads to the aim not only to strive to ensure a quality above the *minimum* standards but also to seek *best* practice, including ethical awareness and accordance to the code. The latter are often referred to as *aspirational* ethics, the very highest standards to which psychologists should aim.

In the reality of health care systems good or minimal standards are common and seen as good enough and not unethical at all. There will often be a gap between the level of standards already reached and those to which professionals should strive. As shown in the example below, the quality of professional activity is related to circumstances and to possible actions and solutions in the community and/or the organisational setting.

This clause also states an obligation for both organisations and individual psychologists to integrate different aspects of ethical behaviour and continuously reflect on professional ethics in their work. It is a question of ethical awareness not only to prevent serious ethical problems and dilemmas in an appropriate way but also to be sensitive to rather minor ethical challenges in daily practice. For the professional organisation this means the promotion of an ethical code, ensuring that training in ethics and counselling on ethical problems are available and that information on relevant conditions, like legal obligations, are provided for the members.

Example 6.3

A school psychologist is employed by a local educational authority. His main task is to assess children with academic, behavioural or emotional difficulties, and to suggest helpful solutions. When the problem is on the psychological level, he can refer the child to good therapists but when the difficulty concerns academic performance, the psychologist finds himself in a difficult situation. He has the choice to suggest an extra lesson per week with one of the two special needs teachers – unfortunately, in the psychologist's view, neither teacher employed by the school is competent , and one lesson per week would not be enough, anyway. Or he can refer the child to a special school in a rather distant town – where the child is liable to stay for several years and to lose contact with his friends in the village. Furthermore, the psychologist is familiar with research findings which show that children with special needs do not necessarily make more progress in a special school than in their regular class where they get extra support. To the regret of the psychologist this school doesn't yet practise adequate inclusion of children with special needs... The psychologist just does not know what to recommend. He cannot offer a solution he is convinced of, and he does not feel free to tell the parents of this child what he thinks of the special needs teachers of this school.

Given the circumstances, the psychologist's decision making process must lead to the result that no best solution could be found. The standards of support by the educational system are not at the level of the scientific knowledge. Therefore the gap between the available standard of support in the community and the desired high standard could not be closed quickly and individual solutions will always be a compromise.

A part of the conflict is the ethical responsibility to the special needs teachers as distant colleagues in terms of fairness and respect; also, the basis for recommending additional support is not strong. But which positive or negative consequences for the child would result from a criticism of the colleagues becoming public, even if it was quite well founded? Or are there better ways of changing the structural conditions of support?

The conflict resulting out of the gap between the standards mentioned above and the lack of competence could not be solved without good co-operation inside the educational system. On the way to high standards carefulness is needed both in strategies to develop organisations and especially concerning the clients' role in raising complaints about the lack of suitable programs and staff quality. There will be a range of cases where clients will want to complain and create a public scandal, whereas others won't. As the improvement of standards often is more relevant to future clients, one should bear in mind that it is, of course, only of secondary interest to the current client in the here and now. Future improvements are of more interest to, and the responsibility of, the psychologist and the local authorities. Another dimension of reflection may be the consideration whether the provision of a high amount of extra support in this area is the duty of the educational system or the parents', responsibility or a shared responsibility.

The tasks of decision making when faced with this tension are, on the one hand, to look for possibilities to promote the implementation of a higher standard and, on the other hand, to find the best possible compromise at this time together with the parents. However, promoting the best interests of the child as the main client requires that the caring parents, who have the responsibility for decisions, know all the possibilities, risks and opportunities. Besides a careful rationale concerning the lack of competence of the special needs teachers, priority should be given in the counselling process to the parents' understanding of their actual choices. Therefore a critical view on the quantity and the quality of support should not be concealed. This may result in activities of the parents ranging from a polite demand for extra support addressed to the school, up to long term political actions.

Based on the explanation that the support available will not be enough and should be extended, solutions for additional support could be sought, for instance from voluntary bodies or by a special choice of games, electronic and media solutions supporting the learning processes.

Avoidance of Harm

i) *Avoidance of the misuse of psychological knowledge or practice, and the minimisation of harm which is foreseeable and unavoidable.*

ii) *Recognition of the need for particular care to be taken when undertaking research or making professional judgements of persons who have not given consent.*

This clause is stated as an alternative formulation of the well known dictum "do good". However, in the case of an ethical dilemma it is not always possible to act in a solely positive way, for example when there are two or more clients and relationships with different wishes, opinions and needs. Furthermore it is hardly possible to draw a clear line defining how much goodness and welfare are to be ensured by meeting the requirements of the code. In some cases one or more principles may be contravened by following one of the other principles which has been considered more important in order to avoid harm.

There may be a conflict in the decision making process between minimisation of harm and avoidance of harm as these two different goals may be difficult to reconcile. The service of a psychologist could be requested for the purpose of minimising foreseeable harm by a third party or even by a person being in the position to suffer harm. Examples of this may be found in the case of a reality TV broadcast format like Big Brother or Jungle Camp where the participants don't know exactly what kind of exposure and amount of harm they will have to face. The service of psychologists may be sought in order to minimise harm and this may be a standard for the broadcast company to deal with their responsibility. In effect, the company shares or largely delegates responsibility to professionals while producing risks by designing effects in the show that could harm participants in order to meet the dominant concern – making money.

From an ethical perspective minimisation of harm as a goal in a future professional role only becomes acceptable if avoidance is impossible or not foreseeable. Where acceptance of some harm rather than avoidance of harm is accepted then this would mean accepting and even, it could be argued, contributing to the occurrence of harm. Decision criteria would include whether the probability of occurrence is very low or high and the extent to which precautions and professional activities could ensure the avoidance of harm. In every case where harm is used in order to make money the conflict between minimisation and avoidance requires the psychologist to reflect before accepting a role of supporting these actions.

A more frequent scenario that requires reflections on the responsibility to avoid harm occurs in the educational assessment of children.

Example 6.4

Mr Scheffer is an experienced educational psychologist working in independent practice. Mr and Ms Turm, who work very hard and are successful, are aiming to prepare and support their five-year-old son Victor for the best life possible. Since they had formed impression that Victor has high potential they want to clarify his IQ because they believe this will help them to decide what kind of support and school would be the best for him. One employee of the kindergarten has given an opinion that Victor has high ability and also a high activity level.

The parents participate as observers when Mr Scheffer assessed Victor. Afterwards he explained to the parents that this test has been well evaluated and that the results are reliable and stable but at this age some of the results may change over time because of children's different speed of development. Mr Scheffer takes 1 1/2 hour time to explain the IQ result of 120 (placing Victor in the top 10% of his age group) and the potential Victor has in the specific domain of mathematical competence. He gives the parents a comprehensive list of the results. The next day Mr Turm comes back and demands a copy of each test item including the test form with the raw data and results. In his opinion some of the items are stupid and have no close relationship to intelligence. Therefore he is sceptical that the overall result is correct and wants to check the test construction himself.

Mr Scheffer explains again the quality of the test and refuses to hand out cop-
ies of the test form or the test materials. He focuses on Victor's needs and ex-
plains that there are risks if Victor were to move to a school for children of high
potential as he has a high potential in only some domains. Mr Turm declares that
he is aware of this but as he has paid for the service he wants a copy of the test
results including the original test form and materials. Mr. Scheffer states that he
is always open to explain the results in an additional paid counselling session or
provide an extensive written report which will provide his opinion supported by
the appropriate data, properly analysed and with suitable caveats such as reli-
abilities of scores. He also advises that the records of the test will be kept 15
years so that Victor as the main client can have an insight into the results when
he is older.

Mr Scheffer is aware that he has two clients: the parents and, as the main client,
Victor who is not able to give informed consent. Since he feels responsible to avoid
harm resulting from misuse of psychological knowledge he does not generally hand
out test materials. In addition he thinks that there is some evidence that the father
may misrepresent the test results to third parties as he is not competent to interpret
the test data.

What would you do in respect of your national ethical code and would it be in
conflict or in adherence to legal regulations governing services and the family?
Would you hand out the whole material; if yes, under what conditions and with
what precautions?

An essential element of assessment services is the detailed and comprehensible
explanation of the test results to the client. There is a basic consensus in Europe
concerning the direct client's right of access to test results as well as concerning the
obligation to retain records for a period of 5-10 years. There are differences, however, concerning the ethical and legal regulations for presentation and delivery of
test results, particularly the delivery of copies of the original documents. Whereas in
Germany the guidance focuses on the original documents remaining the property of
the psychologist, in the Netherlands there are obligations, both by law and the code
of ethics, to deliver copies of the test results to the client (or, in the case of children,
to the parents). In the UK it is expected that a report will typically be provided by
the psychologist setting out the results of the assessment and the psychologist's
opinion. This is a legal requirement in the case of a statutory assessment of a child's
special educational needs but seen as good practice generally. However, as in Germany, the psychologist is expected to maintain test confidentiality and not copy the
test materials, including original test forms.

Arguments against revealing the content of the test, or the raw data arising
from the assessment, include the protection of the test procedure against misuse
and the prevention of misinterpretation of the results by third parties. Furthermore,
there is the danger of a loss of validity due to distribution of the original test to
many people who could then learn its contents and so influence the results of sub-

sequent assessments. On the other hand, provision of a psychological report provides the client with a record of the psychologist's opinion and the evidence that supports it.

In Germany, for example, the major test publishers demand a proof of competence, such as a degree in psychology, before selling a psychological test. With many tests the delivery of copies of test results (or parts of them) to the direct client is unlikely to present an ethical problem. However, there may be an ethical problem with some tests as a matter of principle, or in certain cases with respect to their being passed to third parties, parents or relatives. Therefore a regulation permitting the psychologist to decide on the selective passing on original documents or copies will yield a broader scope to prevent possible misuse. The duty to provide clients with comprehensible and comprehensive information about test results, however, is fundamental, regardless of the decision whether or not to pass on copies of the original documents.

In the example given above, the psychologist's concerns about the risks of misinterpretation and selective (mis)use of test results appear to be concerned with access to the test materials rather than detailed findings. These are separate issues. The latter may be justified whereas the former is unlikely to be. There exist some indications that the father could use results from parts of the test in order to try to have his son placed in a school for children of high potential, where the son might be inappropriately challenged to a damaging degree. However, an admission to such a school based solely on the presented partial test results is improbable. The psychologist's offer for a further extensive explanation of the test results does include the explanation of the limits of interpretation and possible risks of excessive educational challenges for the son. From an ethical perspective an objective and plausible risk of misinterpretation and resulting negative effects would be required to withhold information. In Germany's legal framework this decision remains within the psychologist's ethical responsibility with the purpose of providing accurate information to the client and to prevent misinterpretation.

One measure to prevent or to reduce incorrect understanding of the test results is the extended service of a detailed written report for the client, a common approach in many countries. These reports may provide full details of test results with the psychologist's careful explanation of confidence limits, reliability etc. Results which are hard to understand by lay persons represent a possible risk, but a careful explanation should be part of any psychologist's report. The outcome of the analysis of risk and benefit of providing test results depends on the nature of the client as well as the type of test. Therefore the German code of ethics, for example, does not contain a general recommendation regarding the delivery of copies of the original test results, whereas in the UK, for, example, although the BPS code does not specify this, test results would typically be provided as an example of generally agreed "good practice"; furthermore, in some cases, there is a legal obligation on the psychologist to provide a report to the client and/or parents; for example, the statutory assessment of special educational needs in England

ii) Recognition of the need for particular care to be taken when undertaking research or making professional judgements of persons who have not given consent.

The Milgram[8] experiments on obedience led to a broad discussion concerning the limits of scientific research. Special importance has been attached to the use of deception and compromising the right to information regarding the object of the research, so limiting the participant's ability to exercise self-determination when engaging in deception experiments or failing to acquire the *informed* consent of the participant (e.g., caused by lack of information or explanation). On the basis of specific regulations and their interpretation within the national codes of ethics, the ethics boards of the psychological associations in many countries offer support to researchers with research applications by advising in advance about the compliance with ethical standards of the presented research designs. Also, universities often have their own ethics boards to consider research proposals. In the realm of research which requires a certain minor degree of deception, excessive invasion of privacy can be prevented by some precautions. These precautions include respect for the most intimate core of personality, which is not to be touched without consent, the listing of areas of personality under observation and the subsequent debriefing concerning the details of the object of research. Furthermore, deception as a research method will typically require particular justification (see also Example 7.12).

These preventive measures may not be possible when a psychologist is called upon to make public statements. The role of psychology as an explanatory science for psychological and social phenomena grows as the world of media develops and the interest in social and psychological topics increases. Psychologists are asked more and more often to offer explanations of current events, such as hijacking, kidnapping, taking of hostages, infant homicides and other violent crimes, psychological stress or illnesses of celebrities. In these cases there is regularly no consent of the perpetrator or the celebrity regarding the information given about them. In such cases the psychologist has a greater responsibility to exercise caution.

Example 6.5

The case of Mary Peters, a 17-year-old girl, who was abducted at age 11 and held captive by a man until her escape, received heavy media coverage for several weeks . When more and more details leaked to the media, Ms Peters decided to go on the offensive and gave a TV interview providing details of her story for the first time. The media ran extensive reports and a year later she gave another interview with more details. Again, there was a media hype, and along the way the psychologist Mr. Scholz was interviewed. Scholz emphasised in the preliminary talk before the interview that he wouldn't comment on Mary's inner mental states out of ethical and professional reasons. During the interview the reporter asked repeatedly what conclusions could be

---

[8] E.g., see Milgram (1963), *Behavioural study of obedience.*

drawn from Mary's behaviour regarding her current psychological condition. The psychologist didn't answer the question, but eluded it as he had resolved to do by describing common stresses and strains and coping processes typical for these kinds of situations. When, after the interview, he complained to the reporter about the question, she responded that Ms Peters had knowingly made herself a public persona, and therefore must have anticipated the media coverage and the public response to it.

Psychology as a science has the function to offer explanations to the interested public. In these cases the psychologist's clients are primarily the public and the media representatives. However, it is imperative to respect personal rights. In addition, when a psychologist makes a diagnostic statement about a third person, he implicitly turns that third person into his "client" without his or her agreement. This is essentially a violation of the right of self-determination and of the privacy of the person concerned. Another problem concerns competence, as the question must be raised, if a scientifically based statement can be made without a direct contact with the client. But even if it were possible to provide substantiation neither of diagnostic statements, neither the consent to make these statements nor implicitly to being made a client would have been given. From the professional ethical perspective of psychologists the mandatory respect of personal rights of human beings is not substantively changed by public appearances or status of a VIP.

As journalists typically take a different approach, psychologists run a high risk of finding themselves faced with ethical conflicts while being interviewed. Certain special precautions, like asking the persons for their consent, as a rule will be almost impossible, leaving only the last precaution of not making statements about inner mental states at all. Even if there is a tendency in media coverage for different approaches to be taken with perpetrators and victims, and for different limits to be set, as a matter of principle for psychologists the ethical restrictions will be the same for both victims and perpetrators. A more contentious and somewhat open ethical question concerns statements about deceased persons (e.g., Hitler, Marilyn Monroe or Princess Diana) where the public and historical interest might outbalance their personal rights and/or the rights of their living relatives.

Continuity of Care

i)   Responsibility for the necessary continuity of professional care of clients, including collaboration with other professionals and appropriate action when a psychologist must suspend or terminate involvement.

When dealing with psychological problems psychologists may get into awkward situations where the client's problem isn't yet solved but, because of disturbances to the professional relationship or for other reasons, an untimely termination of the service is necessary, even though the psychologist knows that further help is needed. In this case there is an obligation to organise continuity of care in order to avoid harm and take responsibility for the unfinished process. This obligation also includes the need for collaboration with other professionals or institutions concerning the continuity of care and to ensure that all necessary information is given and actions taken to address the best interests of the client. The responsibility for continuity is also an aspect of competence and respect because competent psychologists are able to anticipate possible negative consequences following early termination of the professional relationship.

Example 6.6

Ms Miller is a clinical psychologist working in the area of psychotherapy in independent practice. After some years she expanded and hired Ms Meyer, a competent clinical psychologist. They made a contract stating that Ms Miller could keep her contracts with the private health services including settlement of accounts. Ms Meyer worked in Ms Miller's rooms in independent practice and received money in relation to clients treated. Given the multiple rates of the special insurance of most of the clients, Ms Meyer received a significantly reduced hourly rate but one that was common in the market. The contract contained the obligation of secrecy concerning matters of practice and a clause in case of leaving the practice to prepare and turn over the clients to another therapist, including the provision of a final report. In case of opening an own independent practice in the vicinity, Ms. Meyer was bound by the contract to not take along any clients from the original to the new practice.

After one year personal conflicts and theoretical differences led to a serious problems and the termination of the contract by Ms. Miller. Ms. Meyer met her obligations by preparing the clients for her leaving office and a change of therapist. However, after the termination of employment it became evident that some of the 21 clients were not ready to change their therapist and additionally not all of the clients could be attended to. There was a discussion between a client, Ms. Miller and Ms. Meyer, where the client insisted that Ms. Miller agreed to the client's being passed over to Ms. Meyer. Afterwards Ms. Miller and Ms. Meyer discussed the handling of unprovided clients. While Ms. Meyer offered to take these over, Ms. Miller suggested that they should be treated in her practice based on the former fee until the end of the therapy.

As Ms. Meyer was still busy in the setup of her own new practice and wasn't willing to work at half of her possible pay, she declined. Ms Miller refused to pass clients to Ms Meyer as she was not willing to assist her competitors and in addition she wasn't convinced of Ms. Meyer's competence. During the following months Ms. Meyer would meet former clients in the street and found out that some of them hadn't started a new therapy or had quit their therapy after a short period of time, due to the long time of waiting for a new therapist. But there was no complaint filed in this case.

In this example the termination of therapy resulted from organisational causes. Both psychologists bear the responsibility for finding a solution for aftercare and continuation of therapy. Ms. Miller is responsible to provide a new therapist as quickly as possible and to refer unprovided clients to her other colleagues. Ms. Meyer bears responsibility to secure the continuation of her clients' ongoing therapy. Unfortunately, both counterparts may see the responsibility as resting on the other side, thus violating their ethical obligation to co-operate with colleagues in order to guarantee a proper continuation of treatment.

From an ethical viewpoint it is hard to decide which of the two psychologists bears the higher degree of responsibility for the continuing treatment of the clients. Because Ms. Miller legally claims the representation of the clients she also is legally accountable to a higher degree for the continuation. On the other hand there is Ms. Meyer's responsibility derived from her (long term) relationships with her clients. Therefore the question arises: was it really unbearable for Ms. Meyer to accept, under the previous conditions of employment, some financial cutbacks and a somewhat delayed business start-up in order to finish the treatment of clients refusing to change therapist or being unprovided.

However, the evaluation of the degree of responsibility is of secondary interest. It is essential that both psychologists accept responsibility and are obliged to find a good solution. The consequences of their personal dispute resulted in the fact that there was no effort to settle for the benefit of the clients. Both psychologists were confronted with the task of coming to an arrangement and to provide a swift continuing treatment, even if some financial cutbacks had to be accepted. In this example the method of mediation would have helped to come to a solution with balanced burdens on each.

On a more basic level it is to be questioned if the employment contract is ethically correct in all aspects. The contract interferes with the right of free choice of therapist as it regulates the interruption of treatment and the referral of clients. However, it can be objected that a psychologist starting a new position at a nearby hospital won't take his or her clients along. Still, a contractual framework which is based too much on economic interests and limits the clients' autonomy doesn't seem appropriate in the realm of psychotherapy. It is Ms. Miller's duty to specify employment contracts and to implement procedures on clients' information in a way that won't violate freedom of consent and the clients' best interests.

ii) *Responsibility towards a client which exists after the formal termination of the professional relationship.*

Example 6.7

Mr Baker a young organisational psychologist works in a company selling proficiency assessment. He carries out the tests for the job of a secretary among 10 candidates and provides a brief counselling session afterwards to each applicant on their results. The interpretation of all the results is done by a senior psychologist in the company and the decision regarding who gets the job is taken by the client of the company. Two months afterwards he met Mary, one of the candidates in a pub, and some days later they come closer to an intimate relationship. Mr Baker asks himself if he is allowed to get in closer contact with her. As he does not remember Mary's results very well and as he has performed no personality or clinical tests he comes to the judgement that it would be ethically acceptable.

Is it ethically acceptable for Mr Baker to go into an intimate relationship with Mary? How would it be if this happens in the following week rather than two months later?

The responsibility to clients persists even after the professional relationship has ended since there is a special history of a professional relationship, including a differential power relationship between the psychologist and the client. This history may interfere in a new relationship whether that is a private or professional relationship. Therefore psychologists have to reflect on this and on keeping professional distance from their former clients. Inequality of power is a characteristic of professional relationships and this may persist.

To address this issue it is often suggested that a time limit should be specified for keeping professional distance. But a time criterion is formal and abstract compared with the real relationship which may take many forms (See also Examples 7.13, 7.15 Integrity). Influences from a short but intense therapeutic relationship dealing with severe psychic problems may exist after years. Influences of a relationship arising from an intervention to reduce a fear of flying, by contrast may reasonably be considered to have, relatively, little influence within perhaps half a year. That does not mean that there is evidence that such clients of psychologists are free from any influence after successful termination of the intervention. There is a need to consider criteria relevant to the *particular* ethical decision in line with both the kind of former relationship and the stage of the personal development of the client. It would not be sufficient to be guided by the time passed.

Important criteria to aid the evaluation of the possible influence of a prior professional role would be the degree of possible dependency caused by theme, type and duration of the relationship and the resulting knowledge about the client. In this current example the professional relationship is defined by a single contact covering job related proficiency assessment. The information obtained about the client is hardly sufficient to constitute or continue a personal dependency or exercise of power. The professional relationship was not personal by nature. No intimate knowledge about the client's personality, problems or other relevant private secrets from her biography had been acquired.

Extended Responsibility

i)   Assumption of general responsibility, for the scientific and professional activities, including ethical standards, of employees, assistants, supervisees and students

The clause on extended responsibility broadens the general responsibility to those working under the supervision of psychologists. Professional and ethical standards as well as awareness are important components of the responsibility and competence of psychologists but to behave ethically is also a necessity for a psychologist's employees, assistants, supervisees and students. Since psychologists bear a general responsibility for actions taken by these groups they also have the responsibility to take care that people involved in their work are well-trained for the tasks they have to fulfil and that they act in accordance with the appropriate ethical and professional standards. Requirements such as the avoidance of harm are also addressed as a responsibility that psychologists have for their assistants, supervisees and students.

Example 6.8

Ms Green is working as a clinical psychologist in the geriatric section of a big hospital providing psychological assessment, intervention and training for all patients. As they see a growing demand, the management of the hospital decides to open a specialised section on dementia and to transfer the psychological service to this section. The former geriatric section will become an independent part of the dementia section and will concentrate on physiotherapeutic and occupational therapeutic interventions only. Therefore no psychologists will work there anymore and the management will be done by an experienced occupational therapist. Since patients regularly come to this former section first it is proposed that a form of minimised assessment of intellectual competence should be done there but without psychological supervision.

The general manager of the hospital asks Ms Green as head of the dementia section and the psychological service within it to provide the psychological tests by ordering them from the test publisher. He claims that, although the staff in this section have no extensive training in psychological assessment, they do have experience with these kinds of tests. He asserts that these staff are capable of performing assessments under supervision of the management who has years of experience as an assistant to a psychologist. Ms Green makes the observation that these staff often do not give enough time and/or skip some items. Ms Green has serious doubts that an adequate performance at the appropriate professional level is assured and refuses to order the tests which, by the publisher's policy of quality management, are restricted to professional psychologists. She argues on the basis of her professional responsibility for the psychological activities involved in the task, the need to avoid harm and the financial risks for damages that could arise as a result of improper test use.

Under what conditions is the delegation of psychological assessment organised in your country and how well does this fit the responsibility to avoid harm?

Given the organisational changes in the health systems of many countries, a tendency can be found to hire cheap labour, in part with only borderline qualifications, in order to deliver services. Psychologists playing a part in this area bear a heavy responsibility for the quality of services and the prevention of damage. In this case a psychologist is asked to obtain psychological tests to be subsequently administered by inadequately trained personnel, thus undermining the common quality standards for test acquisition and administration.

Put into an ethical perspective the psychologist accounts for the quality of the results, damage prevention and quality assurance. As psychological assessment represents a major invasion with extensive consequences for the people concerned, supervision is a central quality measure. Quality control of the assessment results includes the initial training of support personnel, continuing education, supervision and the professional psychologists' monitoring of the interpretation of results, including the taking over of difficult cases and very complex assessment procedures. In the example given this is not guaranteed by the organizational structures of the new department. Therefore the contribution of the psychologist of only the acquisition of tests is insufficient to control quality. Regardless if whether the hospital management is legally liable for any damages and claims, from an ethical perspective there is the necessity to prevent or minimise the risks of possible damage to clients and the standing of the profession.

Resolving Dilemmas

i) *Recognition that ethical dilemmas occur and responsibility is placed upon the psychologist to clarify such dilemmas and consult colleagues and/or the national Association, and inform relevant others of the demands of the Ethical Code.*

Ethical awareness as an obligation for psychologists is defined under the principle of Competence but this must also be considered in combination with the principle of Responsibility, to be open and sensitive to the occurrence of dilemmas. Furthermore this clause clarifies that the responsibility to reflect on and solve dilemmas, in all areas of professional practice, is primarily the task and duty of the psychologist. In addition the national association has a role providing support for the decision-making process. This clause outlines possible steps to deal with ethical dilemmas after having become aware of them. If ethical questions or dilemmas occur psychologists have the task to develop a strategy. They may develop their own approach for this or use a systematic approach developed by others. A very useful list of 10 questions has been published by the Canadian Psychological Association in their *Canadian Code of Ethics for Psychologists (Third Edition)*. At first there are systematic questions dealing with the persons involved, their relationships and which clauses of the ethical code are relevant to consider. These are helpful to find a balanced judgement. Experiences from training and supervision show that regularly five or six of these questions are necessary in a decision-making process to find the most appropriate ethical way forward. Approaches to decision making will be discussed in chapter 9.

Example 6.9

When the psychologists association made a call for members to send in ethical dilemmas to be discussed in its own magazine, a psychologist who was close to retirement replied that she would welcome the endeavour but unfortunately couldn't contribute an example. She continued that this was a result of her being the manager of an organisation, thus not coming into conflict with ethical dilemmas.

This reply illustrates an attitude not infrequent in older psychologists (see also Examples 5.3). During their professional development they have developed certain routines concerning professional and ethical questions that might lead to the conviction to act ethically by default. While evaluating such a statement it would not be fair to imply that there is no sufficient awareness of the fact that ethical problems do occur. On the other hand it is hard to believe that during long years of practical experience no ethical problems should have come up which are worthy of reporting. It could be argued that a heightened degree of self-confidence, accompanied by minor attention and sensibility to problematic developments, is common in leadership positions, whereas a specific characteristic of ethical awareness perhaps is not.

As ethical questions in psychologists' practical experience don't come along as clearly expressed tasks to be carried out, an inadequately developed sensitivity to dilemmas and ethical challenges among those in leadership positions becomes an additional problematic factor. Therefore it is essential for psychologists to pay attention in order to develop and maintain a high degree of awareness and inner readiness to perceive and to seize ethical questions as a self-aware component of their professional role. The maintenance of this level of awareness and a sensitivity towards unknown future incidents is a difficult task, which requires a continuous monitoring of one's inner readiness during everyday practice. Therefore training at the beginning of professional careers is needed in order to sensitise the awareness for ethical questions as a part of the professional role.

But let's go back to the discussion of example 7.6 to illustrate further aspects of the clause. In the run-up to the conflict described here, and the task of ensuring the continuation of treatment, both Ms. Miller and Ms. Meyer had the duty to detect and to grasp the ethical problem that occurred. Both of them had an ethical obligation to make an effort to come to a solution beneficial for the client. The fact that both bear a part of the responsibility does complicate the matter but this should have led to a process of compromise, provided that both of them had awareness of this ethical obligation and a willingness to act appropriately.

Measures have to be taken especially in situations where it can be anticipated that the planned strategies to deal with a problem will turn out detrimental to the clients' interests. Given the background of the psychologists' conflict, it would have been helpful to call in a neutral third party, either within the setting of consultations with the psychologists association, or the services of a mediator before the employment was terminated. This neglect can't be undone a certain time after the event of interruption or termination of therapy. This case study makes clear that even just the lack of activity at the given point of time is enough to create an ethical problem whose consequences can't be easily countered a short time afterwards.

The clarification made in this clause that it is each psychologist's obligation to make efforts to come to an ethical solution is made even clearer by the weak position in which the clients in this example find themselves, and, even worse, are held in by the concealment of their possibilities to change therapists.

Conclusions

Psychologists have a number of responsibilities. These interact with the other three Principles that comprise the Meta-code. These are responsibilities to clients – present and past – and to wider society. These responsibilities including practising on the basis of a scientific evidence base. However, this chapter has also indicated that there may be conflicting responsibilities, for example to direct and second order clients. There may be tensions when it is not clear how to prevent or, at least, to limit harm. These are very real dilemmas. But we have also seen how psychologists, by focussing on their own needs rather than those of their client or wider society, may fail to demonstrate appropriate responsibility.

It is *always* the responsibility of the psychologist to show ethical awareness and appropriate responsibility for practice – whether one's own or that of assistants and students, for example. However, there is also a responsibility on the *profession* in the form of the national association of psychologists and the community of psychologists. The profession has a role in regulating and supporting the optimal, ethical practice of psychologists. The provision of opportunities for Continuing Professional Development is one clear example of how this responsibility can be exercised. Another is the provision of "help lines" to discuss ethical dilemmas. But, furthermore, we have a collective responsibility as individual psychologists to optimise practice. This includes supporting colleagues who are under stress but also – on those rare occasions when this occurs – taking action to report unethical behaviour. Responsibility, therefore while primarily concerned with the individual psychologist is also central to the collective of psychologists.

Chapter 7

The Principle of Integrity

Casper Koene

Psychologists seek to promote integrity in the science, teaching and practice of psychology. In these activities psychologists are honest, fair and respectful of others. They attempt to clarify for relevant parties the roles they are performing and to function appropriately in accordance with those roles

This Principle is elaborated in the following specifications:

- Recognition of Professional Limitations;
- Honesty and Accuracy;
- Straightforwardness and Openness;
- Conflict of Interests and Exploitation;
- Actions of Colleagues.

Including their respective sub-specifications, there are eleven themes to be paid attention to in this chapter, with illustrations from everyday and not so everyday situations and from several national associations' codes of ethics.

The moral concept of integrity has its roots far back, in ancient Rome. The Latin word *integritas* means basically "intact", but already in the first century BC the Roman poet and ethics teacher Horace wrote in his Ode I:22: "*Integer vitae scelerisque purus*", a man of upright life and free from wickedness. Over a thousand years later the medieval Danish historian Saxo Grammaticus defined *integritas* as moral purity, and in western society the concept of integrity has been used in this sense ever since.[9]

In our reflections on the professional ethics of psychologists, it could be useful to keep the ancient Latin origin of the word in mind, as a leading concept in focusing on the ethical principle of Integrity. However, what does "intactness" actually mean in our professional relationships? For instance, never giving up "the independence, necessary for practising the profession", as it is phrased in, e.g., the French code.[10, 11]

---

[9] Saxo Grammaticus (ca. 1150–1220), Gesta Danorum. Liber 7, Caput 4.

[10] Fédération Française des Psychologues et de Psychologie. Code de Déontologie des Psychologues, Titre 1:7.

[11] References to several national psychologists association' codes of ethics will be given, just as

And definitely not harmful "deception, fraud, or intentional misrepresentation of facts", as the Turkish psychologists' association concisely states in article 4 of its Ethics code, which is fairly understandable.

Right from the beginning and even before, psychologists should ask themselves whether they could properly take on a task, a job or a commission, all conditions taken into account.

After all, "the psychologist ensures that he can engage in a professional activity independently and objectively" and his "decision to initiate a professional relationship or to continue it, should always be based on sound professional and ethical criteria", as stated in the chapter on Integrity of the Dutch psychologists' ethical code as an elaboration of this Meta-code subject.[12]

Example 7.1 a

Margaret Miller, occupational psychologist, received a request from the Human Resources division of a big international firm – an important client of hers – to assess one of their middle management employees, Mrs. Stone who applied for a higher management position. It was stated that the company assessment should be focused on the job requirements of the vacant function, but that Mrs. Miller was welcome to give a wider view on the applicant's skills and her personality.

Was Margaret Miller[13] in the given example, acting unethically, if she accepted this commission? Not necessarily, as she was well trained in this kind of assessment and the request was appropriately specified and sufficiently focused within the scope of professional psychology. However, is Mrs. Miller fully aware of what the second part of the request could imply?

Example 7.1 b

In her report Margaret Miller concludes that Mrs. Stone's management capacities certainly meet the job requirements. However, she was of the opinion that a staff position as a senior researcher would be a better fit to her personality profile. Margaret Miller did not communicate this last conclusion to Mrs. Stone before sending the report.

---

some European examples. There is no pretence to give a balanced comparative analysis of the various codes, as this would be out of the scope of this textbook.

[12] Nederlands Instituut van Psychologen (NIP). Beroepscode voor psychologen 2007, articles III.2.1.1 and III.2.1.4

[13] As in other chapters, all names in the examples given in this chapter are fictitious, except for Stanley Milgram's in example 7.12.

Whether or not Margaret Miller was aware of a possible hidden agenda on the side of the commissioning firm, she could have acted more carefully. Even if Mrs. Stone was well informed on the phrasing of the commission, and thereby had given her informed consent [14]the question remains whether Mrs. Stone really was aware of the possible impact of Margaret Miller's report? And, moreover, shouldn't Mrs. Miller have presented her draft report to Mrs. Stone before sending it out, thus giving Mrs. Stone the opportunity to discuss the report with her and eventually to decide not to allow the report being sent if she had substantial objections?

This would have been the case if, for instance, Margaret Miller had worked in The Netherlands, as the Dutch psychologists' association (NIP) has formulated strict clauses on this subject in the articles III.3.2.14 and III.3.2.16 of its code of ethics. It is the Dutch psychologists' opinion that the client's autonomy – except for a judge's request – always requires the right not to have a report being sent to a third party, after having had the opportunity to scrutinise it in advance. However, not every European psychologists association may draw such extreme consequences. For instance, in its article 8:10 the already mentioned Turkish association's ethics code says about this: "if there is a reason for it being inappropriate to report the findings to the person tested (such as in some organisational consulting, pre-employment or security screenings, and forensic evaluations), this condition is clearly explained to the person being assessed in advance."

However, for the moment this last mentioned ethical issue is not our main focus. The question is whether Margaret Miller was ethically right in adding to her report the paragraph on the preferential research position.

Example 7.1 c

After having received Margaret Miller's report, the firm decided to move Mrs. Stone from her middle management function, as some of her superiors were unsatisfied with her style of operating. Neither the higher management function, nor a senior research function was offered to Mrs. Stone, as the former was given to another applicant and no vacancy for the latter was available. The assistant research position offered to Mrs. Stone was seen by her as a downgrading.

Let us assume that Margaret Miller came to her conclusion on a professionally sound base and fully convinced that a research position would be best fitting for Mrs. Stone. Then, she would have acted on a basis of real personal integrity, one would say. However, one's personal integrity might not be enough to ensure professional integrity. Sufficient shrewdness and sensitivity to other people's conceivable motives and perceptions is necessary to avoid one's professional activities unwillingly being corrupted by others or being perceived as such.

---

[14] This subject is elaborately worked out in the chapter on Respect.

On the other hand, one may wonder whether, and if so, to what extent, the psychologist's morality, as shown in their private life, should be taken into account in evaluating their professional integrity. Some may argue that the psychologist's private life is already sufficiently subject to legal scrutiny, and thereby should be kept protected from any judgement by the profession. However, one may wonder whether some private conduct could be seen as incompatible with being a decent professional psychologist.

Example 7.2

Charles Beaufort not only is a clinical psychologist, but also the owner of a first class restaurant, which he himself likes to manage. As an educated cook he frequently takes part in the kitchen work.

Bea Goldstein is a child psychologist, who is also an active member of an opera company, and can be seen on stage several times a year.

Gloria Minelli is a social psychologist. As a student she participated at the time in Miss World elections. She is frequently asked to perform as a photo model.

Gerard de Vries is an occupational psychologist and entrepreneur, owning several "coffee shops", which sell soft drugs. This is not illegal in this jurisdiction.

Karsten Jensen is clinical psychologist and sexologist. He is active in the gay movement and openly frequents dark rooms in gay bars.

Esteban Garcia was starring, as a health psychologist, in a glossy health magazine advertisement, endorsing a new bright light device for treatment of jet lag.

Gabor Ferencz, occupational psychologist, lost his drivers license because of drunken driving and repeated excessive speed driving.

Jaana Viinanen, clinical psychologist, was sentenced with a substantial fine for tax fraud.

Sylvia Pereira, child psychologist, was sentenced to jail because of murdering her mother. She herself claimed to be not guilty, just helping her mother, who suffered from a lethal cancer, to die, at her own request.

Acting as restaurant chef, opera singer, photo model, soft drugs dealer, dark room's activist and health tool advertiser? None of them was involved in any criminal activity. However, which of these activities can be seen as reasonably compatible with being a professional psychologist, and which not? And why not? And what about irresponsible risk taking, tax fraud and euthanasia assistance? Breaking the law and thereby equally incompatible with professional integrity?

Esteban Garcia's advertising could be seen as an infringement of article 52 in the Spanish code that "psychologists must not lend their name, prestige or image as psychologists to be used in advertising for consumer goods [...]", which might not be seen similarly by every European psychologists association. But, even if not open for any scrutinising by the profession, and whether or not any national association has laid down any relevant statement in its code of ethics, it is worth keeping in mind the following phrase from the introduction tot the Lithuanian psychologists code:

"The way of life led by a psychologist must not hinder execution of his/her professional duties, cause damage to the prestige of psychology or psychologists. Psychologists are to observe the rules of society life and understand that their violation may have negative impact upon their professional competence and their colleagues' prestige"

After all these more general considerations, let us look more closely at the specific elements under the Principle of Integrity, as set out in the Meta-code.

Recognition of Professional Limitations

Obligation to be self-reflective and open about personal and professional limitations and a recommendation to seek professional advice and support in difficult situations

It is significant in this aspect, that under the heading Recognition of Professional Limitations personal limitations are mentioned in the first clause. Openness to one's own motives is perhaps the most important characteristic of integrity. Self-reflection is a prerequisite for adequate and competent reasoning on all other aspects. For the majority of us, self-reflection is not always an easy task, as some need for grandiosity might be the secret companion of modesty. Thus, personal dynamics can also hinder us from seeing our professional limitations. Hence, meeting and challenging our inner dark desires and defences in order to come to a real balance of integrity has priority. After all, neglect of limitations too easily leads to false pretence, and thereby dishonesty.

In articles 4.1.1 and 4.1.2 of its Code of Professional Ethics the Irish psychologists' association underlines this clearly as follows:

"Engage in self-care activities which help to avoid conditions (for example, burnout, and addictions) which could result in impaired judgement and interfere with their ability to benefit and not harm others."

"Seek emotional support and/or supervision from colleagues when feeling stressed or vulnerable due to professional dilemmas."

However, to obey the outer-directed obligation to openness about our limitations and shortcomings, and to take appropriate action isn't always easy. Moreover, is it not always easy to decide whether the moment has come to refrain from continuing working or not, especially if others are – to certain extent – counting on our commitments (see chapter 5 on Competence).

Example 7.3

Maria Schindler is working as a health psychologist in private practice. Occasionally she suffers from strong allergic spells for a couple of days. Although she is able to suppress her symptoms reasonably by medication, the overall effect is debilitating.

To cancel appointments for a couple of days will upset her scheme substantially and be unfavourable for at least some clients. Moreover, cancellations do have a certain financial impact. On the other hand, seeing clients in a somewhat impaired condition will, to a certain extent, withhold from them her usual full attention and alertness.

What would we think of Maria Schindler's considerations? To what extent is a certain loss of professional quality detrimental to our clients? Isn't it unrealistic to require psychologists always to be in an optimal condition? On the other hand, would Maria have similar doubts if she hadn't been working in private practice, but in salaried employment? This issue links integrity and competence (chapter 5). The former stresses the need to reflect carefully on this tension; the latter identifies that it is the actual competence to perform the job that is crucial.

Example 7.4

Kuno Jespersen is working as a psychotherapist in private practice at home.

His wife is incurably ill. After previous treatment, a few years ago, it turned out that her brain tumour has started to grow again. The prognosis is that she probably will die within the next 6–8 months, but the precise course of her illness is unclear.

Although being reasonably prepared during the past years, Kuno has to carry a heavy load.

Kuno feels that focusing on his work is helpful – his wife wishes ordinary life to be continued as long as possible – at the same time there is some unavoidable split attention. Kuno considers several options: to stop working for the next several months, to move his practice to another place, or to continue in his practice at home as long as possible. A related issue is to communicate or not his personal situation with his clients.

Kuno decides to consult his former supervisor.

What kind of advice could one give to Kuno?

To give up practising for a couple of months? This would at least ensure his clients are not at risk of getting any treatment, which is (perhaps adversely) affected by Kuno's state. However, at what costs? Apart from what it means to Kuno and to his wife, both financially and emotionally, how should we evaluate such a long therapy pause or premature termination? And what kind of rationale should be given to his clients? What kind of transference would remain not dealt with?

To move the practice? Would putting Kuno at a certain geographical distance really reduce his split attention, or would it increase his tension instead? Hard to say.

And what kind of rationale could be given to his clients in this case?

To continue in his practice at home as long as possible? This would give the best personal conditions for Kuno and his wife, indeed, but with some possible repercussions on the clients, who might be more closely confronted with Kuno's wife's condition. And what to say or not to the clients?

Kuno's supervisor asked Kuno whether he could really be there for his clients without revealing this condition of utmost importance to himself, and whether this would unduly affect his integrity. In thorough self-reflection Kuno found that completely disguising his personal drama would probably lead to serious self-alienation, and thereby disabling him as a person-centred psychotherapist. Kuno's supervisor agreed and advised him to continue practising and to tell the clients about his wife's condition.

Example 7.5 a

Marianne de Vaate treated Willem Vonk in her private health psychology practice. Vonk was referred because of depressive symptoms and possible personality disorder characteristics. His referral came not so long after Vonk's mother had died under suspect conditions. Later, in a very emotional session, Willem Vonk confesses to having killed his mother. Marianne de Vaate is appalled. Based on her personal value system she is convinced that murderers should be punished. Vonk is not willing to give himself up to the police.

What should Marianne de Vaate do in this situation? Taking action by giving Willem Vonk up to the police would be breaching confidentiality. However, not taking any action and just continuing the treatment was seemingly impossible to her.

Thorough self-reflection on what the present situation meant to her, on her own values and on the ethical standards of the profession would have been essential, as it would have been eventually seeking professional advice on what to do. However, she did not.

Example 7.5 b

Since Willem Vonk was not willing to do so, Marianne de Vaate decided to give Vonk up to the police herself. She could not bear the idea that his deed would remain without any consequences. At the police station, and later in court, Marianne de Vaate declared as her conviction that it couldn't be excluded that Vonk would commit another deed of extreme violence.

Willem Vonk was sentenced for murder, mainly on the base of Marianne de Vaate's testifying. Later, this judgement was reversed on appeal.

Marianne de Vaate was severely disciplined by the psychologists association, because of breaching confidentiality.

Honesty and Accuracy

Under the specification of honesty and accuracy, several national psychologists associations explicitly pay attention to the ownership and credits for research, publications etc. in whatever media. They underline that only appropriate ownership or credit can be claimed and that due acknowledgement of the contributions of others to collaborative work should be provided.

Credit should be given in proportion to the professional contribution that they have made, students included. A sound rule of thumb could be the actual weight of each person's contribution to the work to be reflected in the order in which authorship is credited.

The Irish association's code, article 4.2.14, requires furthermore to clarify ownership of documentation, data, and rights of publication with those who commission research and to ensure that those are aware of the rights and responsibilities of all interested parties.

It is not only explicitly the unjustified claiming of ownership which is to be seen as unethical.

The Dutch psychologists' professional ethics code underlines in article III.2.2.7 that psychologists should also avoid implicit claiming of ownership of ideas, when they present the results of their professional activities, whether in written or in verbal form. They should adequately refer to their sources, insofar the results or the ideas aren't the results of their own professional activities. For example, they should adequately refer to relevant work and not, at least implicitly, appear to claim ideas or work that is not their own.

i) Accuracy in representing relevant qualifications, education, experience, competence and affiliations

This element of the Meta-code is clearly outer-directed, contrary to the previous examples. Many national psychologists associations pay due attention to this element in their respective codes, understandably, as false pretences not only are harmful in the direct professional relationships of individual psychologists but also can be seen as detrimental for the prestige of the profession as a whole.

In representing one's qualifications, education, experience, competence and affiliations it is important not only to be accurate in a strict sense, but also to prevent qualifications and competences from being misinterpreted by others, as the British Psychological Society explicitly states in article 4.1(ii) of its Code of Ethics and Conduct. If any misrepresentations are identified, then these should be corrected, quickly, says the Irish association.[15] Psychologists not only have their responsibility to present themselves adequately, but also – to a certain extent – for being represented correctly by others. Members of the Serbian psychologists association, for instance, are required by article 3.5 of their Ethical Code to take action if their qualifications and capabilities are incorrectly presented by others.

---

[15] The Psychological Society of Ireland, Code of Professional Ethics, art. 4.2.1

It might be clear that sometimes representations can be indisputable in terms of accuracy, but nevertheless arouse inappropriate expectations. This cannot be in accordance with an ethical principle of honesty. The German code of ethics pays elaborate attention to this, e.g., by requiring, especially in the field of psychological therapy, not to use pretentious or inadequate grandiose terms in referring to methods or institutes.[16]

Example 7.6

Jean-Louis Legrand graduated as master in psychology and followed a post-academic training as psychotherapist. At the same time, he finished his academic law studies and soon after his law doctorate. From that point, his career was nearly exclusively in law, academically as well as being a successful solicitor. However, he always kept seeing a few psychotherapy clients. In his formal references on letter paper etc., Legrand uses the academic titles professor and doctor. There is no explicit reference to either discipline, law and psychology.

The specification of the Meta-code not only emphasises the need for accuracy, but also the relevance in representing qualifications, education, experience, competence and affiliations.

It might be clear that using titles and qualifications from outside the orbit of psychology might impress people and give thereby an inappropriate aura to the practising of psychology.

Seen in this light, Legrand's representation on the letterhead of professional papers used in his contacts with therapy clients could be seen as questionable.

The code of the Dutch psychologists association underlines in article III.2.2.3 also the converse, namely that also psychology titles and qualifications should only be represented when this is relevant. Once, a psychologist was reprimanded for using his professional letter paper in a fund raising action. As a consequence, as will be shown later in this chapter, psychologists are seen to act as a professional, whenever they use their psychology titles and qualifications.

Example 7.7

The website of the Institut für spirituelle Astrologie gives the following overview of Dipl. Psych. Sonia Mahr's competences:

---

[16] Berufsverband Deutscher Psychologinnen und Psychologen (BDP) Ethical Principles of the German Psychological Society (DGP) and the Association of German Professional Psychologists (BDP) (and Code of Conduct of the Association of German Professional Psychologists), art. D II.1

Channelling Advice, Aura Clearing, Spiritual Astrology, Reincarnation Therapy, Psychological Astrology, Reiki, Life Counselling, Personality Development, Spiritual Initiations.

Web research reveals that Sonia and her husband Peter are the institute's only staff members. Sonia's academic title is accurate.

Is Sonia Mahr's advertising really compliant with the previously outlined ethical standards? Obviously, in this case inaccuracy isn't, strictly spoken, at stake, since Sonia Mahr has been educated in the respective fields.

However, the majority of Sonia's mentioned areas of competence cannot be regarded as endorsed by academic psychology. Hence, also taking into account the institute's name, Sonia Mahr's academic title – which she legally is allowed to use, irrespective of the situation – could be seen as irrelevant in this context, and thereby inappropriate and misleading, as giving an academic aura to non-academic ideas, or the impression that these ideas are solid enough to be used by academically educated psychologists. Besides, in this case the term "Institute" could be seen as disproportionate and grandiose.

ii) Accuracy in representing information, and responsibility to acknowledge and not to suppress alternative hypotheses, evidence or explanations.

The second specification under this section Honesty and Accuracy focuses on the accuracy of the content of information to be represented. National psychologists associations formulate paragraphs in their ethics codes on findings in scientific work, as research, as well as on presenting their professional activities.

Obviously, forgery of research data, test results and findings is not ethical. Neither is presenting such data to individuals or to the public, as the Serbian association states in article 1.5.2 of its Ethical Code. Not only blunt misdemeanours, as fraudulent inaccuracy, are to be seen as unethical. From the perspective of integrity, this is even more so in cases of more hidden deceit. For instance, this could include not mentioning one's own findings, which do not support one's hypotheses or theories. This is the rationale for formulating the second part of the Meta-code specification 4.2 ii.

Of course, if there are any alternative hypotheses, evidence or explanations, then psychologists make their professional judgments on these alternatives explicit. Not only giving one-sided views on the meaning and explanation of psychological findings can be deceptive. This is also the case if giving refurbished presentations on the psychologist's services, with too optimistic expectations of results that are likely following his or her intervention.

Several national associations include paragraphs in their codes of ethics requiring psychologists not to raise unrealistic or unjust expectations regarding the nature, effects and consequences of the services psychologists provide. In addition, the Irish Code of Professional Ethics demands in article 4.2.3 that psychologists make clear whether they are acting as private citizens, as members of specific organisations or groups, or as representatives of the discipline of psychology, when making statements or when involved in public activities.

Under the vigour of the NIP code article I.1.2.1, psychologists are *always* seen to act as professionals, though, whenever they use the designation "psychologist", also when they act in the media. This should be seen in relation to the previous mentioned article, which asks psychologists only to use their psychology titles and qualifications when this is relevant.

In the aforementioned fund raising case the psychologist disclaimed his professional responsibility by denying the professional character of this action. This was not accepted by the disciplinary committee.

In some countries, however, there are limitations on any professional from making informal comments. In these cases the presumption is that, in a sense, the professional is always in a professional role and that opinions given informally to others may still be seen as professional opinions. This places an added burden on professionals. However, from an ethical point of view the issue is for the psychologist to clarify when they are giving opinions or advice *not* as a psychologist but as a friend or member of the public. The onus is on the *psychologist* to ensure that the other person would not reasonably expect this opinion to be a *professional* opinion.

iii) Honesty and accuracy with regard to any financial implications of the professional relationship

This maxim seems to hardly need any further explanation. Or...

Example 7.8

Mirko Kovac, occupational psychologist, is working in private practice offering consulting and coaching services, mediation and assessment. His clientele consists mainly of firms, but occasionally also private persons come to him. As a rule, he sends an informative brochure after the first call, before the intake. One day, a Mr. Roman Musil calls for an intake appointment at short notice. Kovac's diary is fully booked for weeks, but coincidentally there is a short vacancy at the same day, which Mr. Musil happily accepts. During the half hour session Mr. Musil presents his problems and Kovac sets out his fee, amongst other things. Mr. Musil needs to think it over, and eventually calls Kovac not to continue his contact with him, because of the high level of his fees.

Three days later Mr. Musil receives a very steep bill.

Was Kovac acting ethically by sending a steep bill to Mr. Musil for only a half-hour intake session? Of course, there was no reason for Mr. Musil to believe this session was for free. However, since Kovac didn't have the opportunity to inform Mr. Musil beforehand about the financial conditions, and hearing Mr. Musil's financial objections to continue and become a client, Kovac could have reconsidered the billing amount. Therefore, it makes sense to pay attention to article III.2.2.5 of the Dutch code:

"Before or in the earliest stage of the professional relationship the psychologist honestly and accurately informs those involved of the financial and other conditions under which they agree to provide their services, insofar as this information is relevant for those involved to give their consent."

iv) Recognition of the need for accuracy and the limitations of conclusions and opinions expressed in professional reports and statements

The last specification of Honesty and Accuracy given by the Meta-code, is meant to protect people from inappropriate judgements on the basis of psychological reports. After all, there are many situations in which psychological reports play a major role in decision making, as in personnel selection, in educational choices and in the court, to name a few.

Example 7.9

Pieter Post, clinical and forensic psychologist, was heavily censured by the state disciplinary tribunal. In his report on Christine Zwart, suspected of having killed her stepfather, some data were clearly missing and other data were unreliable. His advice was unclear and insufficiently based on evidence.. His test assessment gave only rough, scanty outlines, which hardly contributed to understanding Christine Zwart's cognitive functioning and he ignored contradictory findings. The personality assessment had serious shortcomings: in the selection of tests, in taking into account their limitations and in lacking coherence. A meticulous crime analysis was absent. The fact that the examination and reporting were done under the habitual time pressure, as Post explained, was definitely not regarded by the tribunal as a mitigating condition. On the contrary, it was seen as sinister and ominous.
Christine Zwart's sentence was revised at appeal.

In its verdict on the Post case, the disciplinary tribunal sets out that this kind of report needs to meet the following requirements:
- in a consistent and insightful way, reports set out clearly the premises on which they are based;
- premises, as set out in the report are endorsed by facts, circumstances and findings of the report; this can be sufficiently demonstrated.
- premises justify the conclusion drawn from them.

It is clear that in the context of this last specification, as illuminated by example 9, the aforementioned need for *accuracy in representing information, and responsibility to acknowledge and not to suppress alternative hypotheses, evidence or explanations* is of utmost relevance. Furthermore, it is worth mentioning the Irish paragraph that underlines the need clearly to differentiate facts, opinions, theories, hypotheses, and ideas. After all, especially under time pressure, in one's train of thoughts one may too easily mix up arguments originating from these various levels of evidence, and jump to conclusions.

Straightforwardness and Openness

Straightforwardness and Openness can be seen as the quadruplet siblings of Honesty and Accuracy. Honesty can be corrupted by silence, accuracy by omissions. We all know, however, how not explicitly telling the full truth can be helpful in constructing white lies, in order to make daily life more easy. And what about professional white lies?

Example 7.10

Hannah Silberstein, clinical psychologist, had had a few sessions with a client of hers, when this client started to tell about her obsessive jealousy. She recently got a new boyfriend, and could not bear the idea that he has any interest in other women, and not even that he had had love affairs before. Hannah recognises from her client's description that the new boyfriend is someone with whom Hannah herself had a brief, passionate relationship, ten years ago, at the university.
 After some reflection, Hannah decides not – yet – to reveal this to her client.

Was Hannah Silverstein acting ethically, in being protective to her client by not being open to her, and withholding the information about her own previous relationship with the client's new boyfriend? As such, psychologists should be reticent in self-disclosure.

Hannah considered that bringing in such information at this stage could have been detrimental, by flaring up the client's jealousy to such extent, that she would drop out of therapy. *Not* volunteering this information, however, bore the risk that the client would find out later, which would understandably feed the client's mistrust and her perception of Hannah as dishonest. Hannah's consideration to terminate the therapy immediately, and consequently in an untimely manner, because of some dual relationship of long ago was rejected by her as too far-fetched.

Example 7.11

Back to Margaret Miller, whose case was presented in the beginning of this chapter. Suppose that the formal commission to assess Mrs. Stone did not include yet the invitation to give a wider view on the applicant's skills and her personality. The latter was only communicated in a telephone call after Miller had accepted the commission.

Considering this suggestion as inappropriate, Margaret Miller decided only to assess and report Mrs. Stone's capacities, relevant to the job requirements. Miller does not reveal to Mrs. Stone the telephone call with the Human Resource manager, in order not to upset her unnecessarily.

In this latter scenario Margaret Miller tried to protect her client from unnecessarily worrying. Besides, to inform Mrs. Stone about the Human Resource manager's telephone call could have made things definitely more complicated. And that was something Miller was not so keen on. The outcome of Margaret Miller's considerations can be seen as quite reasonable and not unethical. After all, Miller decided to ignore the suggestion to produce an extended report. And by then the information was irrelevant to her assessment. On the other hand, could the information be seen as relevant for the client to know, in relation to her job application?

i) General obligation to provide information and avoid deception in research and professional practice

This first specification of *Straightforwardness and Openness* especially is about gaining a well informed consent to participating as research participant, as a therapy client or as someone to be assessed etc. Decisions about participating in one of these psychologist's activities should be fairly free, i.e., based on the client's own interests and needs of the client, and not disproportionately on others' interests or on false pretence. The Margaret Miller case should also be seen in this light. After all, agreeing to participate in an assessment focused on a job application certainly does not self-evidently imply agreeing with an assessment of one's fitness for one's present job.

It is obvious that such a morality easily puts some pressure upon psychological testing and research. After all, psychological test construction was – and is, to certain extent – based on only part disclosure of the ideas examined in the test. Lie scores, authoritarianism, paranoia, psychopathy – to name a few – are not likely to be clearly mentioned in the information, provided to research-participants-to-be, or clients to be assessed.

Example 7.12 a

In 1961, Yale University psychologist Stanley Milgram measured the willingness of study participants to obey an authority figure, who instructed them to perform acts that conflicted with their personal conscience.

Research subjects (participants) and the "victim" (in reality a helper of the experimenter) were told by the experimenter that they would be participating in an experiment helping his study of memory and learning in different situations. Research participants were asked to give electric shocks to the "victim", up to 450-volt shocks. In reality, no shocks were given. Research participants' demands to halt the experiment were firmly discouraged.

The research results were alarming: over 60% of the participants administered the experiment's final 450-volt shock, though many were very uncomfortable doing so.

The Irish psychologists association demands in article 4.2.7.of its Code of Professional Ethics that psychologists "conduct research in a way that is consistent with a commitment to honest, open inquiry, and to clear communication of any research aims, sponsorship, social context, personal values, or financial interests that may affect or appear to affect their research", and consequently elaborates in its article 4.3.1 the maxim on providing information and avoidance of deception as follows:

"Respect the right of clients and research participants to receive an appropriate explanation of the nature, purpose and results of investigations, assessments and research findings, in language that these persons can understand."

However, how to interpret appropriateness? To give enough information to enable clients and research participants to come to a balanced informed consent? Or, to ensure the research project or assessment is not biased?

Apart from other ethical dimensions, the controversial Milgram experiments could not simply have been done without being in conflict with the first exegesis of appropriate information: the benefit of the client being at stake. This is not only a reflection with half a century hindsight. Soon after Milgram's first publication (Milgram, 1963) a thorough discussion on research ethics was launched by Diana Baumrind's brief, but influential article commenting on Milgram's study of obedience (Baumrind, 1964) and Milgram's reply to it (Milgram, 1964). Baumrind's criticisms of the treatment of the participants in Milgram's studies stimulated a thorough revision of the American Psychological Association's ethical standards of psychological research.

A major question is, whether the maxim of Straightforwardness and Openness, and thereby issuing information and avoidance of deception, is to be seen as categorical or not. On this, the Meta-code gives the following guidance:

ii) Obligation not to withhold information or to engage in temporary deception if there are alternative procedures available. [...].

Which means that – according to the Meta-code – withholding information and temporary deception *can* be used, as a last resort. It is obvious that the availability of alternative procedures halts withholding information or engaging in deception. However, does the mere absence of alternatives legitimise withholding information and temporary deception sufficiently? The British Psychological Society's Code of Ethics and Conduct says in article 1.3 (xi) about this, *inter alia*, the following:

"Withhold information from clients only in exceptional circumstances when necessary to preserve the integrity of research or the efficacy of professional services, or in the public interest [...]."

One may wonder if *all* "integrity of research or efficacy of professional services" could justify *all* kind of withholding information or deception. Not at all costs. The British Society, not surprisingly, ends the just quoted clause as follows: "and specifically consider any additional safeguards required for the preservation of client welfare." (ibid.)

It is noticeable that, nearly half a century after the Milgram experiments, it is a sort of standard for ethical codes to have included one or more paragraphs on *avoidance of harm*. The Meta-code addresses this subject in the chapter on Responsibility.

Example 7.12 b

The Milgram experiments began in July 1961, three months after the start of the trial of Nazi war criminal Adolf Eichmann in Jerusalem. Stanley Milgram devised his experiments to answer the question if it could be that Eichmann and his million accomplices in the Holocaust were just following orders.

In "The Perils of Obedience" (Harper's Magazine, December 1973, p 62-77), Milgram informs the general public about his experiment, then writes, inter alia: "The legal and philosophic aspects of obedience are of enormous importance, but they say very little about how most people behave in concrete situations. I set up a simple experiment at Yale University to test how much pain an ordinary citizen would inflict on another person simply because he was ordered to by an experimental scientist. Stark authority was pitted against the subjects" strongest moral imperatives against hurting others, and, with the subjects" ears ringing with the screams of the victims, authority won more often than not. The extreme willingness of adults to go to almost any lengths on the command of an authority constitutes the chief finding of the study and the fact most urgently demanding explanation."

After all, the Milgram research is not only to be seen as of great importance because of its contribution to a better understanding of obedience, but also because of the major impetus it gave to the debate on the position of clients' welfare in research ethics.

As the British code does, many European psychologists' ethical codes address in one way or another to circumstantial necessity. However, little attention is paid to the *proportionality* of the disguised objectives and conditions on the one hand and the scientific, societal or personal relevance and importance on the other. Whether the importance of the ends could justify the means.

One approach could be as laid down in the Irish code which, in article 1.3.13, demands psychologists to "seek an independent and adequate ethical review of the risks to public or individual trust and of safeguards to protect such trust for any research, which uses deception or techniques, which might be interpreted as deception, before making a decision to proceed". Weighing scientific benefits against the moral costs could be considered as a parameter of adequacy in such an independent review.

[...] If deception has occurred, there is an obligation to inform and re-establish trust.

As we have seen above, there might be some interpretational noise in the first sentence of the Meta-code's guidance on providing information and avoiding deception in research and professional practice, whereas in the second sentence, on re-establishing trust, there certainly isn't any: a proper debriefing is seen as a necessary part of re-establishing trust. For a proper debriefing, just giving information might not be enough. This technique essentially involves removing any false information (dehoaxing) or negative feelings (desensitising) resulting from deception (Basset, Basinger & Livermore, 1992). For instance, in the aftermath of the Milgram experiments the question was raised, what kind of debriefing could overcome the emotional effects, as described by Milgram in his paper (Baumrind, 1964).

The debate on lying in the name of research has not died down ever since. Arguments about what harm lying can do, both to the liar and to the one being lied to, and the impact it could have on the credibility of the profession continue: "psychologists are suspected of being tricksters" is still thought provoking and an ongoing theme in research ethics (Baumrind 1985). Seen from, for example, Buddhist philosophy standpoint, such harm will be even more widely spread given "the interdeterminate structure of all that exists" (Tarab Tulku Rinpoche, in Tarab Tulku IX & Handberg, 2005).

Apart from the previously mentioned requirement specifically to consider additional safeguards that may be required for the preservation of client welfare, before starting, the BPS code requires in its article 1.3 (xii) that the nature of the deception to be disclosed to clients at the earliest feasible opportunity, whereas the Irish association asks its members to "provide a debriefing for research participants following studies in which deception (or the use of techniques which could be interpreted as deception) has occurred. Psychologists shall clarify the real nature of and rationale for the study, and seek to remove any misconceptions and re-establish trust."[17]

---

[17] The Psychological Society of Ireland, Code of Professional Ethics, art. 4.3.5

Conflict of Interests and Exploitation

This section might be one of those with a high appeal to people's imagination. Not without reason. Although, for example, in The Netherlands, complaints because of alleged exploitation or conflicts of interests turn out to be substantially outnumbered by other alleged infringements of the ethical code[18], many major cases leading to expulsion are often characterised by conflicts of interests or exploitation. However, the latter will not only appear in blunt unethical acting. Subtle exploitation is probably far more common, and often not even seen as such, but rather perceived as innocent and harmless, by the psychologist as well as by the client. As many professional psychologists may have experienced themselves and have seen from others, the risk of sliding down on the slope of personal interest presents itself too easily.

Example 7.13 a

Christian Peters, occupational health psychologist, counselled Mikkel Larsen, 63 years old, expatriate, manager in a multinational corporation, who suffered from the time of his retirement drawing frightening near. Besides, or maybe in the first place, Larsen felt mangled by a rigorous reorganisation process. In the course of the counselling, Mikkel Larsen succeeded to get his perspective on the future more clear, and even started to clear some time to be spent on his old passion, painting.

Mikkel Larsen was clearly very content with his contact with Peters. At the time that Peters rounded off the counselling with this man, whom he had got to appreciate as an interesting, erudite person, Larsen insisted to give him a small painting, bearing Larsen's initials. It wasn't a new one, but forty years old.

Was Christian Peters acting ethically, by accepting this gift from Mikkel Larsen, or should he have refused? This kind of question will rise in the following pages. Let us first see what the Meta-code gives as specifications of the present issue.

i) *Awareness of the problems which may result from dual relationships and an obligation to avoid such dual relationships which reduce the necessary professional distance or may lead to conflict of interests, or exploitation of a client.*

To heighten one's awareness for problems which may arise is perhaps most important as such. Certainly situations may occur in which a specific professional relationship becomes complicated by other relational dimensions with the same person(s). The Meta-code underlines the need for vigilance and obliges psychologists to avoid dual relationships, which reduce professional distance or may lead to conflict of interests, or exploitation of a client.

---

[18] NIP Disciplinary Board annual report 2004, www.psynip.nl.

Several national psychologists' codes, like those of the British and the Dutch, take the same position.[19] [20] In its article 4.4.3, the Irish code points to the need for necessary risk awareness and to avoid dual relationships whenever possible, but states explicitly that it is not always possible to avoid them. The Belgian Psychologists Federation, though, is extremely prohibitive. Its Deontological Code's articles 4.3.1 and 4.3.4 forbid any form of dual relationship with clients. The rationale behind such a rigor might be the awareness of the substantial risks of dual relationships and their possible impact.

Example 7.14 a

Petra Perkins, clinical and occupational psychologist, was commissioned to assess a job applicant, who turned out to be her favourite cousin, who – after two years of fruitless efforts on the labour market – regarded her application as the last chance to get a job matching her level of education. Perkins decides to accept the commission. The test results were just below the limit. In her report, Petra Perkins decided to embellish the results slightly, counting on the probability that one of the better applicants would get the job anyway.

Example 7.14 b

As described in example 7.14 a except for the outcome, in which Perkins decided this time not at all to compromise her professional standards. She launched a realistic report. The relationship with her close relatives was seriously harmed.

These examples make clear that dual relationships may lead to unfavourable consequences such as compromising the profession or creating disturbed relationships. This is not to be seen as restricted to dual personal-professional relationships. After all, professional-professional dual relationships may also lead to unwanted effects. Remarkably, only a minority of the European psychologists' ethical codes, e.g., the Belgian and the Dutch point to the latter explicitly. [21] [22]

Example 7.14 c

Petra Perkins, clinical and occupational psychologist, was commissioned to assess some job applicants. One of these turned out to be a therapy client of hers. Not wanting

---

[19] BPS, Code of Ethics and Conduct, art.4.2.(i).

[20] NIP, Beroepscode voor Psychologen 2007, art.III.2.3.4, art.III.2.3.5

[21] Belgische Federatie van Psychologen – Fédération Belge des Psychologues, Deontological Code art.4.3.4.

[22] NIP, Beroepscode voor Psychologen 2007, art.III.2.3.4.

to do anything that could possibly disclose this professional relationship, or give rise to any speculation, Petra decided to accept the commission. Moreover, the job would be an excellent opportunity for her client. As expected, the assessment results were reasonably satisfying, except for the low score on an emotional stability test. As Perkins thought the latter not being correspondent to her clinical impression during therapy, she decided to ignore these specific test results.

It is worth mentioning, that it is wise to broaden sufficiently the scope of one's awareness of the problems, which may result from dual relationships. Not only actual relationships need to be taken into account, but previous ones too. It is clear that the nature, the quality and the intensity of the (previous) private or professional relationship might be of influence in the decision making whether to risk or not any possible complications in a new relationship. A present neighbour might be even too close to accept for any professional relationship whatsoever, whereas there may be no objections to take in for behaviour therapy, a 25 years old guy, whose parents moved out of your street twenty years ago.

In several psychologists' ethical codes dual relationships (of some kind) are unconditionally forbidden, whereas "occasional lying in the laboratory" (i.e., using deception as a result method) is often considered as tolerable under the condition of temporality. Seen from an ethical point of view, this might be somewhat peculiar. After all, lying cannot be regarded as ethically more acceptable than dual relationships as such.

As already commented on the Belgian code's rigour in these, the rationale must be sought in the level of risks to be avoided. Nevertheless, decision making on the basis of a careful incompatibility analysis seems to be as adequate, or even more, than rigorous rules, since the latter may turn out to in be inappropriately indiscriminate certain situations, and consequently raise the probability of violations occurring.

To illustrate this with the following metaphor: Traffic lights are meant to reduce accident risk, by simplifying human decision-making. Green: drive or ride, red: stop. However, many people feel it as inadequate not being allowed to cross a quiet road when the light turns orange or red, when approaching it at 3 a.m. when no vehicles are due to cross. Passing a deserted road-crossing is not seen as basically immoral, even if it is prohibited at that moment. After all, no harm is done to anyone. In the meantime, many previous traffic light regulated road crossings in Europe have been turned into roundabouts, thereby leading to a dynamic, situation dependent decision making.

To lose professional distance and thereby one's independence and impartiality is a major reason to sharpen the awareness of the risk doing so. However, avoiding losing one's integrity by exploiting a professional relationship deserves a risk awareness of paramount acuity. The Meta-code underlines the nature of exploitation in the following way:

ii) Obligation not to exploit a professional relationship to further personal, religious, political or other ideological interests.

Most ethical codes elaborate this guideline. For example, the Irish association does in giving the following examples in article 4.1.1 of its Code of Professional Ethics:

"... soliciting for private practice clients of one's employing agency; taking advantage of trust or dependency to frighten clients into receiving services; appropriating student's ideas, research or work; using the resources of one's employing institution for purposes not agreed to; securing or accepting significant financial or material benefit for professional activities which are already rewarded by salary; prejudicing others against a colleague for reasons of personal gain".

Remember the Christian Peters case in example 7.13 a. Peters' client, Mikkel Larsen insisted to give him a small painting at the time when the counselling was rounded off.

What should Christian Peters have done? Declined the painting, or accepted it gratefully? After all, accepting gifts as such is not in every psychotherapeutic orientation seen by definition as unprofessional or unethical. What does it mean to the giver if his or her gift is declined? And insofar as the value of the gift shouldn't be out of proportion, what proportion? Should this be seen from the giver's perspective or from the receiver's? Or both?

Example 7.13 b

Three month later, Christian Peters got a telephone phone call from Larsen, who asked to meet Peters again. This time not as a client, but privately. Three months after the last session, this shouldn't be a problem, Larsen said. He invited Peters for an opera performance. Tickets were bought already, and Larsen just wanted good company and couldn't find any better, for the moment.

Christian Peters in fact loved to go to the opera, and he knew that tickets for this particular performance, ranked as one of his favourites, were sold out already a long time ago.

Socialising with an ex-client and accepting being invited, three months after termination of the professional relationship? Should half a year, or two years, after termination be better? Or is socialising with clients or ex-clients as such corrupting the profession? Really?

Is safeguarding the way back to re-open the professional relationship a valid reason to withhold mature people from personal, non-professional involvement? Even if the client prefers to cut off the way to coming back, in favour of staying together non-professionally?

To what extent is the prestige of the profession based on abstinence of personal involvement?

On the other hand, how needy can psychologists be? Need for recognition, need for gratitude, to name a few.

Example 7.13 c

After this re-encounter, other appointments for common cultural events followed.

It was clear that both Peters and Larsen enjoyed each other's company. After a while, Mikkel Larsen asked Peters if he might give him another painting, as a thank you for all Christian Peters meant to him.

This painting, which Larsen had actually brought along already, turned out to be an old one as well. Mikkel Larsen had become very active in painting and was very at ease in giving his works away. However, it was especially this older painting that Larsen wanted to give to Peters. It wasn't an early work of his own, but it was, as was the first given painting, out of a vast collection of his grandfather's works, inherited thirty years ago. What his grandfather actually meant to him, and still did, became especially clear during his sessions with Peters. This is the reason why he chose this one to give away.

Many questions can be raised, and many more questions should one ask oneself, to evaluate one's real integrity and to find the answer whether receiving might be exploitative or not. Mikkel Larsen decided to close off the way back to the psychologist Christian Peters, in favour of socialising with Christian Peters, who happened to be his psychologist. Did it really happen to be to be closed off?

Example 7.13 d

During lunch meetings, Mikkel Larsen sometimes asked Christian Peters' advice, on all kind of subjects, calling him teasingly "my life coach" or "my life psychologist".

How teasingly are Mikkel Larsen's remarks really? Is Christian Peters as much as a psychologist as he is in his relationship with Mrs. Peters? Are some remnants of the past still present? And if so, does it matter? Is any harm inflicted on anybody?

Example 7.13 e

It is clear that Christian Peters and Mikkel Larsen had a great respectful fondness for each other, without much of a claim on each other's private life. Mikkel Larsen was quite a sociable person, with many acquaintances around. However he didn't seem to have real friends and there was no close family. In the meantime it was seven years ago that his partner died and he didn't have any children. He didn't get on very well with his sister and her husband, and cousins and nieces were too distant to be meaningful. Mikkel Larsen considered his relationship with Christian Peters as very special.

Then the moment comes that Mikkel Larsen asks Christian Peters if he is willing to accept to be the executor of his will, the main heir of his capital and the only heir of his collection of paintings. In the meantime, Peters had found out that Mikkel Larsen's grandfather had not just been a meritorious Sunday painter, but had taken a leading part in a famous artists' circle, although this was not very well known in Christian Peters' country.

Was Christian Peters acting unethically if willing to accept Larsen's request? Is the link to the previous professional relationship strong enough not to be ignored? What does it mean if, in hindsight, a gift turns out to be valuable? How should this be balanced against his genuine friendship to Mikkel Larsen, which was just beneficial? The latter argument is especially intriguing if we shift our attention to romantic relationships between psychologists and (former) clients.

Example 7.15

Helen Undritz, a psychology student falls in love with her professor Franz-Peter Wunderlich. The romantic feelings are mutual. Wunderlich is convinced that a personal relationship with this student – an independent and self-confident woman – does not interfere with his supervision of her thesis and being the examiner for one of her exams, which are due in half a year. They agree to have no sex before all the exams are over and the thesis has been accepted. After the exams they are going to live together and finally they get married.

Everyone is happy, nobody complains. But things could have gone differently. Has the professor's behaviour been in conflict with ethical principles?

Whereas a few psychologists' associations even forbid sexual relationships with ex-clients, all European psychologists associations' codes explicitly prohibit sexual relationships with current clients. This is not surprising, since a ban on health professionals having sexual intercourse with their clients is often laid down in national criminal laws as well.[23] However, one may wonder how stringent the ethical rationale is for such a categorical prohibition. After all, consensual love relationships between adult people cannot really be seen as immoral by definition, as could be the case in "lying in the laboratory" (temporarily deceiving research participants) or falsifying research data).

---

[23] E.g., in Austria, Strafgesetzbuch (StGB) § 212, and in The Netherlands, Wetboek van Strafrecht art, 249. The StGB explicitly mentions the clinical psychologist, the health psychologist and the psychotherapist.

A history of patient exploitation in health professions makes draconian rules understandable, especially against the background of not uncommon authoritarian doctor-patient relationships in the past, which certainly may still exist occasionally. On top of that, the patient or client may experience functional intimacy in the professional encounter in health case – whether it is undressing, being touched (breast and genitals not excluded), sharing intimate thoughts and feelings – as containing seductive qualities, if there aren't firm boundaries set, safeguarding the professional relationship. However, does the history of occasional abuse in health care justify categorically withholding from independent and self-confident people, like Helene Undritz? The possibility of intimate, loving relationships with someone of their own choice. Was Franz-Peter Wunderlich acting unethically by responding to Helene's love?

One could argue, that a categorical ban by definition attributes to clients certain incompetence for making responsible, consensual decisions. This is also the case for ex-clients if a ban is specified for certain a period of time; for example, if the ban excludes having sex with the psychologist for two years or even more. But in the history of morality, love and sexuality often was, and still is, not only a matter between two loving persons. The ban on adultery found its place in the Ten Commandments, and incest and adultery have been forbidden, most of the time, in most countries and for most of the people.

In our European society, incest, sex with under aged young people and with persons of who are vulnerable by reason of impaired cognitive ability are still prohibited by laws. Laws protect the moral sense against being offended, the offspring against loss of legal descent, and the vulnerable against abuse and exploitation. This is so even if the vulnerable do not feel vulnerable, don't want any protection and deliberately take the initiative.

From this perspective, love affairs between therapists and clients could be regarded as "therapist incest". But, is this applicable to every psychologist-client relationship? We could consider a hierarchy of power relationships from the very close therapist-client to distant colleagues in an organisation. With respect to students, a supervisory relationship, as with a thesis supervisor and student, may be judged as much closer than a lecturer to a student in a class of 200 for one lecture.

Example 7.16

Nazeer Khalid, clinical psychologist, grew up in a very traditionalistic Muslim family, living in a big European city. During his university education he lost, like numerous fellow students, his attachment to the religion of his childhood. However, unlike many other Muslim-borns, Nazeer could not feel the slightest compassion towards his religious background but turned into a rabid atheist, seeing religion as a danger for mental health. Whenever he perceived clients suffering from imposed despotic religious values, Nazeer volunteered to give his view on religion, wrapped in psychoanalytic terminology.

Even if Nazeer could be right in seeing unhealthy repressive effects of some kind of religious upbringing, one may seriously wonder if his crusade against religion isn't unethical. After all, it seems that Nazeer, masked by authoritative terminology, is trying to convert clients to his personal antireligious view.

ii) *Awareness that conflict of interest and inequality of power in a relationship may still reside after the professional relationship is formally terminated, and that professional responsibilities may still apply.*

Most psychologists will not get into situations where they will meet dilemmas or possible conflicts related to this specification. However, getting referrals of siblings, parents or children of previous clients may need some reflections on the possible consequences of these. Less probable, though certainly not improbable, is the following case.

Example 7.17

Sofia Kontoyiannis, psychologist, is director of a medium sized mental health centre. Personnel affairs are delegated to the personnel manager, except for the formal signing of contracts and dismissal letters.

One day Sofia found a contract to sign, which regarded a former client of hers who had successfully applied for an administrative position in the centre. The position required a responsible and reliable handling of highly confidential material, included those of clients.

Five years earlier, when still working in private practice, Kontoyiannis ceased her professional relationship with this intelligent and sociable person after only few initial therapy sessions because of his clear lack of motivation. At the time Sofia Kontoyiannis was struck by the anti-social personality characteristics of this person, who boasted about a history of successful, and clever fraudulent activities.

Now faced with this contract to be signed, while having serious objections against, Sofia Kontoyiannis decided to invite her ex-client to a meeting, in order to discourage him from taking the post. However, not surprisingly, the ex-client was not willing at all to refrain from his application. Moreover, he threatened Sofia Kontoyiannis with a disciplinary complaint if any of their previous relationship would be revealed.

This case shows that situations may arise, which hardly could have been foreseen, if at all.

Sofia Kontoyiannis is put into the dilemma to take serious risks – in her perception – in signing the contract and employing a person, whose reliability could be seriously questioned and thereby a substantial risk for the centre. On the other hand, there wasn't really a way out, given the ethical, and legal, obligation to keep her professional knowledge about his client confidential, including the fact that this person had been a client of hers. This is one of these situations, so familiar to professional psychologists, which is so strikingly worded by the exclamation of the blind seer Teiresias in Sophocles' classical Greek drama "Oedipus Tyrannus": "… what a misery to have knowledge of something, and not being able to do anything with it" (see Jebb, 1887).[24]

Actions of Colleagues

Obligation to give a reasonable critique of the professional actions of colleagues, and to take action to inform colleagues and, if appropriate, the relevant professional associations and authorities, if there is a question of unethical action.

This very last Meta-code specification pays attention to the need for joint loyalty to clients, to colleagues, to the profession and to professional ethics as such. It should be noticed that this specification is not primarily phrased as an article about "whistle-blowing", but as a moral obligation to support colleagues in helping them to reflect on the ethical dimension of their professional actions and to discontinue unethical actions.

Example 7.18

Anna Lind, child psychologist, receives from a colleague a letter regarding a 6 years old client of hers. The letter is qualified as confidential, and furthermore the colleague asks Anna explicitly not to share the information with the parents of her client, because of the delicate content of the letter. Anna contacts her colleague, verifying her impression that the client's parents didn't have any notion of this sent letter. Then she asks her colleague if he is aware of the fact that clients – in this case the parents as legal representatives – not only have the full right to access their files, received letters included, but that they also should be informed about the content of any information sent out, whether to colleagues or not.

Not giving feedback to a colleague, whose professional behaviour is perceived not to be in accordance with ethical principles, is disloyal to this colleague. A conspiracy of

---

[24] The English translation of this quotation is by the author of this chapter. Teiresias knew that Oedipus – unknowingly – had killed his own father and married his own mother, but could not reveal this to Oedipus and show that it was the reason for the gods' wrath on the city of Thebe.

silence, when psychologists only gossip about a colleague's alleged misconduct and don't take any action, is like passively standing at the riverbank looking at someone drowning. Obviously, in that case there is a high risk that not only the psychologist drowns, but also the client(s). Of course, concerns for clients' welfare and for the profession's reputation aren't of second rank, but indiscriminately hang together with this care and support of colleagues.

Example 7.19

On two separate occasions Marie LeCoultre, clinical psychologist, heard from two clients that they had had a romance with their previous, one and the same, psychologist-psychotherapist. Neither of them seemed to regret the escapade and neither of them wanted to be involved in anything that could lead to complaint procedures of any kind against their former lover-psychologist. Both explicitly claimed confidentiality with respect to their "confession" and did not want their identities revealed.

Marie LeCoultre decided to contact the colleague in question for a sororal appeal regarding professional ethics, thereby strictly avoiding any reference to both of her clients. The colleague did not even try to mitigate or conceal the fact that there had been romantic relationships with some clients, but stated that these were fully consensual and that similar situations might occur in the future too. Moreover, the colleague asked somewhat provocatively if the two of Marie's clients really agreed with this action of hers.

Marie LeCoultre felt shocked, but realised that no evidence could be provided in any formal evaluative procedure, because of the decisiveness of her clients not to co-operate in any complaint procedure.

In this case Marie LeCoultre did what she should do, to confront her colleague with the alleged unethical acting, thereby taking the risk that her clients' identity could be unwillingly revealed. Which turned out to be the case. It is clear, but extremely frustrating, that possible damage to clients or future clients cannot not be prevented if there is no more substantial evidence than hearsay to raise a complaint upon. The only thing to do in such a case is to inform colleagues, thereby risking a lawsuit because of lacking evidence in bringing the particular colleague in disrepute.

Conclusions

Integrity concerns honesty, fairness and respect for others. This Principle has been elaborated to cover a wide range of psychologists' behaviour. It goes beyond competence. It concerns not only how to act but *whether* to act. A request may require knowledge and skills within a psychologist's range but perhaps the purpose is nefarious. Moral choices are involved. Note too that the actions of others are also involved. This can be particularly difficult, dealing with the apparently unethical behaviour of others. Nevertheless, as indicated in this chapter, integrity is central to practice.

Chapter 8

Ethical Problem Solving

Geoff Lindsay

The preceding chapters have provided discussions of the ethical guidance in the Meta-code. The main and most positive approach to developing ethical practice starts with an understanding of ethical principles supplemented by specifications that address more particular aspects of practice. However, even the fullest understanding of the Meta-code cannot be a complete answer. Experience and research show that ethical challenges can arise across a wide range of practice. The task for the psychologist is to deal with these challenges. The Meta-code is sound foundation but also needed is a decision-making approach.

This is, in essence, comparable to problem-solving approaches addressing substantive areas of practice, e.g., the assessment of a person's presenting problems. The task there is to identify key issues, weigh different factors and take action. A similar process is necessary with respect to ethical issues. A number of models have been proposed (e.g., see Pryzwansky & Wendt, 1999, chapter 7 for a review) and guidance will be provided in this chapter using the Meta-code. However, first it is necessary to contextualise decision-making for ethical dilemmas as these comprise only one form of ethically challenging scenarios.

A number of research studies in the US (Pope & Vetter, 1992), UK (Lindsay & Colley, 1995) and elsewhere (Colnerud, 1997; Sinclair, 1998, Waasenaar & Slack, 1997) have shown that ethical dilemmas frequently occur for psychologists. These dilemmas are a subset of a wider range of behaviour whose ethical status is questionable. In addition, studies that have asked psychologists to report ethically troubling events have demonstrated a wide range of conflicts.

A common finding across a range of studies in different countries is that the major area of concern is confidentiality (Pope and Vetter,1992; Lindsay and Colley, 1995). Note the similarities and differences in responses to surveys of members of the British Psychological Society (BPS) and American Psychological Association (APA) – Table 8.1. Whilst confidentiality is a typical issue addressed by ethical codes, dilemmas might arise with respect to limits of confidentiality, especially disclosure of information which might prevent harm. In such cases, ethical principles are in *conflict* and the psychologist must choose, not simply how to behave ethically by following a protocol on confidentiality, but how to behave ethically *weighing up* competing principles and standards.

Table 8.1. Ethically troubling incidents; BPS and APA members

	% BPS	% APA
Confidentiality	10	18
Research	10	4
Questionable intervention	8	3
Colleague's conduct	7	4
Sexual issues	6	4
Assessment	6	4
Organisational	5	1
Dual relationships	3	17
Payments	3	14
Academic/training	3	8

Several studies have also indicated that psychologist practitioners will vary in their agreement with ethical positions (e.g., Haas, Malouf and Mayerson, 1986). Furthermore, even highly experienced practitioners may disagree with ethical positions as laid down by their psychological association, believing their own ethical reasoning is superior (Kalichman, Craig and Follingstad, 1989; Lindsay, 1995). Is this acceptable?

There have also been discussions of the ethics of different types of research methodology. The well established concerns about deception discussed at several places so far in this book are well known. But there are also concerns about the use of interpretive methodologies including ethnography and grounded theory and the use of qualitative methods in such interpretive research. This has become a matter of concern particularly where research ethics committees adopt a positlivist paradigm and where dependency power relations are arguably more equal altering the traditional balance, in an experiment for example, where the psychologist is in the powerful position and the participant is in a potentially much less powerful position. For example, in a research study investigating the opinions of senior politicians, industrialists or university professors using interviews the participants are *de facto* powerful people who will be in a good position to understand and meaningfully consent to, and even control the interview. (Jacobson, Gewurtz & Haydon, 2007).

Unethical Practice

There are a number of reasons why a psychologist may engage in inappropriate behaviour, not all of which represent deliberate and malicious intent:

- *Ignorance* of the ethical code and/or other relevant ethical guidance
- *Carelessness* in interpretation of the code during professional practice
- *Deliberate flaunting* of the relevant code, whether for inappropriate personal bene-fit, or because of disagreeing with the code
- As a result of reduced physical or mental competence
- As a result of *dilemmas* arising in practice whereby ethical principles are in tension or even conflict

Ignorance of the ethical code

Through inadequate training, a lack of maintenance of ethical awareness or memory lapse, a psychologist may act unethically through ignorance of the ethical code. This may be particularly relevant if a code changes – a matter of particular relevance in the US where the APA code has been revised every 5–10 years since the first 1953 edition. This is also a particular problem with highly specific codes. For example, the existence of the internet and psychologists' involvement as consultants to TV "reality" programmes which place members of the public on display in communal living and competitive interaction (e.g., Big Brother in the UK), may not be specifically covered by some codes or may be covered by additional guidance of which a psychologist may not be aware. On the other hand, such developments can be interpreted in relation to the underlying ethical principles and their exemplification in documents such as the EFPA Meta-Code.

Carelessness in interpretation of the code

This is an extension of "ignorance". Here the psychologist has been aware of the code but is insufficiently careful in practice, making decisions which are not sufficiently thoughtful. For example, a psychologist may take a particularly *laissez faire* approach to the code, too ready to make an interpretation which provides the greatest freedom of action rather than thinking primarily of the client. Alternatively, a psychologist may simple be only half aware – knowing the general content of the code but not the detail necessary for a particular situation. Of course, this can be avoided not only by greater knowledge of the code or a readiness to check when in doubt, but this problem may also be addressed by considering the issue relative to ethical principles.

Deliberate flaunting of the code

There are two main sub-classes of deliberate flaunting of the code, deciding not to comply with its requirements or guidance as a result of a reasoned decision and non-compliance in order to benefit inappropriately.

Reasoned disagreement with the Code

An example of disagreements with ethical codes is provided by several research studies which asked experienced psychologists to determine whether certain behaviours were unethical. A particularly important example was the reporting of suspected child abuse. Many jurisdictions have developed laws that require professionals to report suspected child abuse, for example where it is disclosed during a therapeutic interview. Many psychologists at this time, however, objected to this requirement as a breach of confidentiality to the client, or as an impediment to positive therapeutic outcomes in such cases. Such views were found among very senior psychologists, including members of ethics committees. Many others would have sympathy, but not reporting would put the psychologist above the law, which raises other problems. On the other hand, should not psychologists refuse to conduct themselves in ways they consider harmful to clients even if mandated by law? The experience of totalitarian states has made this a very real issue. The major debate within the APA on the role of psychologists in the military following revelations of practices considered to be torture shows that this remains a significant ethical challenge.[25]

Flouting of the Code for self-gratification

This concerns psychologists acting for essentially selfish reasons, leading to their own benefit. Examples may include financial gain, receiving sexual favours, job promotion, or self-aggrandisement. These behaviours are more clearly categorised as unethical, but even here it may be argued that the actions are either not harmful, or even beneficial. For example, a financial arrangement may indeed benefit both client and psychologist. Some clients, and certainly some students, have protested that they do not wish to be safeguarded from an intimate relationship with a senior psychologist such as a research supervisor, but, rather, they wish to determine themselves with whom to develop, and the nature of, a personal relationship.

There is also the delicate issue of a supervisor and student publishing work from a student's thesis. In the case of a doctoral thesis, it is ultimately the student's work and the student who must defend the thesis. However, the designing and carrying out the research and then writing the thesis will be a *joint* effort of student and supervisor, albeit with different roles and the student taking primary responsibility supported and guided by the supervisor. Consequently, joint publications from the research, reflecting the contribution of each, are reasonable. Clarifying this expectation (including also the expectation that the work *will* be published and not left to languish as an unread thesis in a university library and that publications based on a doctoral thesis will normally have the student as first author) may usefully be discussed at the initial meeting between supervisor and student where ground rules and expectations in general are set

---

[25] See chapter 10 for a fuller discussion.

out. Note that this is very different from the senior member of staff (e.g., the director of a centre of the head of department in a university, clinics or psychological service) expecting that their name shall automatically appear on any publication simply because of their position and independent of their input – or lack of input.

Reduced physical or mental competence

This is a common cause of complaints about medical practitioners especially related to alcohol or drugs which are more readily accessed by health professionals. It may also refer to ill health and incapacity related to age which can apply to all professionals. Here the psychologist is seeking to operate appropriately but is unable to do so. This is a challenge for us all – how many of us have worked when not fully fit and well? Working in a supportive environment with "critical friends" is helpful as colleagues can question competence in a supportive non-accusatory manner, helping the psychologists to reflect on their condition and its potential effects on practice.

Ethical Dilemmas

The final type to be considered is the most complex. Professional practice, and a number of research studies, have indicated that there are situations when a psychologist may legitimately be faced with an ethical dilemma such that, whatever action is taken, one or more aspects of an ethical code will be compromised, in order to act ethically in other respects.

A series of studies in countries across the world have demonstrated that psychologists working in a variety of settings are faced by such realities. Typically, the most common type of dilemma concerns confidentiality, (as discussed above) and the challenge of disclosure. In addition to the reporting of child abuse (see above) another common concern is the prevention of harm in general. This issue has a legal dimension as exemplified in the US by the case of Tarasoff v Regents of the University of California (1976). A psychologist was concerned about the disclosure of a student (Poddar), attending the University student health clinic, which made reference to using a gun on his former girlfriend identified only as Tatianna. The psychologist wrote to the campus police who detained but then released the student following evaluation by a psychiatrist, who also ordered the psychologist's notes to be destroyed. A few weeks later the student killed his former girlfriend. The lawsuit alleged negligence by several individuals, including the psychologist because Tatianna was not warned of Poddar's threat. The case went to the Supreme Court which ruled in favour of Tatianna's parents' claim stating:

> The public policy favouring protection of the confidentiality character of patient-psychotherapist communications must yield to the extent of which disclosure is

essential to avert danger to others. *The protective privilege ends when the public peril begins.* (italics added) – (Tarasoff v Regents, 1976, p. 347)[26]

Thus, in the US at least, there is a legal requirement for psychologists (and others) to weigh up the ethical demands of client confidentiality against risk to a third party. However, this case did not specify the duty to protect – what evidence of threat is sufficient or necessary? As such, it provides a clear example of a continuing type of dilemmas which confront many psychologists.

Implications

These different reasons for apparently inappropriate behaviour imply a need for different actions. The *ignorance* and *carelessness* reasons are primarily related to training and maintenance of appropriate professional behaviour. The fourth reason *(reduced physical and mental competence)* suggests the need for action to improve health rather than knowledge and skills, supplemented by a system for challenging by a critical friend. Only the fourth category is concerned with *deliberate* unethical behaviour, but I have subdivided this into two sub-groups. Is one less problematic than the other? If a very experienced psychologist disagrees with part of an ethical code and can convince themselves that they are right, is that sufficient to justify practice that is not in line with the code? The last reason, concerning dilemmas, is a very real problem which also concerns training – not to ensure simply that behaviour will be ethical as in 1 & 2 but rather to ensure the psychologist is aware that there will be times when *no simple answer* is possible and they must have methods to address this, e.g., by identifying and comparing conflicting ethical principles, consulting colleagues.

Decision-making with the Meta-code

This section presents an example of the use of the Meta-code for decision-making[27]. The example raises a number of issues these are discussed systematically. In this section, the approach is to follow the Meta-code section by section, Principle by Principle, so that a comprehensive review of the presenting case is ensured.

---

[26] For further information and a useful discussion see Bersoff (2003)

[27] This section is based on my paper at the European Congress of Psychology, Prague 2007.

Example 8.1

A mental health service in a large European city hires, for a temporary position, an Asian-trained male psychologist to provide mental health services in his native language to immigrants from his country of origin. The psychologist is a refugee himself, and is trying to obtain permission for his family to join him. He is deeply grateful for having been given the position in the mental health clinic.

After he has been on the job for six weeks, his supervisor reprimands him for visiting his clients in their homes and attending social functions in the immigrant community. She informs him that there is a strict agency policy about doing this because it is important to maintain good boundaries with clients and not enter into dual relationships with them. Also, she points out that he can see more clients in a day if he makes appointments to see his clients in the office.

The psychologist is very upset and not sure what to do. He feels great respect for persons in authority and deep gratitude for having employment and money to send home to his family. He cannot afford to lose his employment. He was unable to explain his position to his supervisor. However, he lives in the immigrant community and knows that his people have very different beliefs about the nature of mental health problems and they find services in this country very strange.

He also knows that if he does not participate in community events, he will not be accepted by them and will not be able to help them.

He comes to you as an understanding friend and colleague. How can you help?

All four principles in the Meta-code must be considered for salience, and will be discussed individually. In addition there is also a need to consider *process* issues. The Meta-code sets out the following Key points:

- Psychologists' professional behaviour must be considered within a professional role, characterized by the professional relationship.
- Inequalities of knowledge and power always influence psychologists' professional relationships with clients and colleagues.
- The larger the inequality in the professional relationship and the greater the dependency of clients, the heavier is the responsibility of the professional psychologist.
- The responsibilities of psychologists must be considered within the context of the stage of the professional relationship.

Now, let us consider the relevance of each Principle. In the analysis I shall propose how specifications of each Principle may be relevant to decision-making in this case. This case is also helpful as an example as it includes two different psychologists, so allowing the consideration of the ethical implications for each.

Respect for a person's rights and dignity

General respect

* Awareness of and respect for the knowledge, insight, experience and areas of expertise of clients, relevant third parties, colleagues, students and the general public.

This psychologist, by nature of his cultural background, had experience and insights not shared by the supervisor. These could provide important assistance to practice. Thus even though he is new and of limited experience in his new job, respect for what he potentially has to offer is necessary.

* Awareness of individual, cultural and role differences including those due to disability, gender, sexual orientation, race, ethnicity, national origin, age, religion, language and socio-economic status.

This supervisor may be aware and welcoming of the psychologist's potential to contribute to service delivery on the basis of his linguistic competence. Unfortunately, she does not demonstrate awareness of or sensitivity to cultural differences relating to ethnicity – it may be the case that religious differences are also present. Not only is this problematic with respect to her dealings with the psychologist, it is also potentially a missed opportunity to learn from him and his engagement with the community.

* Avoidance of practices which are the result of unfair bias and may lead to unjust discrimination.

The supervisor may consider she is simply treating the psychologist like everyone else – "rules are rules" and the service has a set of procedures and protocols. This may be so, but equality does not necessarily mean sameness. In this case, although unintended, the psychologist's strengths are not recognized sufficiently and the instructions do impose a restriction on what he might reasonably regard as appropriate behaviour. Consequently, unjust discrimination occurs.

Competence

Ethical awareness

* Obligation to have a good knowledge of ethics, including the Ethical Code, and the integration of ethical issues with professional practice.

Both the supervisor and psychologist would do well to consider this specification. It appears from what has been analyzed so far that the supervisor is not sufficiently aware of the ethical code (or at least the Meta-code, used here). But what of the psychologist? He has important strengths and a potential contribution, but should he not have considered the expectations and protocols of the service? As a new immigrant he also has much to learn if he is to operate optimally. By not checking and discussing differences in expectation before he acted he contributed to the problems that arose.

Limits of procedures

- Obligation to be aware of the limits of procedures for particular tasks, and the limits of conclusions that can be derived in different circumstances and for different purposes.

The service appears to have recognized particular strengths in this new colleague that could help in the delivery of a psychological service to a community that may have been poorly served in the past. In this sense those responsible for hiring the psychologist may have been aware of the requirements of this clause. The supervisor's actions suggest that she may not have been as sensitive to the matter of validity of engagement as she had not considered the psychologist's perspective on maximizing acceptance by the community and individual clients before engaging in specific intervention.

- Obligation to practice within, and to be aware of the psychological community's critical development of theories and methods.

Again, we might ask whether the supervisor was sufficiently thoughtful about the importance of awareness of cultural factors in psychological practice. But the same could be said to apply to the psychologist – did he consider the requirements on professional practice expected of personnel in this service? His focus on the community he knew came at the expense of awareness of the community, the dominant community, into which he was socializing.

- Obligation to balance the need for caution when using new methods with recognition that new areas of practice and methods will continue to emerge and that this is a positive development.

Was the supervisor sufficiently aware of the need to have an open mind? What would this new colleague bring? In addition to the behaviour reported here, what would he bring to the specific practice with clients? The arrival of a new colleague has potential for existing staff to learn and develop from the ideas they bring. In this case there were other cultural and linguistic elements to consider, with great potential benefit to the existing staff. The psychologist also, however, appears not to have thought about this – he was practising on the basis of what seemed appropriate from past experience – fine, but what more could he learn from exploring the practice of those new colleagues he was joining?

Continuing development

• Obligation to continue professional development

As both supervisor and psychologist were qualified the issue raised is that of Continuing Professional Development (CPD) – each has much to give but much also to learn. This may be an opportunity where CPD could be collaborative and collegial, with the new colleague contributing to the development of his colleagues and they, in turn, reciprocating.

Responsibility

General responsibility

• For the quality and consequences of the psychologist's professional actions.
• Not to bring the profession into disrepute.

These clauses are pertinent to both. The psychologist was in danger of creating a significant problem and that could lead to concern in the service. The supervisor meanwhile could be taking action that would offend not only the psychologist but the minority community who would welcome this new, enlightened practice. Neither psychologist was deliberately flouting good practice requirements but neither was sufficiently thoughtful to ensure good practice occurred.

Extended responsibility

• Assumption of general responsibility for the scientific and professional activities, including ethical standards, of employees, assistants, supervisees and students.

The supervisor had an important responsibility to induct her colleague into practice in this service. Induction is a crucial stage even for an experienced practitioner. It is a period of adjustment, recalibration of expectations and norms against which to regulate your own expectations and behaviour. The supervisor could have prevented the difficulties from arising if her approach to supervision had been more sensitive.

Resolving dilemmas

• Recognition that ethical dilemmas occur and responsibility is placed upon the psychologist to clarify such dilemmas and consult colleagues and/or the national Association, and inform relevant others of the demands of the Ethical Code.

Each had an ethical dilemma but it is not clear that either recognized this. Rather, the psychologist appears to have acted in a way he assumed was correct and not appreciated there was a dilemma regarding practice. The supervisor also seems to have adopted a "head down" approach playing by the "rules" – the strict agency policy on not visiting homes. No doubt this was a well intentioned policy and may have been developed by all staff after much consultation but its implementation in this case was unthinking. This is the problem with simply adopting and then requiring all staff to follow policies and protocols.

Psychologists, as professionals, should have a high degree of autonomy. Policies can be helpful but even the best are rarely universally appropriate. Indeed a critical aspect of being a professional rather than a technician is the obligation and ability to think outside the set procedures. The Meta-code recognizes this by highlighting the ethical principles first – the specifications are intended to focus thinking on more specific issues. It does not specify precise and absolute standards. Rather, it specifies issues to consider. As we have stressed throughout this book, this approach also facilitates and indeed encourages individual psychologists to *think* about ethics and not simply follow a "cookbook" approach.

Integrity

Recognition of professional limitations

- Obligation to be self-reflective and open about personal and professional limitations and a recommendation to seek professional advice and support in difficult situations.

Neither of our psychologists thought to be self-reflective or seek further advice until the psychologist came to his friend after the confrontation. This was a wise move but it is a pity it did not occur sooner. One might wonder whether the supervisor had also thought to take similar action – she seems to need to have the opportunity to explore her own thinking on the subject. In fact, as has become evident, each had limitations in their practice – as psychologist and supervisor respectively. Each appeared to have acted in good faith but nevertheless the outcome was problematic. By each opening up about *why* they were adopting their chosen approach then, perhaps with a third person to facilitate, a greater sense of understanding on both sides could be engendered.

Conflict of interests and exploitation

- Awareness of the problems which may result from dual relationships and an obligation to avoid such dual relationships which reduce the necessary professional distance or may lead to conflict of interests, or exploitation of a client.

This is at the heart of the vignette, at least as seen by the supervisor. Protecting against inappropriate dual or multiple relationships is generally seen as good practice – but note the word "generally". In fact this is a much more complex issue. Many psychologists have dual/multiple relationships. This is particularly obvious in small communities where we must shop, take health care, have repairs to cars etc. and indeed generally live our lives. Our children may be friends with the children of clients or, in the case of educational/school psychologists, with the children who are our primary clients. The important issue to recognize is that dual relationships are not necessarily inherently wrong. Rather, it is the nature of the relationship, its purpose, and the degree to which the psychologist considers the ethical implications. There is a wide difference between the therapist who abuses power to seduce a client compared with the psychologist who attends the same church congregation or school Parent Teacher Association in acts of community action.

In this case, the service was no doubt correct to give this issue careful consideration but there was a need to be less rigid and to think through the particular circumstances. The psychologist, however, should also have considered this issue carefully. Visiting homes and attending social functions may well be normal, even expected or necessary in the culture, but the same concerns that led the service to develop its policy are pertinent. The psychologist must still consider where is the appropriate boundary for him as a member of the community as opposed to a psychologist in a professional capacity?

• Obligation to give a reasonable critique of the professional actions of colleagues, and to take action to inform colleagues and, if appropriate, the relevant professional associations and authorities, if there is a question of unethical action.

The supervisor had the opportunity to offer a reasonable critique – this could have been helpful if done in a particular way. But it seems the critique was not an intellectual appraisal influenced by a social-emotional awareness of the dynamics of the situation. Rather it was a negative attack, as seen by the psychologist, on what he thought was not only acceptable but indeed good practice. In this case, was the psychologist acting unethically? Was it not rather a case of differences of view?

But in any case, the important issue is that neither acted in the best way. If each had adopted a position of reviewing the situation from the principles of good, ethical practice, the confrontation that ensued could have been avoided.

Conclusions

The EFPA Meta-code was used as the basis for decision-making in this vignette. Its framework and style actually provided a useful, rather freer model than many national codes. Rather than set out firmer. "bottom line" behaviours to follow the Meta-code encourages psychologists to think about interpretation of principles and specifications. In this example it is important to note that *both* participants had responsibilities – it was not simply one psychologist who would benefit from a better consideration of ethical decision-making. This is not the case normally when a complaint is made about an alleged unethical conduct to an association but it is quite likely to be the case when psychologists have disagreements or conflicts, at least when this occurs for reasons of limited understanding rather than deliberate flouting of the ethical code or indifference.

In terms of using the Meta-code a simple approach might be characterized as follows. Action requires
- Identifying each relevant element
- Analyzing each element in terms of the pertinent issues
- Separating each of these from other factors, e.g., service conventions which are not specifically ethical issues.

In addition, this process benefits in situations such as that addressed here if there is good will, care and good relationships.

A More General Approach

Finally, and to broaden the discussion from a focus entirely on the Meta-code, we draw attention to one particularly useful sequential approach to decision making, namely that developed by the Canadian Psychological Association (2000:3). The CPA propose 10 steps which set out the processes that need to be integrated with the problem solving framework. This guidance is presented in full.

1. Identification of the individuals and groups potentially affected by the decision.

2. Identification of ethically relevant issues and practices, including the interests, rights, and any relevant characteristics of the individuals and groups involved and of the system or circumstances in which the ethical problem arose.

3. Consideration of how personal biases, stresses, or self-interest might influence the development of or choice between courses of action.

4. Development of alternative courses of action.

5. Analysis of likely short-term, ongoing, and long-term risks and benefits of each course of action on the individual(s)/group(s) involved or likely to be affected (e.g., client, client's family or employees, employing institution, students, research participants, colleagues, the discipline, society, self).

6. Choice of course of action after conscientious application of existing principles, values, and standard.

7. Action, with a commitment to assume responsibility for the consequences of the action.

8. Evaluation of the results of the course of action.

9. Assumption of responsibility for consequences of action, including correction of negative consequences, if any, or re-engaging in the decision-making process if the ethical issue is not resolved.

10. Appropriate action, as warranted and feasible, to prevent future occurrences of the dilemma (e.g., communication and problem solving with colleagues; changes in procedures and practices).

Although the style of this approach differs, it is based upon the same premise as that presented for the Meta-code decision making example. Fundamentally, the issue is to *think:* to reflect, weigh up, consider all of the persons (or institutions/organisations) concerned, consider alternatives before acting. When taking action, do so carefully: monitor and evaluate. Note also the strong requirement to accept personal responsibility. This is not to say that all actions must be individual. Consulting peers or more experienced colleagues is highly desirable. Responsibility here refers to the avoidance of blaming others or "dumping" responsibility on them. There may be others who, necessarily, *share* responsibility – but that's different. Finally, the strategy stresses the need to seek to avoid similar situations in the future – not always possible, but certainly something to seek. Where the situation arose from your own error, for example, lessons can be learned from the experience. Even if it comes "out of the blue" there are lessons to be learned that could avoid future problems.

Conclusions

Ethical practice requires initial education learning the ethical code and practising potential challenging scenarios. As a psychologist develops expertise, continuing sensitively will highlight new or recurring ethical challenges. Careful reflection – and here the Meta-code can be very useful – and consultation with another psychologist may be very useful. However, al all costs it is important to avoid a *collusive* relationship where each supports the other uncritically. Rather, the preferred model is that of the *critical friend* – supportive but also challenging. Such approaches can prevent many problems.

Chapter 9

When Things Go Wrong

On Mediation, Arbitration, Corrective Action, and Disciplinary Sanction [28]

Casper Koene

Unfortunately, psychologists' professional actions do not always lead to satisfied customers and happy faces. Sometimes expectations about the psychologist's interventions are exaggerated, sometimes the outcome of an assessment is disappointing, sometimes some doubt has been cast upon the ethical level of the psychologist's behaviour, sometimes this action is experienced as bluntly crossing borders of decent professional behaviour.

If one of these conditions occurs, clients may want to talk about heir unhappy feelings, with the criticised psychologist him- or herself – if they didn't slam the door in definitively leaving the psychologist's office – or otherwise maybe with one of the psychologist's colleagues. Or they just want to raise a complaint to get the psychologist punished. In such a situation, psychologists are faced with possible infringements of their ethical standards: Obviously, the psychologist who is directly involved as the alleged trespasser.

It demands professional maturity and maybe some courage to critically look inside oneself and wonder if the person could be right, and not to slide too easily into defensive behaviour by deliberately wanting to find justifications and excuses, or blaming the other. The profit of such a critical self-reflection might not only be improving the ethical quality of one's work, but also leading towards the best condition to face honestly the other person and to show understanding for his or her objections (see Appendix 4).

However, other colleagues may also become involved, whether or not within a professional relationship with the offended person or as a representative of the psychologists association. In their respective roles, psychologists have the ethical duty to take signs of possible infringements seriously. After all, to keep ethical standards upright is of great importance for the clients' as well as for the profession's interest.

---

[28] In the 3rd EFPA Symposium on Professional Ethics for Psychologists, the author gave a lecture on the significance of mediation for the complainant, as well as for the psychologist and for the professional association as the upholder of professional standards. The text was published as a news item in the European Psychologist (2007). This text is largely used in the present chapter.

Faced with allegations of infringement of its ethical standards, national psychologists associations cannot stay passive. In the Preamble of its Meta-code, the European Federation of Psychologists Associations demands them to have procedures to investigate and decide upon complaints against their members. Taking into account the nature and seriousness of the complaint, this may lead to mediation or to corrective actions or disciplinary sanction.[29] However, to act adequately upon complaints is not just the profession's responsibility. First of all, individual psychologists need to be open to critique of their professional actions and to loyally co-operate with the evaluation of these actions, if these are questioned.

Although not explicitly stated in the Meta-code, this *moral* obligation of openness to *receive* critique can be seen as the logical counterpart of the obligation to *give* a reasonable critique of the professional actions of colleagues, as laid down in article 3.4.5. Deduced from such a moral requirement, one may understand the more legalistic demand as shown in the Appendix of the EFPA *Recommendations on evaluative procedures and corrective actions,* which states that "psychologists should be obliged by the National Association's statutes to co-operate in procedures concerning complaints about professional conduct during their membership" and that members' refusal to co-operate in evaluation procedures should be seen as an offence. Another way to implement this recommendation is to lay down such an obligation in the code of ethics itself, as for instance the Dutch and the Turkish associations did.

Example 9.1

Penny Houtkropper, industrial psychologist, terminated her membership of the psychologists association at the moment it became clear that a complaint would be raised against her. Nevertheless, the disciplinary board decided the complaint was admissible, because termination of membership only can be effected at the end of the year, which was not the case. Mrs. Houtkropper did not respond to any correspondence from the disciplinary board.

After hearing the complainant, the disciplinary board decided to expel Mrs. Houtkropper from membership, not only because of the nature of the primary infringement – which didn't happen for the first time – but also because of her immediate termination of her membership and not responding to any of the board's letters to her. This was regarded as an attempt to withdraw from the evaluation of her professional action.

---

[29] This book is primarily intended to facilitate individual psychologists in reflecting upon the ethical dimensions of the professional conduct. Therefore, only marginal attention will be paid to the more legalistic framework, which regards primarily the profession as a collective, the EFPA Recommendations on evaluative procedures and corrective actions in case of complaints about unethical conduct and the Guidelines on mediation in the context of complaints about unethical conduct. However, the full texts of these documents are available as appendices in this book.

Whether or not psychologists associations may follow the recommendation in this Guideline's Appendix, to "forbid by statutes its members terminating membership during a complaint procedure, to ensure the evaluation of their professional actions may occur with or without their co-operation" might not be of primary relevance for *individual* psychologists, reading this book on professional ethics. However, the particular clause shows evidently the *collectives*, i.e., the psychologists associations, being the addressees of the Recommendations – as well as of the Meta-code – in their responsibilities to safeguard the ethical norms and standards, and the protection of clients by preventing their members from fleeing from the consequences of a misdemeanour, which could be seen as "disciplinary hit-and-run" (Koene 2004).

Openness to critique and loyal co-operation in having one's professional conduct evaluated can be seen as vital conditions for the upholding of ethical standards in the profession. Nevertheless, one may wonder if such an evaluation will give complainants – often clients –enough satisfaction.

Example 9.2

Carry Vermeulen had not worked for quite some time. She had even given up having small temporary jobs, because of the problems with her back. On her general practitioner's advice she applied eventually for a job in sheltered employment, where her impairment would be taken into consideration. But, to be admitted to this kind of employment is not a simple matter. An assessment needs to be done to verify whether the person has physical, mental or intellectual disabilities to such an extent that working in a normal job is impossible.

When the authorities finally let Carry Vermeulen know the outcome of the assessment, it turned out that she was considered to belong to the target group for sheltered employment. However, Carry's joy was tempered, to put it mildly, because of the basis of this decision. Not only she was supposed to have physical impairments due to the back issues. During the examination some evidence was found that Carry had had special education and had suffered from severe test anxiety. The psychologist involved in the assessment procedure reported on the basis of these findings that Carry Vermeulen was intellectually and mentally impaired as well.

To be seen as a "cretin" and a "nut" was too much for Carry, and she raised a complaint against the psychologist. According to Carry, he should never have drawn such conclusions without his own psychological examination, and the report should never have been sent to the authorities without her permission.

It eventually did not become a disciplinary court case, since after further reflection Carry decided to withdraw her complaint.

What could have brought Carry to her last decision – was she afraid of repercussions? She had been put on the waiting list, but she didn't yet have a job in the sheltered workshop. Or, did she have a talk with the psychologist, who might have made clear to her that the probability of eventually getting a job in sheltered employment had increased by also being labelled as mentally impaired as well as intellectually handicapped? We do not know.

Furthermore, about the quality of the psychologist's judgment we may only guess. As we may guess about the procedure, in which the judgment was based purely upon documents. And we may wonder if Carry Vermeulen had been given the opportunity to read the report before it was sent.

However, Carry's reality at the time is not our issue at this moment. The point is what it would have meant if the psychologist involved really didn't act according to professional standards. Say, it was the true that his evaluation was below standard and say, that the procedure was unfit and say, that Carry didn't get the opportunity to read the advice, prior to it being reported. The main issue in this present chapter is: whose interests have been infringed in cases of unethical behaviour, and whose interests have been damaged most seriously. Those of the client, who is primarily the injured party, or those of the psychologists' community, whose professional ethics rules are violated and whose reputation might be at stake? Which party's interest is mostly served by a disciplinary evaluation and an eventual sanction?

Evaluative and disciplinary procedures are to a certain extent comparable to criminal law procedures. In spite of the fact that complainants usually are the accusatorial party in front of the disciplinary tribunal[30] – unlike criminal law cases, where the public prosecutor and not the complainant is the antagonist of the accused – the outcome of the evaluative and disciplinary procedures exclusively concerns the relationship between the censured psychologist and the professional collective. Be it a warning, a reproach, a suspension or an expulsion from membership, acquiring satisfaction from these sanctions is all that the complainant may get out of it.

There may be violations of norms, which justify a community to take action to protect others against being victimised. There also may be violations of norms which justify a community feeling deeply harmed and determined to impose punishment, even if this is not, or not any more in the victim's interest, nor in the interest of others in his or her direct environment: An example is the avenging of the murder of a lonely vagabond, because of the fundamental unacceptability of this crime. Upholding norms by the collective is meant to prevent individuals feeling outlawed. And this is even more important if it concerns individuals in a relatively weak and vulnerable position. The psychologists associations' disciplinary procedures may find their *raisons d'être* especially in this last condition.

However, insofar as client vulnerability provides justification for a special complaint procedure in psychologists association one may wonder if the individual client is served in the best possible way by disciplinary procedures. If a sanction is imposed after a disciplinary procedure – which is often long and drawn out – in which discrep-

---

[30] This is not always and not everywhere the case. In The Netherlands, the Health Inspector may act as prosecutor in legal disciplinary pursuit and in the British Psychological Society the individual complainant is not a party any more in front of the tribunal, after the preliminary investigation. Then, the BPS takes the role of public prosecutor.

ancies will rather be accentuated rather than diminished, will such a sanction bring the satisfaction which the complainant is waiting for? Sometimes it does, sometimes certainly not – far from it. Some complainants want to see blood, but not all of them. Some of these could feel more and better understood in their complaint if a well-meant apology was given. However, after a formal evaluative and disciplinary process an explanation and apology – if appropriate as such – will often be further away than ever. And how often could this count for the psychologist as well?

Mediation

As mentioned before, EFPA not only demands national associations to have investigative, corrective and disciplinary procedures to decide upon complaints against members and to determine necessary action. In the same paragraph the option of mediation is mentioned.

In mediation, the complaint can be seen as an expression of a problem or conflict between the complainant and the accused psychologist. Seen from that point of view, the interests of the psychologists association are not at stake. In an informal, semi-structured process an impartial mediator assists the disputing parties to work through and resolve problems or conflicts together. It is a non-judgmental, voluntary process that focuses on helping parties to find mutually satisfying resolutions to their problems, consistent with the interests of each party. Whether or not by one's own initiative, participation in mediation is on a voluntary basis. Each person, complainant and psychologist, is autonomous and able to determine their own actions. This requires that each party is free to close the mediation process at any moment, if they no longer consider the mediation as being helpful.

As conflicting parties are facilitated to come to a solution themselves and have the freedom to terminate this process at any time, mediation conditions are essentially different from binding oneself beforehand to a final decision of any authority, as in arbitration.

The involvement of a third party may be seen as a complicating factor. Such a person may have their own interests in the solution of the conflict and may interfere, or perhaps their approval of the outcome must be required. Therefore, possible juridical or complaint procedures, which had already been started, must be deferred in order to be able to start with mediation.

Solutions found in mediation may well be better – for the complainant and the accused – than a judicial judgment. After all, both parties carry the outcome, which is certainly not the case if the disciplinary tribunal rules against one party. Therefore, it might be preferable to choose mediation instead of a formal complaint procedure for the client to be understood in his or her complaint by the psychologist involved and not by the disciplinary court on behalf of the profession.

In Carry Vermeulen's case for instance, the psychologist's recognition of *blame* and his *atonement* would give a better opening for paying off and reconciliation than a conviction for a "*crime*" and an imposed *punishment* would do. However, even if there is no violation of any professional ethics principle, mediation will probably give the psychologist a better opportunity to come to an understanding of the client's objections and to be able to show this, than standing in front of a tribunal.

Mediation – in the framework of an ethics complaint procedure – begins with the psychologists association's willingness to refrain from further investigation and evaluative procedures during the period of mediation and to recommend the opportunity for mediation to the complainant and the accused psychologist. This implies that the association should not interfere in the process or need to be asked for agreement on the mediation outcome. As a party of indirect interest, the association puts itself so to say on the "reserve bench".

In considering whether the opportunity for mediation should be offered or not, the fundamental question arises: how should the client's individual interest of atonement should be weighed against the interests of the psychologists association in upholding norms by evaluating the professional behaviour and eventually sanctioning trespassers.

A consideration in the decision whether to offer mediation or not, should have regard for the seriousness of the alleged infringement. Thereby, the nature of the complaint should be taken into account, as well as the potential for further risk to the public and the reputation of the profession. This means that in certain cases the profession – embodied in the psychologists association – may decide that its collective responsibility doesn't allow it to stay passive. This is the case when the possible infringement of the profession's ethical standards is such a serious offence that other clients' welfare or the profession's standing are seriously at stake. In that case the association will not abstain from formal evaluation of the alleged misconduct.

Not to take away the vital importance of what has just been stated, nor questioning its eventual impact, it is challenging to reflect upon another perspective. Seen from a moral point of view one may wonder if, in its ultimate consequence, the complainant and the accused shouldn't *always* be offered the opportunity to come to an agreement by themselves. In its ultimate consequence, it could be taken for granted that, for instance, even serious breaches could be compensated financially, and psychologists thus have a lucky escape from being sanctioned heavily. After all, it is not unthinkable that some complainants will choose such options. One may wonder which principle informs objections that may arise against such a solution. Doesn't a direct atonement for distress or compensation for harm outweigh formal sanctions? Isn't a direct paying off the debt superior to punishment for breaching norms? And why should the possibility of a more satisfactory settlement be given to someone who raises a minor complaint, and not to someone raising a serious one? One might argue that cases of serious harm in particular deserve the best possible atonement.

Until now, these reflections were mainly focused on the significance mediation could have for the complainant. However, for the psychologist involved the significance of mediation is probably as large as it is for the complainant. To explain one's point of view and to show understanding for the complainant's angle is more easily done if one is not being put in a defensive position. Thus, mediation gives opportunities, which are less likely in a formal exchange of documents or a hearing in front of a tribunal. This is especially so if the real motives to complain are hidden behind formal objections: the implosion of high expectations, the disappointment about the outcome of an examination, the confrontation with painful developments in life. Sometimes the client holds the psychologist, the messenger, responsible for these and seeks pretexts for a complaint.

The fact that in cases of mediation the profession steps back and doesn't have any influence on the outcome doesn't mean that the outcome of the mediation is not in the interest of the profession. After all, mediation could well contribute to restoring the complainant's confidence in the profession and, moreover, it is conceivable that more understanding for the complainant's point of view could bring the psychologist to an improved reflection on the ethical dimensions of their professional actions, maybe more than disciplinary sanctions will do.

Up to this point mediation seems to be the morally ideal means to bring conflicting parties together in order to find a solution, agreed by both of them. By its nature mediation could contribute to raise the psychologist's ethical awareness and the client's appreciation of the psychologist's profession's ethics. However, this is a wishful view. Realistically, expectations should unfortunately not be too high. Options for mediation, as offered in running complaint procedures, are generally chosen by only a minority of the complainants. The majority prefers a formal complaint procedure. Moreover, certainly not all mediations lead to an end which is acceptable for both parties. As mentioned before, parties are free to close the mediation process at any moment if they no longer consider the mediation as being helpful. Therefore, there will be instances where a mediation procedure is closed in an untimely manner and consequently a formal complaint procedure is opened or reopened.

Arbitration

This possibility to open or reopen formal complaint procedures will not be the case after arbitration, if an association has chosen to offer this instead of mediation. In arbitration too, the situation is seen as a conflict between the complainant and the accused psychologist. As in mediation, in arbitration also the position of the profession is formally marginalised and evidence of an infringement of ethical principles will not lead to disciplinary measures. The fundamental difference between mediation and arbitration is that the latter will give an outcome, whether or not parties find it agreeable, since both parties bind themselves beforehand to accept the arbiter's decision.

Example 9.3

Anna Fischler was referred by her family doctor to a psychologist for an exploratory psychological assessment. At her first appointment, Mrs. Fischler arrived 20 minutes late because of problems in finding the location of the practice. Since no previous agreements had been made, no fee for the time lost due to the delay was charged. Shortly before the set hour of the second appointment, Mrs. Fischler cancelled because her child was suffering from a headache. During this phone conversation, the psychologist told her that she would be charged the cost of this appointment, whether she would arrive or not. Then, she decided to come anyway, be it with substantial delay. A few days later, Anna Fischler received the psychologist's invoice.

In her complaint Anna Fischler contended that she had been under the impression that the psychological diagnosis would be established under the national health insurance scheme and thus would not be payable by her. In the complaint investigation, the psychologist stated that the appointment with Mrs. Fischler for a clinical-psychological diagnostic assessment had been made by phone. A time period from 10 a.m. to noon was reserved for her and she had been requested to be punctual. In this very telephone call the psychologist had told to Mrs. Fischler that, if she were unable or unwilling to keep the appointment, to cancel the set appointment 48 hours in advance, otherwise the full fee of the session would be charged. After Mrs. Fischler arrived at her first appointment with a thirty-minute delay, he had again called her attention to the aforementioned cancellation conditions. To accommodate Mrs. Fischler, the psychologist did not charge any fee for this thirty-minute delay. Furthermore, the second appointment was cancelled by phone, 40 minutes before its scheduled beginning. Mrs. Fischler claimed that she could not attend because she had to appear in court. The psychologist had reminded her again that appointments should have been called off 48 hours before, underlining that appearances in court are not communicated only 30 minutes before the beginning of a hearing. Then, Mrs. Fischler decided to keep her appointment after all and arrived at 11.30 a.m. The psychologist charged her only for 90 instead of 120 minutes.

After several phone conversations with both parties, the arbitration board decided that Anna Fischler should pay the outstanding fee.

Disciplinary Procedures

Whether or not after the complainant's or the psychologist's refusal of mediation, an untimely closing a mediation or the association's decision not to offer mediation, complaint may lead to formal disciplinary procedures. Then, an investigation will take place through the formal complaint procedure, be it a separate stage in the process or not. The investigation will involve gathering evidence from the complainant, the psychologist who is the subject of the complaint, and any other source, which will provide assistance.

From the very beginning of a complaint procedure, the psychologist needs to be aware of the prevailing ethical principles and code regulations that still pertain in such a challenging situation.

Example 9.4

Anton Berg, clinical psychologist, was not amused, when he got a letter from the Disciplinary Committee that Mrs. Groen had raised a complaint against him because of breaching confidentiality in his contact with her general practitioner. Berg was invited to give a first reply, in the context of the investigation.

Berg wrote an angry letter, stating that such a complaint by "someone with clear histrionic personality characteristics, which the Disciplinary Committee indubitably must have recognised, has to be seen evidently as a revengeful acting out of despair due to a collapse of her erotomaniac fantasies (see Mrs. Groen's enclosed record). Thereby Mrs. Groen's complaint should immediately be dismissed."

Justified by the principle of equal arms, psychologists *may* decide to breach confidentiality to be able properly to found the defence against allegations. However, psychologists aren't completely free in doing so. Ethical principles should still guide actions and psychologists are still subject to their code of conduct. Therefore, revealing data from the client's record should be done respectfully and restricted to those which are relevant and necessary for the defence. However, using psychopathological labels in this context can only be seen as complainant bashing by attempting inappropriately to disqualify complainants and bluntly neglecting to pay appropriate respect. It does not only happen that psychologists try to disqualify complainants in such a blatant way. At least as serious are attempts to exclude more categorically certain people from raising complaints in the first place.

Example 9.5

Paula Hermanides, forensic psychologist and manager of a large forensic experts bureau, contacted her association, claiming immunity for the members of her team, since forensic expertise too easily leads to disciplinary complaints. Paula Hermanides argued that it happens all the time that unsatisfied parties, supported by their lawyers, try to seek ways to disqualify unfavourable forensic reports by misusing disciplinary procedures. These procedures bring along an excessive extra workload and a substantial strain for the psychologists involved. In her opinion, this should be an argument for the psychologists association no longer to burden the staff members of this respectable expert bureau with disciplinary procedures.

The association's reply was not particularly welcomed. It said that the association's members are obliged to co-operate loyally if there is any reason to evaluate their professional conduct. This obligation is fully incompatible with any claim on immunity. As the association did acknowledge the higher complaint rates in forensic psychology, it recommended Mrs. Hermanides to set up special ethics courses for her staff members, in order to sensitise her colleagues to the special pitfalls in the practice of forensic psychology. In this way the ethical quality of their work could be improved and the prevention of complaints could be maximised. An additional recommendation contained initiat-

ing in corporate trainings to prepare her colleagues to appropriately defend their cases in front of the tribunal.

The second recommendation, given to Paula Hermanides, brings us to the point that many psychologists are ill-prepared, when faced with a complaint. Even in countries as for instance The Netherlands, where disciplinary cases are regularly publicised, the idea of having to show up for a hearing is rather disturbing for many colleagues. Arguments that disciplinary procedures could be seen as part of one's personal quality assurance system may be valid in theory, but in practice having one's conduct being scrutinised easily brings highly uncomfortable feelings, even in case of a good conscience. Standing in front of a tribunal *is* standing in front of a *tribunal*. This is a situation where one cannot count on just friendly fraternal understanding, since such a tribunal should be impartial, in every respect. However, psychologists should realise that they, as much as the plaintiffs, are protected by fair procedures as hearing both parties, by the tribunal's impartiality and by maxims as *actori incumbit probatio* and *affirmanti incumbit probatio* [31], although the latter principle is not always fully applicable. After all, psychologists do have an obligation to implement proper record keeping, which may shift some of the onus of proof to the psychologist.

This does not take away that, as long as the tribunal is not convinced by the plaintiff's arguments and evidence, the complaint will be regarded as unproven. The standard of proof in a tribunal's operation may vary. In the UK, for example, the standard is the "balance of probabilities" unlike in criminal cases in court where the standard is "beyond reasonable doubt". Also, there is a requirement that the implementation of this standard takes into account the seriousness of the case *for the psychologist*. So, if a guilty verdict will lead in all probability to the psychologist being struck off the register, the bar is set higher.

What does it actually mean, hearing about a colleague against whom a complaint was lodged? Do we have a tendency to avoid him or her, not to refer clients any more, or are we still open to give fraternal support? Though not mentioned in the Meta-code, being supportive to colleagues could be seen as a consequence of the general responsibility for the profession: not to protect colleagues unduly, but to contribute personally to the support system of the profession. From this perspective, it is not on simply to ostracise colleagues just because of complaints being raised against them. As the Turkish Association states in article 17 of its Ethics Code: "Psychologists do not discriminate against people who are being investigated nor jeopardize their employment. However, they take the necessary steps following the conclusion of the ethical investigation according to the requirements of the verdict." Unproven complaints may not be untrue. However, we must rely on the tribunal's verdict.

But even evidence doesn't necessarily mean that it was more than just an error. In its Recommended procedure for ethical decision-making, the Psychological Society of

---

[31] "The burden of proof lies upon the plaintiff" and " the burden of proof lies upon him who affirms, not upon him who denies".

Ireland says: "professional bodies and the law accept that practitioners may make errors of judgment, and that such errors are distinct from malpractice." Furthermore, there is no justification to see minor infringements as capital sins. After all, a *warning* doesn't imply more than the word says. Let us have a look at a relevant paragraph in the explanatory memorandum on the Dutch Individual Health Care Professions Act (Wet BIG), which says that a warning is "an suitable reprimand, which posits the incorrectness of the conduct, without qualifying it as reprehensible".

Judging in Europe

Just imagine the following story. You are on holiday, travelling by car through a foreign European country. Suddenly a dog is crossing the road. Breaking doesn't sufficiently help and you hit the dog, that is seriously wounded after the collision. While you are taking care of the dog, the police come and bring you to the police station. You are clearly in trouble. After considerable delay and a substantial fine for lacking vigilance, you may continue your journey. Two weeks later, when you come home, your own dog, overjoyed crosses the street to welcome you and is hit by a car. While you are taking care of the dog, the police come and give you a fine for not keeping your dog under control and thus being responsible for the accident. Eventually you have to pay the damage to the car. End of holidays.

Apart from the sorrow for wounded dogs and additional nuisance, you might feel unjustly treated, by being held responsible for similar accidents twice, whether you were the victim or not. To prevent comparable situations in professional psychology, the EFPA did not only conceive the Meta-code as common European ethical standard, but also laid down its *Recommendations on evaluative procedures and corrective actions in case of complaints about unethical conduct,* formulated by its Standing Committee on Ethics. After all, in an opening European labour and consumer market, it would be good for the profession if similar complaints and similar facts would lead to similar actions, whether the psychologist's services are received in Estonia, France, Portugal or Austria, to name a few.

It is significant that the Recommendations not only refer to *disciplinary actions*, which involve sanctions as a reprimand or suspension from a register. As important are *corrective actions*, designed to improve future performance, for instance requiring specific additional training or re-training and supervised practice. Even taking all this taken into account, one may still wonder whether European psychologists associations really deal in similar ways with alleged infringements of these standards.

Unfortunately, recent comparative data about complaint procedures are not available. The only study on this subject (Koene, 1997) is over ten years old, and published in Dutch after being orally reported at the 5th European Psychology Congress, held in Dublin, July 1997. Though disciplinary procedures in several associations may have progressed since, especially after the mentioned EFPA recommendations were adopted, and though the response rate doesn't allow drawing firm conclusions, it might be worthwhile getting an impression of the results of this study.

A questionnaire was sent to all EFPPA [32] member associations, in order to get information about their disciplinary procedures and sanctions. In a second part of this inquiry statistical information was gathered. In the third part, eighteen short vignettes were presented, giving "facts" of possible violations of professional ethics. The associations were requested to give their opinion about the appropriate measurements to be taken in the given cases. Outcomes of the latter were compared with data from samples of Dutch psychologists and civil servants at the Dutch Ministry of Social Affairs, giving their opinion on the same vignettes.

Fourteen associations filled out the first part of the questionnaire. Already at that time, nearly all associations had a disciplinary committee to investigate and decide upon alleged infringements of their ethical codes. In a small number of associations it wasn't possible to have a hearing attended by both parties; their disciplinary committees only decided on the basis of circulated documents above.

Half of the responding associations formally forbade their members to terminate membership during a complaint procedure. A third of the associations, however, didn't even require their members to co-operate with the scrutiny their professional conduct. One out of seven associations did not have any power at all to impose a sanction on members for proven infringement of their ethical code, which contrasts with nearly half of the committees whose verdicts not only could lead to disciplinary sanctions, but could also play a role in civil court cases as well as in criminal court decisions. A minority, although non-marginal, of the associations did not have an appeal procedure, even though disciplinary actions may have such a substantial impact for psychologists, a reason why access to a review of the verdict is certainly recommended.

As such, one may wonder whether complaints are easily lodged or not. Publications about the Dutch legal healthcare disciplinary system suggest that the number of complaints is substantially fewer than the estimated number of medical errors made. It is not very likely that the dynamics would be considerably different in complaining about psychologists.

An experience of being incorrectly treated seems to be a necessary, but certainly not always sufficient condition to decide to complain. In our daily life we often take certain misery for granted. The burden of writing a letter…, claiming a guarantee for something we bought somewhere far away…. After all, the expected retribution should be in reasonable balance with the invested effort, as is the case with the expected probability of retribution. Obviously the extent to which we are aggrieved or hurt play a role too. On top of it, dependency and loyalty often plays a role in client-psychologist relationships, which may put up an extra barrier against complaining.

In the associations responding to the survey, whose combined membership totalled 96.740 members, only 360 complaints were raised in the year of the inquiry, i.e., about

---

[32] The European Federation of Psychologists Associations (EFPA) was previously called European Federation of Professional Psychologists Associations (EFPPA), and counted at that time 26 member associations.

0.4% of the membership.. One out of five of these complaints were judged as inadmissible and in nearly half of the cases no evidence for unethical behaviour was found. In five cases corrective measures were taken to improve professional procedures or skills. Three persons – out of 96.740 – were expelled from membership of their association.

Most of the verdicts concerned incompetence and irresponsibility, less frequently did they concern informed consent and confidentiality. One out of twenty judgements regarded dishonesty, as was also the case for harmful dual relationships and for sexual relations with clients. One out of four judgements concerned clinical psychologists as was the case for forensic psychologists. One out of seven decisions was about work- and organisational psychologists. Both psychotherapists and child psychologists brought about a tenth of the verdicts, twice as many as assessment psychologists. The last ten percent (miscellaneous) included researchers.

Psychologists in some sectors of their profession seem more easily to slide into violating certain ethical rules than others do. Sexual relationships with clients more often occur in clinical or psychotherapeutic relationships, or are at least more clearly felt as boundary transgressing. In other niches, as in providing a report as an expert in forensic psychology, conflicting interests often are at stake and lawyers are already involved. These conditions may raise the probability for clients feeling unjustly treated and lower the threshold for lodging complaints.

Example 9.6

A psychologist consulting to a secondary school was asked to give counselling to a 15-year-old girl. Before the start of the professional contact the girl insisted on absolute confidentiality as a condition sine qua non. Even her parents weren't allowed to get any information.

Rather soon the girl turned out to be suicidal. The psychologist consulted a colleague and a psychiatrist and found that the situation wasn't so dangerous that other interventions were necessary, nor did he find a reason to breach confidentiality by contacting the parents.

After a while, the guidance of the girl could be finished successfully. Later on, the parents found out what had happened. They furiously lodged a complaint to the disciplinary committee.

Please, give your opinion on this case and choose one option from the following tariff:

- *the psychologist's conduct should be regarded as being within the ethical standards;*
- *the reason for the complaint should be acknowledged, but no sanction will be imposed;*
- *the psychologist needs to be given some advice on professional ethics;*
- *a warning should be given;*
- *a reprimand should be given;*
- *a reprimand should be given, as well as a conditional suspension of membership;*
- *a fine should be given;*
- *the psychologist should be expelled from his association's membership;*
- *other ....*

In the third part of the questionnaire mentioned earlier eighteen vignettes were presented, to be evaluated by disciplinary committees of the national psychologists associations. The committees were asked to regard all the showed details as – the only – facts of the cases and to come to a "verdict" and to give a sentence, to be chosen out of a tariff, as in the above given example. For several reasons only six associations responded on this part of the questionnaire, reason why the results should be seen as highly tentative, not even taking into account the considerable time lag between the survey and writing this present chapter. Nevertheless the results may give some insight into how disciplinary board members think about ethics infringements.

The overall inter-rater agreement was very reasonable. Not surprisingly, the psychologists were more coherent in their opinions than the non-psychologists. As a group the latter were more lenient about some issues as sexual relationships with clients immediately after termination of therapy. Apart from a striking discordance on the case described in example 9.6, the inter-rater agreement between the international disciplinary board members was even higher than the Dutch psychologists', notwithstanding that cultural differences easily could have interfered. Generally the board members' opinions were somewhat milder than those of the Dutch psychologists.

Although the findings presented here are not very up-to-date, they may promise the likelihood of fairly equal treatment of complaints against psychologists, wherever they practise in Europe.

Conclusions

Things can go wrong. Errors are made. Infringements will occur. Psychologists need to face this and to take the consequences. Individual psychologists need to be open to look critically into their own behaviour and thus comply with the professional ethics requirement to be loyal in having their professional conduct scrutinised, if a complaint is raised. Or, sometimes better, to come to a settlement as a result of a mediation process.

The profession needs to take responsibility to maintain its high standards of professional ethics by having solid procedures to investigate and to decide upon complaints. In criticising the psychologist's professional conduct in retrospect, the imposition of sanctions may be unavoidable. However, to take corrective actions to ameliorate the ethical quality of future professional conduct, like requiring additional training, might be more constructive in promoting good ethical behaviour.

Looking into the future, it would be a good thing for the profession if the upholding of its ethical standards could be similar in all European psychologists associations. Some research findings suggest that such is not necessarily just a dreamscape.

Chapter 10

Ethical Challenges for the Future

Geoff Lindsay

In this final chapter I shall attempt to explore some likely ethical challenges for the immediate future. Each of these is rooted in the present but likely to take on more salience over the next 5–10 years. In exploring these I shall also invite readers to consider the degree to which our current approaches to ethics are fit for purpose to meet the challenges ahead.

National Security

Probably the most acute and serious issue is that which is concerned with national security. I use this term as a general label to cover a range of aspects of the way societal changes are impacting now on psychologists and how the impact may be predicted to intensify. In the past, most of those of us working in Western liberal democracies have not had to consider the issues raised here to any great extent. We have worked as researchers or practitioners facing the kinds of ethical issues which have been explored in this book. The group that has mainly had to deal with these issues has comprised those psychologists working for the military. Concerns about abuse of control by the state were largely linked to totalitarian regimes. That is now changing. The rise of the use of extreme violence for political ends has been associated with increasingly severe reactions by some states. This raises the question: *Is a psychologist's ability to act ethically compromised when national security is threatened?*

In the UK, for example, the government has extended the time period for which those suspected of terrorist offences may be kept in custody without trial. As this chapter is written there remains a major debate about this: there is resistance among Members of Parliament to a further extension of this time limit from 28 days, already the longest in Europe, to 42 days. In the US there have been substantial concerns about the alleged use of torture and the nature of imprisonment without trial. These matters are not limited to these two countries.

It is already evident that these socio-political developments are having an impact on psychologists. Perhaps the most evident has been the furore within the American Psychological Association (APA) about the role of psychologists working with or within the military. This led to the APA setting up a group to consider the ethical challenges and the fitness for purpose of the APA ethical principles and code of conduct. The Presidential Task Force on Psychological Ethics and National Security (PENS) reported in June 2005. Its remit was to examine whether the Ethics Code adequately addressed the ethical dimensions of psychologists' involvement in national security related activities. The Task Force produced 12 statements setting out their view of the ethical obligations of psychologists in national security-related work, drew several other conclusions but failed to reach consensus on three issues (www.apa.org/releases/PENSTaskForceReportFinal.pdf Retrieved 25 March 2008). The report was endorsed by the APA Council in August 2005, but there then followed a substantial controversy. For example, The British Psychological Society's monthly journal, *The Psychologist* (April 2008, pp. 282–283) reported that there had been resignations from the APA, including such members as Kenneth Pope, former chair of the Ethics Committee, in protest over the APA's position on interrogation and torture. Further information including various press releases and resolutions, may be examined by accessing the APA website (http://www.apa.org/topics/topicethics.html)

I offer the following brief comments on the 12 statements in the PENS report:

1. *Psychologists do not engage in, direct, support, facilitate, or offer training in torture or other cruel, inhuman, or degrading treatment.*

This is an absolute statement which clearly sets a prohibition on psychologists' involvement in torture. At a time when some politicians modify language and so "torture" is not used as a term, the reference to "other cruel, inhuman, or degrading treatment" is helpful. It does, of course, depend on the definition of such behaviour but this statement has the benefit of clarity.

2. *Psychologists are alert to acts of torture and other cruel, inhuman, or degrading treatment and have an ethical responsibility to report these acts to the appropriate authorities*

This statement may be seen as relating to the ethical principles of respect and avoidance of harm. Protection of civil and human rights is also addressed here. Note the responsibility is on the psychologists to report such actions, as has been the case in other ethical codes for some time when a psychologist is believed to have acted unethically, "whistle blowing".

3. *Psychologists who serve in the role of supporting an interrogation do not use health care related information from an individual's medical record to the detriment of the individual's safety and well-being.*

Statement 3, however, poses problems. Normally it is good practice for psychologists to be aware of, and to use, health information if available. For example, a child's hearing loss is important information for an educational/school psychologist referred a child with reading difficulties. The problem here is that in some cases a psychologist may be asked, overtly or not, to use (i.e., misuse) health information. For example, knowledge of a prisoner's susceptibilities may be important to increase the chance of successful interrogation. This statement prohibits use of medical information that leads to the detriment of an individual's safety and well-being, but in practice this may be a fine judgement.

4. *Psychologists do not engage in behaviours that violate the laws of the United States, although psychologists may refuse for ethical reasons to follow laws or orders that are unjust or that violate basic principles of human rights.*

Statement 4 is the kind of statement often debated in discussions on ethics. To what extent should the law of the state override the psychologist's ethical judgment? In the past, this has been seen as less of an issue for psychologists working in benign democratic states, unlike repressive regimes. However, the situation now has changed. Firstly laws have been passed in the US, UK and elsewhere that are less liberal and more constraining, resulting in diminution of civil liberties. It is not my role here to question whether this is right or wrong but rather to consider the implications. I suggest that this societal shift towards greater restrictions ("for the common good") is likely to increase the challenge to accommodate ethical judgments within a legal framework in an increasing number of professional actions.

5. *Psychologists are aware of and clarify their role in situations where the nature of their professional identity and professional function may be ambiguous.*

This is a sound principle, and one which is often found in ethical guidance. The difference here concerns the nature of the psychologist's employment, particularly but not limited to those working for the military. It echoes the dilemma faced by psychologists working in prisons except that in that case the clients are convicted of crimes (although a psychologist may see some clients on remand prior to conviction). Is the psychologist working for the good of the individual, or to help the state protect its citizens?

6. *Psychologists are sensitive to the problems inherent in mixing potentially inconsistent roles such as health care provider and consultant to an interrogation, and refrain from engaging in such multiple relationships.*

Again, this is a sound principle but I wonder how easy it is to put into practice, particularly for psychologists engaged with the military. Can a "multiple relationship" be avoided? Or should one psychologist aid intrusive interrogation and a second psychologist provide health care to the detainee?

7. *Psychologists may serve in various national security-related roles, such as a consultant to an interrogation, in a manner that is consistent with the Ethics Code,*

and when doing so psychologists are mindful of factors unique to these roles and contexts that require special ethical consideration.

This comes out clearly in support of psychologists having a role in national security-related roles. As such it links to historical roles in law enforcement. However, it is again important to ask how easy and practical this is. Can a psychologist maintain respect for a "client" if consulting in interrogation of an unconvicted detainee, in detention for years without trial, and even without formal charges? Can such professional action be ethical?

8. *Psychologists who consult on interrogation techniques are mindful that the individual being interrogated may not have engaged in untoward behaviour and may not have information of interest to the interrogator.*

This is also interesting and challenging especially given the public statements of those in charge of facilities such as Guantanamo Bay that the detainees are "guilty". There have been reports, albeit by journalists with little substantiation because this is rarely possible, of detainees facing well over 100 interrogation sessions but protesting innocence. More recently inmates have been released, without charge, but with insinuations from the authorities and/or politicians that they are indeed guilty

9. *Psychologists make clear the limits of confidentiality.*

This is a clear statement but I wonder what confidentiality is possible in the situation detailed above?

10. *Psychologists are aware of and do not act beyond their competencies, except in unusual circumstances, such as set forth in the Ethics Code.*

This is clear. However, it raises the question of the competencies needed for some methods used and where these are learned and whether there is a research bases for their validity and effectiveness. If there is such evidence, has it been published in the public domain or is it limited by a restriction on the basis of national security?

11. *Psychologists clarify for themselves the identity of their client and retain ethical obligations to individuals who are not their clients.*

This is rather complex dealing as it does with the individual, the organisation (e.g., a detention facility of dubious legality) and the national government whose actions may not clearly have the backing of the current law. The PENS document usefully directs readers to specific parts of the APA code, as it does in other sections, showing that there is much relevant guidance in the existing code. However, again one may wonder how easy it is to follow an ethical line in these restricted environments, especially where they are themselves of questionable legal status.

12. Psychologists consult when they are facing difficult ethical dilemmas.

Throughout this book we have urged the need to consult other colleagues as well as to examine texts such as this and the ethical code itself. This advice is welcome here – but who is an appropriate colleague? Would another psychologist also in the same detention facility, for example, be appropriate? An important issue in peer consultation is the need to avoid unintended collusion arising from too similar a perspective shared by each psychologist and a lack of critical position, standing outside the shared beliefs and responsibilities. In such examples, it would be advisable also to seek consultation with a peer, and/or a more experienced colleague who is *detached* from the situation and can bring a dispassionate perspective.

My comments are relatively gentle and benign – the debate that has taken place within the APA has often been at a much higher temperature. But the central issue concerns the *change in* the *societal baseline*. When the state adopts behaviours that are of dubious legality the frame in which psychologists work alters. Citizens may choose to support more extreme measures being taken which threaten or undermine civil liberties if they believe they are under a real threat. But states may also go further and exaggerate threats: the international furore over the Iraq war is a current example with infamously untrue representations of the threat from "weapons of mass destruction" to be delivered with little warning.

The focus has generally been on those psychologists who are confronted directly with dilemmas, primarily, those working for the military. But it can be argued that there is a more pervasive impact. If societal perception of degree of threat changes so, it may be argued, will the acceptance of actions previously considered unacceptable. Notions of civil liberties may change.

A good example is the increasing use of surveillance. This has been aided by the development of new technology such that cameras are now relatively cheap and effective. The UK in particular has taken to surveillance in a way previously unheard of. If private behaviour is now not really very private, how does a psychologist conceptualise confidentiality?

If medical practitioners can be charged with placing bombs, as was the case in the UK, what price the *assumption* of ethical integrity of those professionals, including psychologists, working for the good of society, as has been the traditional view?

There are complex issues that touch upon politics and personal values. The point I wish to make is that the development of "national security" as a powerful organizing factor in societal affairs poses a broad ranging challenge to psychologists, *all* of us, not only those working in the security field. There is a need for strong leadership from our professional associations (see also the British Psychological Society's condemnation of torture www.bps.org.uk/media-centre/press-release/releases$/2005/declaration.efm. However, ultimately we need, individually, to have vigilance in pursuing ethical practice.

The Development of a Common Ethical Code?

The second issue is more positive in intent. The purpose of this book has been to build upon the work of the EFPA Standing Committee on Ethics in promoting sound ethical practice throughout the national Associations that are members of EFPA. The development of the Meta-code has been highly successful in supporting new and emerging Associations. This book takes a further step and aims to help individual psychologists.

But how far should we go? The original EFPA idea of a single ethical code for all member Associations was abandoned for practical reasons (see chapter 1). However, this may be seen as a fortunate turn of affairs as it led to an intellectually stimulating focus on international comparabilities and differences. The development of the Meta-code was *collegial*. The Standing Committee on Ethics and its predecessor, the Task Force on Ethics, worked collaboratively not simply to find common ground – as in many political processes. Rather, the endeavour was to identify ethical principles and how these are applied in practice. The proof of the success of this approach has been in the acceptance of the Meta-code by all EFPA Associations in 1995 and the relatively few changes needed for the Revised edition in 2005. Furthermore, national Associations have either amended existing, or developed a new code, on the basis of the Meta-code. A strength, therefore, is the collegial process whereby the Meta-code was developed, optimizing agreement. A second strength was the format which specified what a national code should address, leaving specific language to each country.

A more recent initiative attempts to take this process further. The *Universal Declaration of Ethical Principles for Psychologists* is being developed by a working group set up by the International Union of Psychological Science (IUPsyS) at its 2002 General Assembly. This initiative seeks a more substantial coverage than EFPA: a worldwide applicability. It has the support of IUPsyS, the International Association of Applied Psychology and the International Association for Cross-Cultural Psychology.

This initiative has a more demanding task as the Declaration seeks, by definition, to have applicability and relevance for *all* countries. The development of the Universal Declaration has been a series of drafts discussed at international conferences, a cautious and reflective approach which is still on-going at this time. Although having slightly different aims – a Declaration rather than a Meta-code – it shares the objective of supporting the development of optimal ethical practice. Furthermore, in both endeavours, there has been an intention of seeking a collegial approach and common ground.

The challenge for the future is to develop further this search for a common approach to ethical practice while respecting individual cultural variations that need to be taken into account but not allowing the domination of the most powerful or common code(s). This was achieved within Europe; it is to be hoped that a similar outcome can be achieved world-wide. The challenge will be particularly acute in developing countries, as has been found within Europe. Limited resources, especially training, and a lack of infrastructure such as that provided by a national Association present difficulties. However, a collegial, respectful approach can lead to psychologist from countries with well established training and support systems working with colleagues from newly developing countries. The emphasis here is a collegial as each has much to learn from the other.

Specific Technical Developments

A review of the first 100 years of psychology as a profession reveals enormous changes in knowledge and skills based in that knowledge. New methods for assessment and intervention, for example, have continually been developed. Research has supported the use of some but shown the limitations of others. The scientific basis of psychology has served the discipline well.

It may be predicted that new techniques will continue to come into play. Many will be variations on an existing themes but occasionally there will be a quantum leap forward – or backward! A good example is the use of the internet. This has greatly enhanced the possibility for practice at a distance whether assessment or intervention. There are a number of challenges that follow: is the "client" the person I think it is? how can I tell if the person is really competent, legally and/or developmentally to give informed consent? how can I ensure valid and reliable responses? how do I protect the security of the data? These are but a few of the issues raised by the internet. But these are not necessarily new ethical challenges in a fundamental sense. In the past, psychologists have used telephones and even the postal service to work at a distance. Rather, the difference is one of degree.

The use of the internet was examined by the EFPA Standing Committee on Ethics and determined to raise the same ethical issues as traditional practice (see the ethics section of the EFPA website www.efpa.eu). Nevertheless, there may be a sharpening of these issues. For example, a security lapse in a psychologist's office may result in an unauthorized person catching a glimpse of a client's private file. A miskeying of a command on a computer may lead to an email being sent to many people. This is easily done – but not easily rectified.

New research and practice methods may also push back boundaries. In the past this occurred with, for example, the use of aversive treatments. More recently there have been concerns about the use of psychology in the making of "reality" programmes where participants are deliberately humiliated for the pleasure of the audience. But, again, are these issues new, or rather variations on the traditional themes?

Regulation or Education?

The final issue to be considered in this look into the future concerns a relatively recent phenomenon. The first step in developing ethical practice is to identify the ethical principles that should guide practice and then to specify exemplifications. At this point training can be developed on a structured foundation rather than be limited to personal reflection or discussion among peers or a between senior and junior psychologist (mentor and mentee). Ethical codes such as the Meta-code can support both reflective practice and systematic training. The Canadian Psychological Association's approach is an excellent example of putting education at the centre of the rationale for developing an ethical code (Sinclair & Pettifor, 1991).

A second development, however, uses an ethical code to support a regulatory system. In many countries professionals are regulated by law. Only accepted persons are allowed to practise. Regulation may be *functional* or *indicative*. In the former case the defining feature is the practice itself, e.g., extracting teeth (dentists) or psychotherapy (psychologists – and others). This is not-easy to execute in psychology. First other professions may have an historical basis for claiming the function as theirs, wholly or partly. Psychotherapy is a good example where psychologists and others (even priests) *may* claim this. Second, and again psychotherapy is a good example, the definition of the function may be difficult – when does a psychologist's psychotherapy differ from a priest's practice? Indeed the history within Europe of trying to define psychotherapy, and of trying to limit its use to psychologists has been fraught with problems. Third, functions may vary over time. Procedures once considered to require high levels of skills may be delegated to less qualified practitioners. Also, professions such as psychology make use of many different functions.

In many countries the preference has been for *indicative* regulation: that is, regulation by title. To practise as a *psychologist* a person needs to demonstrate the ability to carry out safe and effective practice. This requires training and education to achieve competencies and ethical knowledge. The state regulates the legal use of the title – only those on a legally defined register may practise.

Some professions, including medicine and law, have been statutorily regulated for many years but to achieve this for psychology requires the relevant government to allocate time to devise and pass a law. In the UK, for example, the attempt to achieve statutory regulation can be traced back at least 40 years to the granting of the British Psychological Society Royal Charter in 1965. It is likely that statutory regulation will finally be enacted in early 2009.

The purpose of statutory regulation is to have the power of the law to protect the public from unethical psychologists or to punish those who act unethically. From my experience leading the BPS's attempts to gain statutory regulation for about 15 years, and my experience on Conduct Committee Hearings, I fully support the need for statutory regulation as a means of public protection. However, it is also my view that this is not where the main energy is needed. Rather, the need is to ensure the *avoidance* of unethical behaviour by psychologists rather than the punishment or correction of unethical behaviour that has already occurred.

In this book we have referred to these matters, and to the use of mediation as well as corrective and disciplinary approaches. There is a challenge for the future, however, as newly developing Associations decide where to put their energy. There is a need to develop systems to address concerns and complaints (see chapter 9) but I suggest that the primary need is to support the development of ethical behaviour in new psychologists and the maintenance and improvement of ethical behaviour in experienced psychologists.

Conclusions

In this final chapter I have tried to highlight some of the main challenges facing national Associations and individual psychologists (see also Koocher, 2007). They do not stand in isolation. The impact of "national security" may become even more pervasive and have increasing influence on practice in traditional fields way outside obvious security-related situations.

The message of this book and of the final chapter, however, is over-whelmingly positive. Yes, there are challenges, but that is how it should be. Psychologists have the opportunity to exercise power and influence many people's lives. This carries with it the necessity to behave ethically.

This book developed out of the work of the EFPA Standing Committee on Ethics. That work continues to support the further development of ethics across Europe, and beyond: to enhance psychologists' practice, whether as applied practitioners or researchers; and to contribute to the enhancement of the well-being of individuals and societies.

References

Arendt, H. (1978). *Life of the mind*. London: Secker and Warburg.

Bassett, R., Basinger, D. & Livermore, P. (1992). On ethics, lying in the laboratory: Deception in human research from psychological, philosophical, and theological perspectives, *Journal of the American Scientific Affiliation 34*, 201–212.

Bauman, Z. (1993). *Postmodern ethics*. Cambridge: Blackwell.

Baumrind, D. (1964). Some thoughts on ethics of research: After reading Milgram's *Behavioural Study of Obedience*. *American Psychologist, 19,* 421–423.

Baumrind, D. (1985). Research using intentional deception: Ethical issues revisited. *American Psychologist, 40 ,* 165–174.

Bersoff, D.N. (2003). *Ethical conflicts in psychology* (3rd edition). Washington, DC: American Psychological Association.

British Educational Research Association. (2002). Report of BERA ethical guidelines working group. *Research Intelligence, 80,* 10–11.

Canadian Psychological Association (2000). *Canadian code of ethics for psychologists*. Ottawa, Ontario: Canadian Psychological Association.

Colnerud, G. (1997, July). The patient died but we did not break the principle of confidentiality. Paper presented at the 5th European Congress of Psychology, Dublin.

Crafts, L.W., Schneila, T.C., Robinson, E.E., & Gilbert, R.W. (1938). *Recent experiments in psychology*. New York: McGraw-Hill.

European Federation of Professional Psychologists Associations (1995). *Meta-code of ethics*. Brussels: Author.

European Federation of Psychologists Associations. (2005). *Meta-code of ethics (2nd Edition)*. Brussels: EFPA (www.efpa.eu, accessed 8.4.2008).

Eysenck, H.J. (1971). *Race, intelligence and education*. London: Temple-Smith.

Gladstone, D., Johnson, J., Pickering, W.G., Salter, B., & Stacey, M. (2000). *Regulating doctors*. London: Institute for the Study of Civil Society.

Haas, L.J., Malouf, J.L. & Mayerson, N.H. (1986). Ethical dilemmas in psychological practice: Results of a national survey. *Professional Psychology: Research & Practice, 17,* 316–321.

Hall, C.S. (1952). Crooks, codes and cant. *American Psychologist, 7,* 430–431.

Jacobson, N., Gewurtz, R., & Haydon, E. (2007). Ethical review of interpretive research: Problems and solutions. *IRB, 29,* 1–8.

Jebb, R. (Ed.). (1887). *The Oedipus Tyrannus of Sophocles*. Cambridge: Cambridge University Press.

Kalichman, S.C., Craig, M.E. & Follingstad, D.R. (1989). Factors influencing the reporting of father-child sexual abuse: Study of licensed practicing psychologists. *Professional Psychology, 20,* 84–89.

Kamin, L.J. (1974). *The science and politics of IQ*. Potomac, MD: Erlbaum.

Koene, C. (1997). Op de stoel van de tuchtrechter. *De Psycholoog, 32*, 511–517.
Koene, C. (2004). Opgezegd. *De Psycholoog, 39*, 569–573.
Koene, C. (2007). Blame and atonement. *European Psychologist, 12*, 235–237.
Koocher, G. (2007). Twenty-first century ethical challenges for psychology. *American Psychologist*, 62, 375–384.
Landis, C. (1924). Studies of emotional reactions: General behaviour and facial expressions. *Journal of Comparative Psychology, 4*, 447–450.
Levinas, E. (1981). *Otherwise than being or beyond essence*. The Hague: Martinus Nijehov.
Lindsay, G. (1992). Educational psychologists and Europe. In S. Wolfendale, T. Bryans, M. Fox, A. Labram & A. Sigstone (Eds). *The profession and practice of educational psychology*. London: Cassell.
Lindsay, G. (1995). Values, ethics and psychology. *The Psychologist, 8*, 493–498.
Lindsay, G. (1998). Are educational psychologists serious about research? *Educational and Child Psychology, 15*, 74–85.
Lindsay, G. & Colley, A. (1995). Ethical dilemmas of members of the Society. *The Psychologist, 8*, 448–451.
Mackintosh, N.J. (Ed). (1995). *Cyril Burt: Fraud or framed?* Oxford: Oxford University Press.
Milgram, S. (1963). Behavioral study of obedience. *Journal of Abnormal and Social Psychology, 67,* 371–378.
Milgram, S. (1964). Issues in the study of obedience: A Reply to Baumrind. *American Psychologist, 19*, 848–852.
Øvreeide, H. (2002). *Fagetikk I psykologisk arbeid*. Kristiansand: Høyskoleforlaget
Phinney, J.S. (1996). When we talk about American ethnic groups what do we mean? *American Psychologist, 51*, 918–927.
Pope, K.S. & Vetter, V.A. (1992). Ethical dilemmas encountered by members of the American Psychological Association: A national survey. *American Psychologist, 47*, 397–411.
Pryzwansky & Wendt (1999). *Professional and ethical issues in psychology*. London: Norton.
Rice, C.E. (1997). Scenarios: The scientist-practitioner split and the future of psychology. *American Psychologist*, 52, 1173–1181.
Sinclair, C. (1998). Nine unique features of the *Canadian code of ethics. Canadian Psychology, 39*, 167–176.
Sinclair, C. & Pettifor, J. (2001). *Companion manual to the Canadian code of ethics for psychologists* (3rd ed.). Ottawa: Canadian Psychological Association.
Tulku, T.XI., & Handberg, L. (Eds.) (2005) *Einheit in der Vielfalt. Moderne Wissenschaft und östliche Weisheit im Dialog*. Stuttgart: Theseus.
Waasenaar, D.R., & Slack, C. (1997, July). Ethical dilemmas of South African clinical psychologists. Paper presented at the 5th European Congress of Psychology, Dublin.
Zimbardo, P. (2007). *The Lucifer effect: How good people turn evil*. London: Rider.

Appendix 1

European Federation of Psychologists Associations (EFPA):

Meta-code of Ethics
(2nd edition)

Accepted by EFPA General Assembly, Granada 2005[*]

1. Preamble

Psychologists develop a valid and reliable body of knowledge based on research and apply that knowledge to psychological processes and human behaviour in a variety of contexts. In doing so they perform many roles, within such fields as research, education, assessment, therapy, consultancy, and as expert witness to name a few.

They also strive to help the public in developing informed judgements and choices regarding human behaviour, and aspire to use their privileged knowledge to improve the condition of both the individual and society.

The European Federation of Psychologists Associations has a responsibility to ensure that the ethical codes of its member associations are in accord with the following fundamental principles which are intended to provide a general philosophy and guidance to cover all situations encountered by professional psychologists.

National Associations should require their members to continue to develop their awareness of ethical issues, and promote training to ensure this occurs. National Associations should provide consultation and support to members on ethical issues.

The EFPA provides the following guidance for the content of the Ethical Codes of its member Associations. An Association's ethical code should cover all aspects of the professional behaviour of its members. The guidance on Content of Ethical Codes should be read in conjunction with the Ethical Principles.

The Ethical Codes of member Associations should be based upon – and certainly not in conflict with – the Ethical Principles specified below.

National Associations should have procedures to investigate and decide upon complaints against members, and mediation, corrective and disciplinary procedures to determine the action necessary taking into account the nature and seriousness of the complaint.

---

[*] Original Meta-code accepted by General Assembly, Athens 2005. Revised edition accepted by General Assembly, Granada 2005. (Reprinted by permission of EFPA (IVZW), European Federation of Psychologists Associations, Grasmarkt 105/18, B-1000 Brussels, www.efpa.eu)

2. Ethical Principles

2.1 Respect for a Person's Rights and Dignity

Psychologists accord appropriate respect to and promote the development of the fundamental rights, dignity and worth of all people. They respect the rights of individuals to privacy, confidentiality, self-determination and autonomy, consistent with the psychologist's other professional obligations and with the law.

2.2 Competence

Psychologists strive to ensure and maintain high standards of competence in their work. They recognise the boundaries of their particular competencies and the limitations of their expertise. They provide only those services and use only those techniques for which they are qualified by education, training or experience.

2.3 Responsibility

Psychologists are aware of the professional and scientific responsibilities to their clients, to the community, and to the society in which they work and live. Psychologists avoid doing harm and are responsible for their own actions, and assure themselves, as far as possible, that their services are not misused.

2.4 Integrity

Psychologists seek to promote integrity in the science, teaching and practice of psychology. In these activities psychologists are honest, fair and respectful of others. They attempt to clarify for relevant parties the roles they are performing and to function appropriately in accordance with those roles.

3. Content of Ethical Codes of Member Associations

In the following Meta-Code the term 'client' refers to any person, patients, persons in interdependence or organisations with whom psychologists have a professional relationship, including indirect relationships.

Professional psychologists' ethical codes must take the following into account:

- Psychologists' professional behaviour must be considered within a professional role, characterised by the professional relationship.
- Inequalities of knowledge and power always influence psychologists' professional relationships with clients and colleagues.
- The larger the inequality in the professional relationship and the greater the dependency of clients, the heavier is the responsibility of the professional psychologist.
- The responsibilities of psychologists must be considered within the context of the stage of the professional relationship.

Interdependence of the four principles

It should be recognised that there will always be strong interdependencies between the four main ethical principles with their specifications.

This means for psychologists that resolving an ethical question or dilemma will require reflection and often dialogue with clients and colleagues, weighing different ethical principles. Making decisions and taking actions are necessary even if there are still conflicting issues.

3.1 Respect for a Person's Rights and Dignity

3.1.1 General Respect

i) Awareness of and respect for the knowledge, insight, experience and areas of expertise of clients, relevant third parties, colleagues, students and the general public.
ii) Awareness of individual, cultural and role differences including those due to disability, gender, sexual orientation, race, ethnicity, national origin, age, religion, language and socio-economic status.
iii) Avoidance of practices which are the result of unfair bias and may lead to unjust discrimination.

3.1.2 Privacy and Confidentiality

i) Restriction of seeking and giving out information to only that required for the professional purpose.
ii) Adequate storage and handling of information and records, in any form, to ensure confidentiality, including taking reasonable safeguards to make data anonymous when appropriate, and restricting access to reports and records to those who have a legitimate need to know.
iii) Obligation that clients and others that have a professional relationship are aware of the limitations under the law of the maintenance of confidentiality.

iv) Obligation when the legal system requires disclosure to provide only that information relevant to the issue in question, and otherwise to maintain confidentiality.

v) Recognition of the tension that can arise between confidentiality and the protection of a client or other significant third parties.

vi) Recognition of the rights of clients to have access to records and reports about themselves, and to get necessary assistance and consultation, thus providing adequate and comprehensive information and serving their best interests and that this right to appropriate information be extended to those engaged in other professional relationships e.g., research participants.

vii) Maintenance of records, and writing of reports, to enable access by a client which safeguards the confidentiality of information relating to others.

3.1.3 Informed Consent and Freedom of Consent

i) Clarification and continued discussion of the professional actions, procedures and probable consequences of the psychologist's actions to ensure that a client provides informed consent before and during psychological intervention.

ii) Clarification for clients of procedures on record-keeping and reporting.

iii) Recognition that there may be more than one client, and that these may be first and second order clients having differing professional relationships with the psychologist, who consequently has a range of responsibilities.

3.1.4 Self-determination

i) Maximisation of the autonomy of and self-determination by a client, including the general right to engage in and to end the professional relationship with a psychologist while recognising the need to balance autonomy with dependency and collective actions.

ii) Specification of the limits of such self-determination taking into account such factors as the client's developmental age, mental health and restrictions set by the legal process.

3.2 Competence

3.2.1 Ethical Awareness

Obligation to have a good knowledge of ethics, including the Ethical Code, and the integration of ethical issues with professional practice.

3.2.2 Limits of Competence

Obligation to practise within the limits of competence derived from education, training and experience.

3.2.3 Limits of Procedures

i) Obligation to be aware of the limits of procedures for particular tasks, and the limits of conclusions that can be derived in different circumstances and for different purposes.
ii) Obligation to practise within, and to be aware of the psychological community's critical development of theories and methods.
iii) Obligation to balance the need for caution when using new methods with a recognition that new areas of practice and methods will continue to emerge and that this is a positive development.

3.2.4 Continuing Development

Obligation to continue professional development.

3.2.5 Incapability

Obligation not to practise when ability or judgement is adversely affected, including temporary problems.

3.3 Responsibility

3.3.1 General Responsibility

i) For the quality and consequences of the psychologist's professional actions.
ii) Not to bring the profession into disrepute

3.3.2 Promotion of High Standards

Promotion and maintenance of high standards of scientific and professional activity, and requirement on psychologists to organise their activities in accord with the Ethical Code.

3.3.3 Avoidance of Harm

i) Avoidance of the misuse of psychological knowledge or practice, and the mini-misation of harm which is foreseeable and unavoidable.
ii) Recognition of the need for particular care to be taken when undertaking research or making professional judgements of persons who have not given consent.

3.3.4 Continuity of Care

i) Responsibility for the necessary continuity of professional care of clients, including collaboration with other professionals and appropriate action when a psychologist must suspend or terminate involvement.
ii) Responsibility towards a client which exists after the formal termination of the professional relationship.

3.3.5 Extended Responsibility

Assumption of general responsibility for the scientific and professional activities, in-cluding ethical standards, of employees, assistants, supervisees and students.

3.3.6 Resolving Dilemmas

Recognition that ethical dilemmas occur and responsibility is placed upon the psycholo-gist to clarify such dilemmas and consult colleagues and/or the national Association, and inform relevant others of the demands of the Ethical Code.

3.4 Integrity

3.4.1 Recognition of Professional Limitations

Obligation to be self-reflective and open about personal and professional limitations and a recommendation to seek professional advice and support in difficult situations.

3.4.2 Honesty and Accuracy

i) Accuracy in representing relevant qualifications, education, experience, competence and affiliations.
ii) Accuracy in representing information, and responsibility to acknowledge and not to suppress alternative hypotheses, evidence or explanations.

iii) Honesty and accuracy with regard to any financial implications of the professional relationship.

iv) Recognition of the need for accuracy and the limitations of conclusions and opinions expressed in professional reports and statements.

3.4.3 Straightforwardness and Openness

i) General obligation to provide information and avoid deception in research and professional practice.

ii) Obligation not to withhold information or to engage in temporary deception if there are alternative procedures available. If deception has occurred, there is an obligation to inform and re-establish trust.

3.4.4 Conflict of Interests and Exploitation

i) Awareness of the problems which may result from dual relationships and an obligation to avoid such dual relationships which reduce the necessary professional distance or may lead to conflict of interests, or exploitation of a client.

ii) Obligation not to exploit a professional relationship to further personal, religious, political or other ideological interests.

iii) Awareness that conflict of interest and inequality of power in a relationship may still reside after the professional relationship is formally terminated, and that professional responsibilities may still apply.

3.4.5 Actions of Colleagues

Obligation to give a reasonable critique of the professional actions of colleagues, and to take action to inform colleagues and, if appropriate, the relevant professional associations and authorities, if there is a question of unethical action.

Recommendations on Evaluative Procedures and Corrective Actions in Case of Complaints About Unethical Conduct

1. Preamble

These recommendations on evaluative procedures and corrective actions in cases of complaints about unethical conduct build upon the EFPA Meta-code on Ethics approved by the EFPA General Assembly, Athens, July 1995. The Meta-code on Ethics provides guidance on the content of member Associations' on codes of ethics. The Meta-code, therefore supports Associations, and ultimately psychologists, by its guidance on ethical behaviour. However, complaints of alleged unethical behaviour by psychologists may arise. Member Associations should have procedures for investigating and evaluating such complaints and deciding any action considered to be appropriate. The term disciplinary refers to actions that involve sanctions including, but not limited to, a reprimand, suspension from a register or expulsion from the Association. The term corrective actions refers to actions designed to improve performance including, but not limited to, requirements for specific additional training or re-training and supervised practice. Both kinds of action are important but address different issues: punishment of the psychologist's past behaviour which was the subject of the complaint compared with improvement of future behaviour. These guidelines have been produced as a comparable document to the Meta-code of Ethics. That is, the guidelines are for Associations. They respect different national contexts by focussing on principles and general procedures arising there from, rather than presenting a single, detailed system, which all Member Associations would be required to follow. However, to provide assistance to Associations, an Appendix provides a more detailed and specific system, which might be helpful as a model. The nature of any Association's role in evaluative and correction actions will be affected by the presence or absence of a statutory body within the country and its statutory responsibilities for these matters.

2. Introduction

2.1   The European Federation of Psychologists Associations (EFPA) adopted its European Meta-code on Ethics at its General Assembly, Athens, July 1995, as guidance for the content of the Ethical Codes on its Member Associations. This should provide – in the common interest of clients, psychologists and the profession of psychology all over Europe – one ethical frame of reference for Psychological Associations to develop their ethical codes and to provide assistance in the evaluation of their members' conduct.

2.2   In accepting the Meta-code, EFPA Member Associations ensure the national codes are not in conflict with the Meta-code. As a result the ethical code of each member Association will be based on the same principles and have comparable content.

2.3   According to the Meta-code, Member Associations can contribute in several ways to the appropriate ethical level of their members' professional conduct. One of these ways is by instituting evaluative and disciplinary procedures in case of complaints about alleged unethical conduct of their members.

2.4   Individual members are expected to comply with their Association's code. Consequently the ethical behaviour of individual members of any EFPA Member Association can be evaluated against a common framework.

2.5   There are four main means whereby Member Associations may seek to ensure their members act appropriately and ethically:
   •   The formulation and publicising of the ethical code.
   •   The regulation of initial training
   •   Requirements for members to maintain and develop their ability to practise competently and ethically
   •   The provision of evaluative and disciplinary procedures in cases of complaint

2.6   The present guidance addresses the fourth of these functions, namely the responsibility of Member Associations to have procedures for the evaluation of members' practice in cases where a complaint is made, and to have the disciplinary procedures which may follow there from.

3. Need for Evaluation of Alleged Unethical Conduct

3.1   Psychologists may behave in ways, which are considered unethical and may be subject of complaint for several different reasons including:

- Ignorance of the national association's ethical code and/or other relevant ethical guidance;
- Carelessness in interpretation of the code during professional practice;
- Deliberate flaunting of the relevant code, whether for inappropriate personal benefit, or because of disagreeing with the code;
- As a result of dilemmas arising in practice whereby ethical principles are in tension or even conflict;
- As a result of reduced physical or mental competence.

3.2 Psychologists will inevitably meet situations in which professional ethical principles will be in conflict with one another or with the law. Then, it is impossible to act in accordance to all ethical principles equally. Thus psychologists are faced with ethical conflicts, which bring them into dilemmas concerning how to balance the relative significance of relevant ethical principles in the given situation.

3.3 Ethical conflicts not only may arise if professional ethical principles are incompatible with one another in a given context, but also if personal values or generic ethical principles would be violated by acting in accordance with specific principles of professional ethics. Although these cases could not strictly be seen as professional ethics dilemmas, they can still be powerful and may influence substantially the psychologist's ethical decision-making.

4. Principles

4.1 Access to information

The psychologist should be informed of the details of the complaint and the possible violation of the ethical code. Members of the public and psychologists should have easy access to information explaining the procedures concerning the making of a complaint; the process of evaluating the complaint and the psychologist's behaviour; and the decisions and range of sanctions that are available. During any evaluation and disciplinary procedure, both psychologist and complainant should have easy and equal access to all information and evidence.

4.2 Equity

All aspects of the process of evaluation and discipline should be open, transparent, fair and equitable for any complainant or psychologist. Comparable cases should lead to similar outcomes in evaluation and in corrective actions.

4.3 Equal arms

A complaint should not be pursued unless the complainant accepts that evidence necessary for the evaluation of the complaint will be required and therefore must be made available.

4.4 Avoidance of trivial or inappropriate actions

There should be a facility to reject complaints that are not related to the ethical code, are trivial or are mischievous.

4.5 Expert evaluation

The evaluation of complaints about a psychologist's professional behaviour and its alleged contravention of the Association's ethical code will require experienced psychologists to contribute to the evaluation of the complaint. Associations should incorporate into their evaluative procedures the possible use of psychologists expert in the domain of practice of which the complaint is made. Such experts should provide evaluations of the psychologist's behaviour about which a complaint has been made, and in particular should advise on the degree to which it is acceptable or not acceptable psychological practice.

4.6 Integrity

All who are involved in the evaluation and discipline procedures should act with integrity, honesty and fairness. They should not take on any role if there is conflict of interest. If a conflict of interest should occur during the process, then this should be brought to the attention of those with a need to know and the person concerned should withdraw from further involvement.

4.7 Confidentiality

Complaints and evidence should be treated as confidential during the process of investigation. Where a complaint is dismissed or not upheld, the matter should remain confidential. The psychologist who is the subject of a complaint may use information which is confidential for the purposes of defending him or herself, but must limit any release of such information with discretion and expressly for this purpose.

4.8 Public confidence

The Association's procedures should inspire public confidence. This will be achieved by the thoroughness and efficiency of the procedures, the integrity of all those concerned with operating the evaluative and disciplinary procedures, and necessary transparency in the procedures. All procedures should be carried out as quickly and expeditiously as possible. Confidence may also be enhanced if a hearing (Tribunal) is held in public, and if the outcomes of evaluated complaints are published.

4.9 Involvement of non-psychologists (lay persons)

Public confidence may be enhanced if non-psychologists are involved in the judgement of the complaint and the decisions regarding whether the complaint should be dismissed or upheld, and in decisions regarding corrective action if a complaint is upheld.

4.10 Separation of investigation, evaluation and corrective procedures

Associations should determine whether and how the three stages of investigation, evaluation and disciplinary action should be related.

a) Investigation

There should be a stage of investigation. This will involve the gathering evidence from the complainant, the psychologist who is the subject of the complaint, and any other source which will provide assistance.

b) Evaluation

The evidence is assessed to reach an evaluation of whether the complaint, and the alleged infringement(s) of the Association's ethical code are upheld.

c) Actions

If a complaint is upheld, decisions are required regarding what, if any, action(s) should follow.

4.11 Disciplinary and corrective action

Disciplinary actions should take into account the nature of the infringement of the ethical code, including the degree of harm resulting from the unethical behaviour, together with information presented in mitigation. Even where disciplinary actions are determined, the need for corrective actions in addition (e.g., further education or supervision) should be considered. Member Associations should develop and state publicly their tariff of sanctions.

4.12 Appeal

There should be an appeal procedure.

4.13 Monitoring

The investigation evaluation and disciplinary procedure should be monitored and considered by the appropriate body within the Association on a regular basis.

4.14 Publicity

Publication of the outcomes of evaluated complaints may be helpful in promoting the content of and the adherence to the ethical code. Statistics regarding investigations, evaluations, and corrective actions should be reported to the Association's members annually.

4.15 Interface between the Association and the State

Where another body has a legal responsibility for the regulation of psychologists, that body would normally be expected to hear complaints about unethical behaviour. The nature of such relationships differs across Europe from there being no statutory body, in which case the Association must take full responsibility for acting on complaints, to a statutory body with full powers to judge such complaints and make decision which are legally binding on the psychologist. Even in the latter case, the Association should maintain and promote its ethical code and ensure that the whole range of ethical questions is open to complaints and evaluation. Irrespective of the particular legal circumstances in any country, the Association has a responsibility to ensure the public are aware of the system(s) for dealing with complaints.

4.16 Models of practice

The Appendix provides a more detailed exposition of the principles outlined in the main part of this Guidance. It sets out a model for a system of investigation, evaluation and discipline.

Misconduct Resulting from Ill Health

Associations should have a separate procedure for evaluating complaints if the behaviour complained about is either alleged or found to be a function of a psychologist's ill health. This difference should apply also to the sanctions and other corrective actions that might follow the evaluation. The procedure should include the requirement for appropriate medical evidence on the psychologist's health.

Appendix 3

Guidelines on Mediation in the Context of Complaints About Unethical Conduct

1. Preamble

1.1 These *Guidelines on mediation in the context of complaints about unethical conduct* build upon the revised EFPA Meta-code of Ethics approved by the EFPA General Assembly, Granada, July 2005 (www.efpa.eu). The Meta-code of Ethics provides guidance on the content of member Associations' own codes of ethics. The Meta-code, therefore, supports Associations, and ultimately psychologists, by its guidance on ethical principles.

1.2 Complaints of alleged unethical behaviour by psychologists may arise. Consequently, Member Associations should have procedures to investigate and decide upon complaints against members. Separate guidance has been developed to aid National Associations in developing their evaluative and disciplinary systems[33]. These procedures may result in a decision to require supervision and/or disciplinary measures.

1.3 In addition, mediation[34] might be offered as an option to the complainant as a means of attaining a resolution between the complainant and the psychologist. This would normally be instead of supervision and/or disciplinary action. Its use would depend on the nature and seriousness of the alleged infringement.

1.4 The present *Guidelines* give additional guidance to EFPA Member Associations on the use of mediation as a means for the complainant and the accused psychologist to come to a settlement by themselves, facilitated by a third party, in such cases where the Association judges this appropriate.

1.5 National Associations should first set up the overall framework for evaluation and discipline, of which mediation may be an option, to ensure that mediation is part of the total system.

---

[33] Recommendations on evaluative procedures and corrective actions in case of complaints about unethical conduct (www.efpa.eu).

[34] In other languages a different term which represents the process described here may be more appropriate.

2. Mediation Characteristics

2.1   In mediation, the complaint can be seen as an expression of a problem or conflict between the complainant and the accused psychologist. The interests of the Association are not at stake. In an informal, semi-structured process an impartial mediator assists the disputing parties to work through and resolve problems or conflicts together. It is a non-judgmental, voluntary process that focuses on helping parties to find mutually satisfying resolutions to their problems, consistent with the interests of each party.

2.2   Whether or not by one's own initiative, participation in mediation is on a voluntary basis and in autonomous self-determination. This requires that each party is free to close the mediation process at any moment, if they no longer consider the mediation as being helpful.

2.3   As conflicting parties are facilitated to come to a solution themselves and have the freedom to terminate this process at any time, mediation conditions are essentially different from binding oneself beforehand to a final decision of any authority, as in arbitration.

3. Mediation Requirements

3.1   In implementing its procedures for dealing with complaints the National Association should take account of both the nature of the complaint and the potential for further risk to the public and/or the standing of the profession and of the Association itself.

3.2   Mediation is an option to be considered following a complaint alleging unethical conduct by a member of the Association. Consequently, decisions regarding the option of mediation should be part of the Association's system of addressing such complaints.

3.3   Adequate information about all relevant conditions of mediation in the context of complaint procedures against psychologists should be available for both psychologists and for the public. This should include both the criteria for complaints that the Association considers suitable for mediation and the process of mediation.

3.4   In the case of an actual complaint the complainant should be given details of the Association's total system for dealing with complaints, including mediation.

3.5   If mediation is found suitable by the Association, full details of the mediation procedure should explicitly be given to both the complainant and the psychologist.

3.6 Mediation requires special strategies and intervention techniques. Mediators do need not necessarily need to be psychologists, but they do need to have appropriate skills to undertake this role.

3.7 The mediator should be accepted as impartial by both the complainant and the psychologist.

3.8 All information about the complaint that is discussed during mediation will be treated as confidential by the mediator and will not be shared with the Association.

3.9 No formal record will be made of the mediation by the mediator.

3.10 If an allegation of a separate ethical violation is made during the mediation, the mediator should consider a) whether to stop the mediation and b) whether to advise the complainant of their right to make a new complaint.

3.11 The report of the mediator to the Association should be agreed by the complainant and the psychologist and may be limited to the outcome of the mediation process. This may be limited to a statement that the mediation has been successful and the complaint has been withdrawn.

3.12 Only anonymised statistical information concerning mediation should be made public by the Association.

4. The Mediation Process

4.1 The Association should see that its mediation process attempts a proper balance of power. Properly trained mediators are well prepared to handle mediation settings in which substantial differences in power between parties may occur. However, in order to give weaker parties sufficient confidence in mediation, the Association should ensure that in its mediation regulations attention is paid to the subject of power balance.

4.2 The Association may allow the mediator to decide upon arrangement strategies and techniques.

4.3 Mediation begins with the Association's willingness to refrain from further investigation and evaluative procedures during the period of mediation and to recommend the opportunity for mediation to the complainant and the accused psychologist. A decision to offer mediation should be made taking regard of the seriousness of the alleged infringement.

4.4 Mediation may end with the insight of the complainant that no ethical violation took place, the psychologist's expression of remorse or any other formal, written agreement between parties to 'close the books', or with a recompense. However, as parties are free to close mediation at any time, mediation may end without any result being satisfactory to both parties.

4.5 The National Association may decide to offer mediation early in the complaint process, or may prefer to do so after more thorough investigation, or even after a decision on a corrective action is made. However, it should be noted that the willingness to participate in mediation might decrease as its possible outcomes are limited by formal judgements or decisions.

Appendix 4

When Confronted with a Complaint[35]

When an ethical psychologist is confronted with a complaint, it is often natural at first to feel defensive possibly even to dismiss the possibility of a basis for the complaint. However, this is not an ethical reaction. Instead, it is incumbent upon the psychologist to reflect on the complaint and to try to see the situation from the point of view of the complainant.

The following actions are suggested as responses in the rare cases of being subject to a complaint whether for a client or a fellow psychologist:

- Acknowledge the complainer and accept the questions raised as, in principle, a legitimate response to your professional actions. To complain about professional practice is a legitimate action.
- Give your response and explanation whether oral or written by describing your actions in concrete terms.
- Make clear any limitations that may need to be observed be in relation to confidentiality or the like if you have commitments to people and legal restraints that may prevent you from being able to answer or give certain information to the complainer.
- Try to make understandable the considerations you have made without attacking and blaming others. Explain any ethical principles that may support and have guided your practice. If not, be modest and admit insufficient awareness of relevant ethical issues.
- Do not use your professional knowledge and theory to make attributions about complainer, the complaining or complaint. If psychology is used in response and defence to the questioning of one's own professional actions this could be a misuse of power and in itself be an unethical action.
- If you find that you may have acted unethically, make your regret clear to the complainer and take action to restore any damage that may have occurred or to prevent such damage that could occur.

---

[35] Translated from the Norwegian: Øvreeide, H. (2002). *Fagetikk I psykologisk arbeid.* Kristiansant: Høyskoleforlaget.